Decentring
Work

EDITORS:

Heather Mair, Susan M. Arai,
and Donald G. Reid

Decentring Work

CRITICAL
PERSPECTIVES
ON LEISURE,
SOCIAL POLICY,
AND HUMAN
DEVELOPMENT

UNIVERSITY OF
CALGARY
PRESS

University of Calgary Press
2500 University Drive NW
Calgary, Alberta
Canada T2N 1N4
www.uofcpress.com

LIBRARY AND ARCHIVES CANADA CATALOGUING IN PUBLICATION

Decentring work : critical perspectives on leisure, social policy, and human development / editors: Heather Mair, Susan M. Arai, & Donald G. Reid.

Includes bibliographical references and index.
Also available in electronic formats.
ISBN 978-1-55238-500-5

1. Leisure—Social aspects—Canada. 2. Canada—Social policy. I. Mair, Heather II. Arai, Susan M., 1968- III. Reid, Donald G.

GV14.45.D43 2010   306.4'8120971   C2010-906957-9

The University of Calgary Press acknowledges the support of the Alberta Foundation for the Arts for our publications. We acknowledge the financial support of the Government of Canada through the Canada Book Fund for our publishing activities. We acknowledge the financial support of the Canada Council for the Arts for our publishing program.

Printed and bound in Canada by Marquis Book Printing Inc.
∞ This book is printed on FSC Silva Enviro paper

Cover image: Bees on Honeycells by Irina Tischenko (www.istockphoto.com)
Cover design by Melina Cusano
Page design and typesetting by Melina Cusano

Contents

Introduction

Susan M. Arai, Heather Mair, and Donald G. Reid

The role of leisure in social development has long been at the roots of our profession – a calling to which many suggest we return. In this book, we take up this challenge and shed light on the importance of leisure in the context of social issues that touch the everyday lives of people in our communities. We examine the potential of leisure in contributing to the health and well-being of individuals and society and discuss the positioning of leisure within social policy. Central to this book is a critique of social policy that narrowly defines social issues as individual problems with economic solutions. How has it come to be that paid work is the only avenue available for attaining sustenance, self-esteem, and human dignity? Given the intractable nature of issues such as poverty, homelessness, patriarchy, racism, and exclusion, we ask: why not investigate options outside of this scope? We encourage a broader scope for examining social problems, one that de-centres work and opens up a space to consider the role of leisure. While work and paid employment are often viewed as the primary way to achieve individual health and well-being and define human value, this emphasis excludes many people and limits our vision for (re)creating community. In this book we encourage scholars and practitioners to explore and re-think the relationships between leisure, social policy, and human development.

This book represents a coming together of some of the most innovative and provocative thinkers in our field. The authors draw on research and theoretical expertise from a wide range of subject areas, including federally sentenced women, aboriginal youth, new immigrants, women living in poverty, and older adults. The authors bring their many years of research, practice, and writing to bear on topics such as homelessness, stigma, dementia, marginalization, inclusion, and ethnicity. Each chapter stands alone as an in-depth investigation, and yet, woven together, they grow into a treatise on notions of work, leisure, power, and social change. Using a mix of approaches from in-depth empirical studies to more conceptually driven discussions, the authors in this book help us take some important steps towards rethinking the positioning of leisure in social development and social policy.

To begin this rethinking, Part One of the book – *Leisure and Social Policy* – explores the complexity of social policy and its implementation, with an eye on the resultant impact on individual citizens, community, and the public good. In Chapter 1, Don Dawson describes different understandings of social policy and social welfare and the roles envisioned for government and the non-profit and private sectors. Then in Chapter 2, Janna Taylor and Wendy Frisby examine policy-making efforts of local government to develop inclusive leisure services; specifically, the communication of leisure access policies through information and communication technology on the web. In both of these chapters, the concept of social inclusion is introduced and an argument is made for the participation of citizens in the social policy process. Don Dawson concludes that postmodern and global contexts require leisure (and social) policy that is incremental and flexible, arising through conversations from the "ground up" to meet the needs of diverse and changing communities. Similarly, Janna Taylor and Wendy Frisby argue that public recreation remains one of the few remaining places for democratizing participation for all citizens; however, they note that current leisure access policies reflect an ongoing policy approach that is racialized, gendered, and ageist and contributes to the ongoing systemic exclusion of citizens on low income. Taylor and Frisby outline opportunities and strategies for active citizen engagement to create the incremental paradigmatic change or radical policy change needed to overcome systemic oppression and see the return of democracy in leisure.

Picking up on these themes, we aim to broaden the lenses used to examine marginalization, equality, access, and power and explore the ways leisure may play a role in addressing these issues. Marginalization is understood here as the processes by which individuals are excluded from full and equal participation in mainstream society. While the reasons for this exclusion may emanate from physical, social, psychological, or economic challenges (or some combination thereof), in many cases these individuals experience discrimination or are portrayed as deviant. Thus while other arguments position issues such as poverty, homelessness, racism, and patriarchy as individual issues, we encourage readers to examine these as social issues and to consider the ways policy both contributes to and alleviates these challenges. We pick up these ideas in Parts Two and Three of the book.

In Part Two, *Leisure and Alternative Policy Frameworks for Health and Social Development*, the authors speak to the ways current social policy and approaches further exclude people who are already marginalized in Canadian society. These chapters offer three alternative policy frameworks, which challenge us to reconsider the situation of leisure within policy and to understand individuals in the broader relational and community contexts in which they live. In Chapter 3, Don Reid, Leigh Golden, and Leah Katerberg examine the role of leisure policy in poverty reduction. The authors argue the need to consider issues of human development, self-worth, and dignity – accomplishment over accumulation – in poverty reduction strategies. They present a transformational model for social policy, emphasizing social and psychological aspects of human development through both work and leisure. Sherry Dupuis (Chapter 4) then challenges traditional planning and policy models that have defined Canada's care for persons with Alzheimer's disease or a related dementia (ADRD). Like Dawson and Taylor and Frisby, Dupuis highlights the importance of citizen participation in social policy. She presents an innovative planning framework that emphasizes active personal and community engagement of persons with dementia and their families and involves recreation and leisure professionals in challenging current perceptions and approaches to deinstitutionalization. Susan Arai and Rishia Burke then examine the life concerns of women living in poverty in Chapter 5. Using a framework built on critical race and feminist theory, Arai and Burke challenge the individualization of poverty and explore how new definitions of social policy may move us beyond a culture of blame, employment numbers, and welfare statistics. Examining poverty from a relational and community perspective, they examine leisure as a social determinant of health and, importantly, question how we respond to difference in community and provide critical reflections on the notion of social inclusion from the perspective of difference.

The aim of the book is also to further our understanding of leisure and social policy from the experience of people who are often marginalized in community; this is taken up in Part Three, *Social Policy from the Perspectives of the Margins*. With a neo–Marxist lens Susan Tirone (Chapter 6) underscores the relationship between social policies focused on immigration, multiculturalism, and leisure and highlights the historical interplay of cultural pluralism, control, and capital accumulation throughout Canada's immigration policies. In Chapter 7, Darla Fortune, Alison Pedlar, and Felice Yuen discuss the role of leisure in the lives of federally sentenced women drawing on their experiences with an innovative project that engages community volunteers in recreation activities with women serving their sentences. Heather Mair and Dawn Trussell (Chapter 8) then examine leisure in the context of homelessness and social housing in Canada, challenging broader debates about social policy and public responsibility for social welfare. While many of the authors use their understanding of a seemingly intractable social problem as entry into discussions about the role of leisure, in Chapter 9 Karen Fox and Brett Lashua start with what they know about leisure (urban, Aboriginal hip-hop) and use that as an entry into discussions about how social policy and social change might be reconceptualized. Fox and Lashua challenge our assumptions about marginalization and social inclusion and argue for the importance of maintaining the margins and the potential of leisure to challenge dominant production systems.

These chapters take up the notion of *difference* and re-vision the ways leisure and social policy can contribute to a healthy, inclusive society. Susan Tirone reviews contemporary theories guiding cultural and leisure policies and reveals the challenging relationship between them, including examples such as the presence of social exclusion and behavioural control in leisure policies, and the existence of racialized barriers preventing access to leisure. Tirone then recommends improvements in recreation supports for newcomers and people labelled as ethnic minorities through the generation of a deeper understanding of the intended and unintended impacts of multiculturalism policy. Darla Fortune, Alison Pedlar, and Felice Yuen describe policy shifts in federal corrections and the expectation of women's social inclusion upon release. They argue that these hopes are often at odds with society's notion of the "offender" and the oppressions characterizing the lives of women who are incarcerated. Fortune, Pedlar, and Yuen argue leisure may be one area where women who are incarcerated maintain some semblance of dignity and respect and participation and inclusion in society, and the women with the volunteers are able to realize common interests and accomplishments and celebrate difference. In their critical rethinking of homelessness and social housing policy, Heather Mair and Dawn Trussell argue that social policy discussions about access to safe, secure, and stable housing must be re-injected with a sense of our *societal, collective obligation* to address these issues. They describe leisure as the context where issues of homelessness and reclaiming the revanchist city may be discussed, debated, confronted, and reconsidered and societal collective obligation restored while respecting diversity, privacy, and control. Fox and Lashua then argue for a rethinking of marginalization in a way that embraces issues of difference, multiplicity, and expressive diversity, rather than marginalization as something *to be fixed* and intentions to create one "normal" system. For Fox and Lashua, margins can be both "safe havens" for difference and sites of oppression. They argue that expressive initiatives underpinning leisure by urban Aboriginal youth may create alternative resolutions and strategies necessary for dynamic diversity.

In the final chapter, we provide a summary and conclusion to the book. Here we wrap up the discussion by pulling out the main themes running through most of the chapters by focusing on a number of key assumptions. In this way, we also set the stage for future research, exploration, and discussion in these areas. Furthermore, we posit the idea of *the leisure imagination* and call on others to embrace, challenge, and push forward both our language and our understanding of the issues raised throughout the book.

Who the Book Is For, and How to Use It

The book is meant for anyone conducting research, writing, or engaging in community practices that address social issues, marginalization, and difference. While we hope this book will be taken up in leisure studies and kindle a rethinking of leisure theory and critical perspectives on leisure studies, the book also has broader applications in disciplines such as labour studies, health promotion, and critical social work. This is the first time in our field that a collection of works has directly addressed these large social issues. In the name of difference we encouraged the authors to each take their own road to bring their expertise and contribution onto the page. Some authors approached the task with a grounded and empirically driven account; others worked at an abstract or conceptual level – all attempt to break new ground in articulating the connections between leisure, social policy, and social development. We feel that this approach was essential since successful social change demands both thinking practically on the ground and thinking with a broader vision. To this end, the chapters in the book can certainly stand on their own, or in combination, as case studies. People interested in specific topics (i.e., poverty, corrections, health care, youth, immigration) may want to read selected chapters. We only ask that you read, debate, and consider for yourselves what needs to be done and how leisure may play a more significant role.

Acknowledgment

Parts of the research presented here as well as an initial conference held at the University of Guelph in May, 2007, (the impetus for this book) were supported by a generous grant from the Ontario Ministry of Agriculture, Food and Rural Affairs. The editors would like to thank each of the contributing authors for their commitment to this process.

PART ONE:
LEISURE AND SOCIAL POLICY

Part One is an attempt to provide the reader with an understanding of the complexity of social policy and its implementation, with an eye on the resultant impact on both individuals and the broader community. These chapters explore the relationship between understandings of social policy, values or normative foundations, and the relationship of these to the development of leisure policy and the provision of leisure at the local level.

In making the connection between social policy, social welfare, and leisure, Don Dawson describes the ways social policy and social welfare are understood in Canada and the roles envisioned for government and the non-profit and private sectors. Dawson describes the relationship between social policy and social inclusion and debates the role of leisure in social inclusion policy. Dawson argues that leisure and recreation are recognizable and valuable elements of social welfare policies. Tracing the distributive, redistributive, and accumulative functions of leisure in Canadian social policy, Dawson concludes postmodern and global contexts require leisure (and social) policy that is incremental and flexible, arising through conversations from the "ground up" to meet the more specific needs of diverse and changing communities.

Chapter 2 extends the discussion and addresses inadequate leisure access policies through citizen engagement in the process. Janna Taylor and Wendy Frisby examine the policy-making efforts of local government to develop inclusive leisure services. Examining the communication of leisure access policies through information and communication technology on the web, Taylor and Frisby identify the many pitfalls associated with this approach. Arguing that while public recreation remains one of the few remaining places for democratizing participation for all citizens, current leisure access policies reflect an ongoing policy approach that is racialized, gendered, and ageist and contributes to the ongoing systemic exclusion of citizens on low income. Taylor and Frisby outline opportunities and strategies for active citizen engagement to create the incremental paradigmatic and radical policy change needed to overcome systemic oppression and to see the return of democracy in leisure.

– I –

Leisure and Social Policy

Don Dawson

The place of leisure in social policy is widespread yet ill-defined. In order to make some sense of the varied assortment of leisure-related policies, the notions of *public policy* and *social welfare* will be introduced along with *social inclusion*. The role of governments and the non-governmental sector will be discussed. Finally, trends in leisure and social policy will be presented.

PUBLIC POLICY, SOCIAL POLICY, AND WELFARE

The concept of "policy" can be applied to the setting of goals and the means of achieving them in a variety of sectors, such as the government or state sector, the business or commercial sector, and the not-for-profit or voluntary sector. Policy made in the name of the "public," usually by governments, is *public* policy. Public policy is generally conceived of as decisions made by government to pursue a course of action in addressing societal concerns. State policy is also evident in government decisions to reject certain initiatives and "do nothing" about a particular question. *Social* policy is a subset of public policy that has to do with social issues such as education, health, and recreation. It can be contrasted with foreign policy and economic policy, although all policy areas are interrelated at some level. Social policy relates to guidelines or plans for creating, maintaining, or improving living conditions that are conducive to human welfare. Thus, social policy generally applies to developing the welfare or well-being of citizens.

Welfare, in this regard, is associated with basic needs (food, housing, clothing, and security), but it extends beyond these to foster the conditions that allow people to exercise the freedom to take advantage of opportunities and participate fully in the life of their community. The debate around social welfare policy in the public sector is not whether collective social provision should exist but about how much provision there should be and how it should be directed. Painter and Pierre (2005) explain that governments have varying levels of "capacity" to formulate and deliver public services. They argue that in addition to the *administrative* capacity to manage resources efficiently, and the *state* capacity to mobilize support for public social goals, governments must also have sufficient *policy* capacity to make intelligent collective choices about, and set strategic directions for, public policy means and ends. The choices made concerning public policy, what to do and what not to do, may require intelligence, but they are also normative decisions.

Public policy is always relative to some implied norm and is usually intended to reproduce dominant cultural norms (e.g., universal public education). In this sense all social policy is norm-based. Clearly, some norms may result in social policies that are more inclusive and tolerant and others that are more divisive and exclusionary (Schram 2000). For example, the policy goal of social inclusion, broadly defined as the ability of all citizens to develop their talents and capacities to the fullest, to actively participate in society, and to enjoy a measure of equality of "life chances" is a normative position based on a set of values. Thus, one can "believe" in social inclusion or view it as infringing, for example, on individual rights and as undermining personal initiative and general economic performance. Of course, there are many "good" reasons for developing effective policies to address problems of social exclusion that go to the very heart of the kind of society people want.

By their nature, social welfare policies ostensibly strive to promote the well-being of all, but unintended consequences of adopted policies and the fallout from "non-decisions" or inaction, as well as misguided policies and deficient implementation, may result in outcomes that exacerbate social divisiveness and further exclude marginalized groups. In any case, one can conceive of four broad categories of public policy; distributive policy, redistributive policy, constituent policy, and regulative policy (Henry 2001, 4). Distributive policies benefit all citizens indiscriminately while redistributive policies favour one segment of the population at the cost of other segments. Constituent policies define laws and democratic procedures while regulative policies control the behaviour of community members. Historically leisure policies have been distributive and redistributive as well as regulative, but not constituent. Social welfare policies may be further construed as directing provision according to three different principles; *residual* welfare, *solidarity*, and *institutional* welfare (The Robert Gordon University Center for Public Policy and Management 2007). Residual welfare directs policy and services toward the poor, providing a "safety net" for those unable to manage otherwise. Solidarity is based on a principle of mutual responsibility of people to take care of others in their society. Thus, policy based on both the residual welfare and solidarity principles is directed to individuals or groups seen to be socially excluded or marginalized from their communities. Institutional welfare views social welfare as a normal part of everyday life, and provision is indiscriminately made for the population as a whole.

Within these approaches two methods of welfare provision are evidenced; universality and selectivity. Universal benefits are available to everyone or broad categories (e.g., children or seniors) as a right. Selective benefits are reserved for specific people judged to be in need. While universality is a key to much public welfare policy, many states take recourse to selective policies and programs in particular circumstances to ensure that needs are met. In this way the principles of residual welfare and solidarity can coexist with institutional welfare principles.

Whatever the policy principles or methods (universality or selectivity), social inclusion remains a critical aspect of welfare policy.

SOCIAL INCLUSION POLICY

Social inclusion policy should be recognized as not being static or fixed; it must adapt to circumstances and develop over time. Richmond (2004) holds that social inclusion exhibits three essential features: (1) it should address the structural roots of exclusion, (2) it should be rooted in community organization, and (3) it should lead to real policy changes which transform structures that promote exclusion and limit inclusion. This view is in keeping with critics who suggest that too narrow a focus on social exclusion is a "risk orientation" that distracts from redistribution policies (Freiler 2003). Levitas (1996) objects to the "interventionist agenda" in that policies aimed at reintegrating people into the labour market often focus on their lack of skills and resources and as such tend to blame them for their failings and emphasize the personal over the systemic.

Nevertheless, social inclusion policies can make a significant contribution to all policy areas by serving as a "lens" through which policy agendas and decisions are assessed and acted upon. While social inclusion is understood as a means "to create and sustain inclusive communities for the mutual benefit of all people" (Social Planning and Research Council of British Columbia 2006, 2), it is a complex concept that has many dimensions. Among these dimensions are included *value recognition* (conferring recognition and respect on individuals and communities), *opportunities for human development* (nurturing the talents, skills, capacities, and choices of people), *involvement and engagement* (having the opportunity to be involved in community decision-making and being engaged in community life), *proximity* (reducing the social distances between people and sharing public spaces), and *material well-being* (having the resources to participate fully in one's community) (Freiler 2003).

These dimensions of social inclusion underscore the normative basis of social policy. In order to support such a policy of social intervention, people must share common principles and objectives: ensuring access for all to essential programs and services; providing assistance to those in need; and ensuring adequate, stable and sustainable funding for social programs (Canadian Council on Social Development 2004, 4). Indeed, the Canadian Council on Social Development (2003, 1) holds that these principles "resonate with the values of Canadians" that support the setting in place of "social policies that will knock down the shameful barriers of exclusion." Obviously these are value-laden and norm-based assertions to which not everyone may easily adhere. For example, the following "values that serve as a foundation for work on social inclusion" have been identified by the Social Planning and Research Council of British Columbia (2006, 6): social justice, valuing diversity, opportunities for choice, entitlement to rights and services, and working together. Some may argue, for instance, that the values of *social justice* (distribution of social and economic resources of society for the benefit of all people), *entitlement* (universal entitlement to rights and services) and *working together* (building common interests and shared goals) are not necessarily compatible with *diversity* (recognition and respect for the diversity in society) and *choice* (the right of individuals to make their own choices). Regardless, proponents of social inclusion policy, such as the Canadian Council on Social Development, argue that inequality and marginalization are persistent, if not growing, social problems that require critical social investment in order to create a more inclusive society.

The impact of values and norms extends beyond the debate over whether social inclusion policy is desirable or not into disagreements as to how social inclusion can be achieved. Some advocates of social inclusion policy are convinced that governments should "move away from neo-liberal economic policies emphasizing the universal benefits of general universal growth and into ... social supports and policy reforms needed by specific excluded communities" (Richmond 2004, 76). Whereas this view supports selectivity in locating and transforming specific forms of exclusion, others, equally committed to social inclusion goals, are confident that social inclusion must take a human development approach that moves away from "a focus on marginalization and targeting to a struggle for solidarity and universalism" (Freiler 2003, 1). The latter view holds that selectively targeting specific "at-risk" or needy groups will result in a patchwork of band-aid programs and services that ultimately do little to address the fundamental long-term socio-economic basis of exclusion and marginalization. Still others anticipate that some combination of universal and selective policy initiatives can best reduce social exclusion.

LEISURE POLICY

In any case, a policy of social inclusion must result in actions, programs, and services that reduce exclusion, or it is mere rhetoric. In Canada, for example, the 2006 federal government budget plan included programs such as the Universal Child Care Plan for all families and a Children's Fitness Tax Credit available to all. Funding for Affordable Housing was provided to the provinces and $50 million was granted to the Canadian Council for the Arts. As well, the government announced increased funding targeted to Aboriginal communities for programs to reduce disparities between Aboriginal people and other Canadians. Such policies, the government asserted, would help in "building a better Canada" (Government of Canada 2006). The Canadian Council on Social Development (2003), in an earlier pre-budget submission, sought a "fairer" tax system benefiting lower income citizens, a higher minimum wage, and increased benefits to the unemployed. While these initiatives were justified by trying to find a balance between work and family life, in promoting children's fitness, and tax relief to put more discretionary income in people's pockets, there were no policies explicitly directed toward leisure. Why is that the case? Is it because leisure policy is not seen to be an important policy domain?

Searle and Brayley (2000, 6) hold that public policy-makers do not perceive the need for leisure services to be a "frill": instead, they see recreation as "an essential service." Coalter (1988, 130) believes that of those publicly organized, controlled, and subsidized services for which access is largely non-market, leisure provision, "although not ... of the same significance," ranks alongside health and education. Similarly, Bramham, Henry, Mommaas, and van der Poel (1989, 280–81) posit that, while leisure policy is "an important element in improving the quality of life of the deprived and disadvantaged, ... leisure initiatives have only a limited impact on tackling and redressing social and economic problems." In this sense, "leisure policy has remained at the margins of political debate" (Coalter 1988:1) in most instances. Indeed, for many public social policy initiatives "recreation development activities are of secondary or ancillary concern" (Searle and Brayley 2000, 82). Nevertheless, recreation is a recognized social policy area that has a long history in the provision of public services and the discourse on state intervention (see Bramham, Henry, Mommaas, and van der Poel 1993). The goals for public policies in the area of recreation and leisure are many and varied. A Canadian investigation into the significance of public recreation policy focuses on youth, but its hypotheses apply to recreation and leisure participation in general (Canadian Council on Social Development 2001a, 2):

- **The Human Development Hypothesis**

   Recreation and leisure participation contributes to long-term socio-emotional human development.

- **The Civic Competence Hypothesis**

   Recreation and leisure develops civic competency and improves the quality of democracy.

- **The Insufficiency Hypothesis**

   Significant numbers of people are not participating in recreation and leisure activities enough to receive its full benefits.

- **The Inadequacy Hypothesis**

   Non-participation is related to the inadequacy of existing public recreation and leisure provision.

Thus, recreation and leisure may be seen as potentially important areas of public social policy and service provision.

There are many other perspectives and justifications for the development of government leisure policy and state intervention in leisure. One such justification, crucial to the welfare state model (discussed more fully below), relates to "market failures" with respect to *positive externalities, preservation values, economic development,* and *merit goods* (Gratton and Taylor 2000). The market does not account for externalities experienced not by the individual but by society as a whole. Positive leisure externalities might include increased productivity at work and reduced health costs as consequences of improved fitness and health through recreation participation, or reduced crime attendant to expanded involvement in recreational facilities, programs, and services. There are, however, negative leisure externalities such as noise and pollution from boating or snowmobiling. Preservation values relate to things that individuals value but don't necessarily use themselves, such as national parks, wilderness areas, heritage sites, or facilities for the arts. Leisure provision can also stimulate economic development in many ways; through allied support services, tourism, and employment. As well there are numerous examples of merit goods that are under-consumed if left to private demand and market mechanisms. These would include museums and libraries, for instance.

Over and above these market failures, a fundamental justification for public recreation lies in the affirmation that leisure is a right of citizenship. This argument holds that all people are entitled to the opportunity of a certain amount of leisure participation. Questions concerning the right to leisure have focused on the level of provision to which people are entitled, how such policy is best implemented, and the extent to which any apparent lack of participation is a matter of choice, freely chosen. Nevertheless, the notion that people should have equal access to recreational facilities, services, and programs is widely held. This view has historically been used to justify selective recreation policies targeting particular disadvantaged groups, but the social inclusion motivation traditionally placed great emphasis on provision for the poor generally.

The beginnings of public recreation in North America stem back to the early 1900s where playground programs were provided for under-privileged children and their families. Low-income families still face many barriers to recreation participation. These include user fees, equipment costs, lack of transportation, lack of awareness of opportunities, and inadequate safe facilities. These barriers are at the root of social exclusion in leisure and, it is argued, they must be removed and "policy makers need to see structured recreation as a public good" (Canadian Council on Social Development 2001b, 1). Recreation and leisure are a public good – merit goods – because of the significant social benefits, including social inclusion, they are said to foster. Although empirical support is limited in some areas, the following are often cited as terms under which recreation might promote social inclusion (Donnelly and Coakley 2007):

- *Accessibility* – access to recreational opportunities
- *Agency* – an active, determining role for participants
- *Competence* – enhancement of participant self-esteem and confidence
- *Continuity* – consistency of pro-social impacts and results
- *Integration* – bringing together of people from different backgrounds
- *Leadership* – leaders developed among participants
- *Motivation* – inclusion goals are emphasized in programs

STATE POLICY AND THE LEVEL OF GOVERNMENT

If recreation and leisure are public goods that provide for the welfare of people, how does the state deliver these "essential" services? In countries such as the United States and Canada, there are multiple levels of government; federal, state/provincial, and municipal. The Canadian situation, for example, situates the "primary role" for recreation development at

the provincial level, and various provincial governments have made as-
sorted public policy pronouncements over the years (Searle and Brayley
2000, 93). Yet "primacy does not mean exclusivity" (Searle and Brayley
2000, 93) and the federal government along with the provinces recognized the need for shared policy with respect to recreation. Moreover,
as Mirecki (1992, 9) pointed out, while recreation and leisure initiatives
may originate at the federal and provincial levels, "municipalities are the
principal providers and architects of recreation and leisure opportunities." This "municipalization" of leisure (Harvey, Andrew, and Dawson 1990) has been evident across the twentieth century in virtually all
Western nations. In Britain and Europe as well, it is at the level of local
government, or municipality, where state leisure policies and practices
are expressed (Coalter 1988, 4).

A "serious flaw" in Canada's recreation system (Mirecki 1992, 9)
and elsewhere is a lack of coordination of recreation and leisure policy
among the levels of governments. Commentators underline that there
has been little coherent "national" level policy in either North America
or Europe (see Freysinger and Kelly 2004; Coalter 1988). The absence
of firmly established national leisure policies may suggest that wide
variation is possible at local levels. As well, leisure programs are almost
uniformly non-mandatory in nature. That is to say, there are few legislated, mandatory obligations for municipalities to provide for leisure.
The legislated role of local government in leisure provision is "permissive" in that it is permitted to provide recreation services and facilities
but rarely has any legal obligation to do so. The lack of coordination
between levels of government, diffuse leisure policies at the national and
regional (state/provincial) levels, and the permissive nature of municipal
leisure provision would seem to allow for considerable independence
in these regards at the local level. However, Coalter (1988, 142) warns
that one should not "over-emphasize" the possibility of "particularism"
in policies and practices at the local level. Indeed, various models of local state leisure provision point to varying degrees of control by higher
levels of government (Dawson, Andrew, and Harvey 1991).

Nevertheless, multilevel governance arrangements do present distinct challenges as well as opportunities for municipal recreation policy

and practice. On the one hand, involving multiple levels of government in leisure policy may enhance the capacity of local authorities to mobilize resources and leverage action from a number of different sources. On the other hand, the complexity engendered by these multiple levels may encumber the municipality's capacity to set policy and take action, given the number different actors involved. The key to success depends, perhaps, on the ability to manage bargaining situations and engage in productive negotiation (Painter and Pierre 2005). In this way municipal recreation providers may enhance their power if they can mobilize local resources and work to direct policy agendas.

Recent experience suggests that local leaders can be overwhelmed by decreased budgets and increased demands. Over the last few decades, much of the burden of dealing with problems such as social inclusion has been downloaded to municipalities who often know what the problems are but do not have the necessary resources to respond adequately. Nevertheless, it is frequently held that the decisions of local government are those that make the most difference to people's leisure activities and opportunities because it is in the best position to respond to local needs and preferences. This notion that problems should be dealt with at the lowest possible tier of government is sometimes referred to as the "subsidiarity" principle and is often in effect with regard to leisure policy (Bramham, Henry, Mommaas, and van der Poel 1993, 10).

The history of local leisure provision shares many similarities across Western democracies in North America and Europe. In the nineteenth century, a broad range of government policy was "leisure-relevant" in that it was not leisure policy *per se* but had effects on leisure (Coalter 1988). Policies on transportation and housing, for instance, had implications for the structure and content of leisure facilities and services. When policies were directed toward leisure opportunities, they tended to be largely *ad hoc* and reactive, resulting in a fragmented policy area with little coherent policy on leisure. This fragmentation and lack of coherence was further complicated by the fact that leisure refers to a diverse array of sporting, recreational, artistic, and social activities that take place in a wide range of contexts. Still, by the end of the nineteenth century, the broad elements of public leisure policy were evident. These elements include (Coalter 1988, 15–16):

- Recreation provision to counter urban deprivation.
- A concern for the health and productivity of the workforce.
- A campaign against morally suspect working-class leisure through the provision of wholesome recreation opportunities.
- The use of leisure to build "community" through social integration and social control.
- A utilitarian ideology that the dominant use of leisure was for self-improvement.

Despite these elements of public leisure policy a non-interference or "hands-off" approach is often seen by historians as the prevailing attitude of government toward leisure in the 1800s (Borsay 2006). Although the role of the state was not entirely "laissez faire," the state's role in providing leisure was residual and enabling up to the first half of the twentieth century. It was "residual" in that governments most frequently intervened in leisure only if the private or philanthropic sectors could not supply services to meet community needs and "enabling" because the state was often more comfortable in helping the other sectors meet needs rather than doing so directly itself.

In the mid-twentieth century, social policy shifted to goals of achieving equality of recreational opportunity within a broader social welfare. The overarching notion of the democratization of culture and leisure was predominant in the rhetoric of the day, and the welfare theme played a prominent role. The extension of leisure opportunities was seen as a means of meeting needs, contributing to individual and social welfare and achieving equality. During this period the preoccupation of leisure policy gradually shifted from social welfare for those in need to one of improving the quality of life for all (see Freysinger and Kelly 2004 for the U.S. case; Searle and Brayley 2000 for Canada). After World War II, leisure policy in Canada, for instance, was used to promote the fitness of all citizens, to contribute to economic growth, to provide a sense of national pride, and to protect the natural environment (Searle and Brayley 2000). The principle of provision for the disadvantaged, the very foundation of the early playground movement in both the United States and Canada, was often subsumed by these broader policy directions.

Further "questioning of the welfare state" came about in Canada and elsewhere when governments in the 1970s began to experience mounting costs and falling or stagnant revenues and embarked on a series of expenditure cutting exercises. This also led to the downloading of responsibilities to municipalities and privatization of hitherto state functions. The emphasis was no longer on the social welfare ideal of equal provision but more so on a model of consumer choice and a logic of service delivery based on market forces.

Although social welfare programs were scaled back in the 1980s due to public fiscal woes, expectations have not changed dramatically since the inception of post-war welfare statism. Indeed, people's "expectations for themselves, their children, and their fellow citizens have probably increased over the years" (Scott 2006, 1). In the leisure arena, calls for policies assuring the "essential benefits of recreation" for all are persistent and vigorous (Mirecki 1992). In Canada, the Canadian Parks and Recreation Association (2001, 2) continues to lobby for a National Policy on Recreation for low-income families to remove barriers to participation. In 2005 the Canadian Parks and Recreation Association (2005, 2) endorsed an inclusive National Recreation and Sport Infrastructure Program that sought to meet the needs of "vulnerable populations" and to "improve the quality of community life and health status" of targeted communities.

Leisure Policy and the Non-Governmental Sector

Painter and Pierre (2005, 7) warn, however, that "to focus on the government alone as the source or even the instrument of policy capacity would be misleading." They adhere to the broader notion of "governance" as denoting a wide variety of social networks, public-private partnerships, professional associations, and the policy community that spans formal jurisdictions. Although the state is typically identified as the key actor in defining policy goals and deciding policy priorities, much policy design is seen to evolve through an interactive governance process of consultation, coordination, and bargaining across boundaries. At a more complex theoretical level, the balance between the role of the state (collective) and non-governmental sectors (individual) in governance and policy formation can be seen to encompass a range of consumption processes. Dunleavy (1980) conceives of four categories of forms of public-sector involvement in social services. These vary from completely *collective* consumption that is publicly organized and subsidized and has non-market criteria for access; *quasi-collective* consumption that is privately organized but is publicly subsidized and has non-market criteria for access; *quasi-individualized* consumption that is privately owned (i.e., with market criteria for access) but publicly subsidized, and entirely *individualized* consumption that is privately owned, requires market criteria for access, and is not publicly subsidized. It is important to note that quasi-collective consumption, despite being publicly subsidized (to allow for non-market criteria for access) is essentially a private process wherein day-to-day control of the resource, facility, or service remains largely in private hands. Only a strategy of complete collective consumption maintains full policy control in the hands of the government.

In a practical sense, the major players in recreational collective/individual consumption processes are the commercial (private) sector, the not-for-profit (often publicly subsidized) sector, and the public sector. According to Henry (2001), recent history, particularly in liberal welfare states such as Canada and the United States, has seen reductions in state involvement in leisure policy and an increasing significance in the commercial and voluntary not-for-profit sectors. This is a result of the decline of the welfare state as governments "around the world are looking for new ways to deliver public services at lower costs to taxpayers and users" (de Bettignies and Ross 2004, 135). In this regard many public sector decision-makers are turning increasingly to partnerships with the private sector. These "public-private partnerships," or P3s, are rapidly expanding in many jurisdictions. P3s are defined as public-private partnerships that "are contractual arrangements between government and a private party for the provision of assets and the delivery of services that have been traditionally provided by the public sector" (de Bettignies and Ross 2004, 136). Today, recreation facilities and services are frequently included in such public-private partnerships.

P3s lie somewhere between traditional "contracting out" and a private market approach. De Bettignies and Ross (2004, 138) suggest that there are three main characteristics of the "new wave" of P3s. First, all P3s are really extensions of contracting out, but secondly, they are characterized by a "bundling" of several responsibilities to the private sector (such as the design and construction of a facility in addition to its management). The third dimension of a growing number of P3s is the allocation of the financing task to the private partner. Thus, modern public-private partnerships go beyond the contacting out of some elements of collective consumption to a pattern of quantitatively and qualitatively larger and growing privatization of consumption. However effective P3s may be as mechanisms for the provision of public services, their impact on social inclusion policy initiatives needs to be understood.

The main implication of P3s for social inclusion policy is that the emphasis on the provision of services, including leisure opportunities, is placed on profitability rather than accessibility (Smale and Reid 2001). The imperatives of profit (capital accumulation) mean that access is determined by the market, or the ability to pay (individualized consumption). Thus, the shifting of services from the public (publicly subsidized collective consumption) to the private (market-based individualized access) is of benefit only to those who can "pay the price" and perpetuates market inequalities. In any case, the more "narrowly defined" interests – lower costs and higher profits – of private-sector partners do not favour social inclusion goals and objectives nor make them priorities. Indeed, Richmond (2004, 77) assails the "destructive trend" of transferring public community services to the non-governmental sector through such contracts and laments the negative impact of public-private partnerships on equitable access.

In addition to the private commercial sector, the notion of governance includes a role in policy development for voluntary not-for-profit organizations and professional groups. It is the case that a good number of community-level social services are delivered by voluntary agencies, usually publicly subsidized, whose mandate is to identify and meet the needs of particular communities. These community-sector agencies can act as advocates for disadvantaged or marginalized groups and be efficient and effective providers of quality services that are closely tailored to the needs of communities and client groups (Johnson 2002). Because they are non-profit and voluntary, profit-taking and market criteria for access are customarily eschewed. As well, social inclusion through leisure is a specific mandate for many of these bodies. The Canadian Parks and Recreation Association (2001), the national voice of the recreation profession in Canada, advocates that all levels of government engage all "stakeholder organizations" in addressing the exclusion from recreation of low-income families and their children. With regard to public-private partnerships, the Canadian Parks and Recreation Association (2001, 4) argues that the government should adopt a policy such that "infrastructure programs develop eligibility requirements that include community recreation facilities that support participation by low-income families." This would contractually bind private partners to providing the poor access to leisure facilities and services. This is an illustrative example of "strong professional support for leisure initiatives" in removing barriers to participation (Bramham, Henry, Mommaas, and van der Poel 1989, 280) and of a "professional community with a common interest in developing particular policies" (Coalter 1988, 133).

LEISURE, SOCIAL POLICY, AND THE FUTURE

What specific policies targeting leisure can people look forward to in the near future? Painter and Pierre (2005, 7) point to a "dilemma of growing instability, complexity and uncertainty in the policy environments of modern governments." With particular reference to leisure policy, there is an added dimension of uncertainty in that public leisure policy is fragmented because it reflects a traditional ideology in which provision and subsidy were largely reactive and residual. As well, leisure policy entails a wide range of collective, quasi-collective, and private consumption processes in an array of spheres that are relatively independent of each other. Thus, Coalter (1988, 192) questions "the degree to which a coherent, integrated and detailed public policy for leisure could be developed." Clearly, the instability of present global socio-economic conditions and the very complexity of "leisure" itself render contemporary leisure policy-making a difficult challenge to those concerned with social inclusion and development.

Present and future leisure policy will evolve within the context of *post-modernity*, *globalization*, and the information-based *New Economy*. In a treatise on "Postmodern Public Policy," Miller (2003) argues that any hope for a rational, consensual public dialogue leading to universal public social policy is futile. The best that can be hoped for in the post-modern era is a never-ending "conversation" in which local communities need to continuously negotiate and constantly revise policy on diverse social problems. This kind of locally based, "bottom-up" discourse leaves little room for central government policy development. This is one consequence of "the erosion of the social democratic consensus" inherent in post-modernity (Henry 2001, 66). A concurrent social transformation accompanying post-modernity is globalization.

As the world economy globalizes, the interconnectedness of international and transnational politics, according to many observers, means that there is less space in which national governments can manoeuvre. It is said that the interpenetration of global markets is such that the state is "deprived of some of its former control and leverage, while policy choice is conducted within a narrower range" (Painter and Pierre 2005, 13). Domestic policy under this new globalized political economy is more often reactive to transnational pressures than proactive with regard to internal social development needs. Consequently, it is said, the balance between the increasingly global market, the state, and civil society has been reset; there is "less opportunity for intervention at the level of nation-state to 'make a difference' in people's lives" (Henry 2001, 100). However, globalization has, in a perverse way, meant a growing role for local state policy as a "defender" of locality and localism. Hence, the national government's growing preoccupation with the transnational exchange "may also allow more policy space at the local (particularly the city) level" (Henry 2001, 238).

A third key contemporary social development linked to post-modernity and globalization is the emergence of the "New Economy" accompanying the explosive growth of information technology. The old industrial-based economy is in rapid decline and as the digital revolution takes roots globally, a new knowledge-based economy is on the rise. There is optimism that this New Economy "promises better educational opportunities, better capacity to access government, better and more responsive state services, and a host of other facilities that promise to integrate individuals into the broader society through information technology. For individuals living in disadvantaged communities ... these benefits could prove to be extremely important" (Mackenzie, Sheldrick, and Silver 2005, 5). Yet, there is little evidence that this is happening. On the contrary, the New Economy is seen to facilitate market outcomes rather than challenging market inequalities. While the state remains active in the New Economy, it is clear that state policy in this area is designed to operate within the logic of the market. "Consequently, there is very little state policy attempting to direct the benefits of the New Economy ... into historically disadvantaged communities" (Mackenzie, Sheldrick, and Shaver, 2005, 23).

Social development advocates call for state policies that consider how the benefits of the New Economy are distributed and that engage disadvantaged communities in order to develop their New Economy competencies (Mackenzie, Sheldrick, and Shaver, 2005). Development goals of social welfare and equity can be infused into the development of the New Economy but only through policies that are created through consultation and partnerships with disadvantaged communities; it cannot be "left to chance (i.e., the market)" or such communities risk further marginalization (Mackenzie, Sheldrick, and Shaver, 2005, 25).

Post-modernity, globalization, and the New Economy all present challenges for public policy aimed at social development and inclusion. All three socio-economic trajectories make for an increasingly "open market" to which public policy must adapt and find ways of reinventing itself. What worked in the welfare state era of the past will not necessarily work now. At the same time, "letting the market work" isn't working according to the Canadian Council on Social Development (2001c).

How can a society provide for social equality and equity in a rapidly changing, post-modern, globalized New Economy? The Canadian Council on Social Development (2001d, 2) believes that "there is a need to increase the provision of social security outside the market through new programs and services. Social investment now is crucial if we want to create a more inclusive and more prosperous society."

In order to meet the new challenges facing governments with respect to social policy, many have embraced a "third way" as an alternative to free market liberalism on the one hand and active state intervention on the other (Kapstein 1999). This is proposed as a new balance between the state and the market. Kapstein (1999) sees sharp reductions in social programs and rising income inequality as consequences of the present world economy. States, he argues, are failing to meet their obligations to those who are most vulnerable. A "progressive" third way strategy should, then, focus on mechanisms to assure that transnational, mobile capital pays its fair share for goods and services provided by governments and that "a substantial share of those revenues must be devoted to social policy" (Kapstein 1999, 12). This, however, is not simply a call to return to the old welfare state model (Battle, Mendelson, and Torjman 2005).

Scott (2006) advises that policies that served counties well a generation ago may no longer fit the dynamic social and economic realities of today. Factors such as post-modernity, globalization, and the New Economy are altering the old assumptions about labour markets, families, communities, and the primary institutions of the welfare state. Consequently, "a new fundamental rethinking of the post-war welfare edifice is needed, a new 'social architecture' to build an inclusive and prosperous Canada" (Scott 2006, 28). The welfare state is no longer relied on to protect people from the extremes of the market. Rather, the new idea is for the state to increase people's capacity to better compete in the market as a means reducing inequalities.

The accent now is not on regulating the market to ensure social welfare, but to empower people so that they are better equipped to satisfy their welfare needs in the market. The emphasis, then, is on furnishing people with the requisites needed for individual success. The attendant logic holds that inequalities that emanate from the markets can be overcome if we target policy so as to allow all to compete on an equal footing. Responsibility shifts from the state to the individual. The old welfare state fostered dependency, it is argued, while the new approach in policy is based on helping people accumulate financial assets, human capital, community resources, as well as information and knowledge such that they become more self-reliant. Proponents see this as a "hand-up" rather than the "hand-out" of the welfare state era. Greater weight is given to equality of "opportunity" than to equality of "condition" or "outcomes." Critics (Scott 2006; Myles 2005) argue that providing equal opportunities for people who start from a disadvantaged position (inequality of condition) does not lead to equality of outcomes. Policies need to address all aspects of equality – opportunity, condition, and outcome – if they are to succeed.

Despite "new architecture" policies to increase equality of opportunity for people, the market, by its very nature, still runs counter to the goal of promoting high levels of social inclusion. The realities of the current market environment (post-modernity, globalization, the New Economy) will continue to relegate the disadvantaged to the margins of society unless inventive policies are brought to bear. What is needed, according to Scott (2006, 30), are innovative policies and programs that work toward social inclusion:

> Ultimately, it is an extraordinary waste of human potential to relegate members of our community to the social and economic margins. Providing support to meet basic needs, respecting human rights, promoting the active participation of community members in social, economic, cultural and political life, and affording opportunities to learn over the life course are the key building blocks of a new social architecture for the 21st century.

It should not be forgotten that any policy of social inclusion is normative. The commitment to inclusion and equity is at odds with competing perspectives that are more exclusive and divisive in outlook. One can envision a continuum of social policy outlooks from inclusive/equality to exclusive/divisive. The degree to which one adheres to, or disagrees with, the aims of social inclusion rests on normative decisions that individuals, communities, and nations must make. The extent to which a state prioritizes social inclusion policy goals can be seen in its "will to act" on these convictions.

The old style welfare state promoted universal social programs as a kind of "insurance" against the vagaries of the market. Social assistance and unemployment insurance are examples of this universalistic approach to social welfare. In the post-modern, "post-welfare state" (Battle 2001) era, however, universality is construed, ironically, to be discriminatory precisely because it treats everyone the same, in an age where people are said to be increasingly different one from the other. Universal standards, then, should not be imposed comprehensively across an entire population because they fix norms *a priori* in theory and do not respond to particular contingencies in practice (Schram 2000). Contrasted with universal policies are those that address specific disadvantaged communities with targeted compensatory programs. Schram (2000) agrees that the state should not try to treat everybody alike according to liberal welfare state notions of equity. Instead, state policies should embrace a "compensatory" process that would be ready "to continually make exceptions and account for anomalies" (Schram 2000, 164).

Governments would have to let go of the "normative ethic" of the welfare state and embrace an "ethic of contingency" wherein society can respond as circumstances change. This is the post-modern condition. Consequently, policies of social inclusion need to move away from rigid universalism toward more compensation-based social inclusion policies. Notwithstanding this assertion, "universalism versus compensation" and "norm-based policies versus contingency policies" are false dichotomies. Schram (2000) outlines a "hybrid" approach that maintains the fundamental, universal, normative programs that insure security but combines them with compensation programs contingent on the specific circumstances of marginalized groups, not some elusive collective social norm.

In moving from one case to the next, programs should compensate those who do not qualify for universal programs, in an effort to deal with "more people, more problems, and more risks" (Schram

2000, 177). Schram (2000, 177) views this process as "Incremental Universalism" that combines universal programs and singular compensation programs such that compensation is "provided on a piecemeal basis, one group at a time, each justified according to a principle that legitimates their deservingness and invalidates their being left out." It supports universal welfare in that "many small programmatic changes could be initiated with the cumulative effect of creating a more universalistic welfare" approach (Schram 2000, 178).

The traditional welfare state model was universal and comprehensive as it was founded upon a widely held normative consensus. As has been discussed, this normative consensus has eroded and the welfare state has gone through a period of crisis such that the very notion of universality is under question. Paternalistic welfare, wherein the needy depended on the charity of the state or other agencies, predates the modern welfare state, and incremental compensatory approaches are nothing more than emergency social assistance. The new era, dominated by post-modernity, globalization, and the New Economy, necessitates a new approach to social inclusion policy, one that responds to specific needs in order to bring disadvantaged, marginalized communities up to universal standards of equity and quality of life. Schram (2000) characterizes this Incremental Universalism as being an elaborated social safety net. With specific reference to Canada, Battle (2001, 229) refers to this gradually but cumulatively evolving new architecture of social programs as "relentless incrementalism." Battle (2001, 229) posits that, despite opposition from some social advocacy groups, this new approach will ultimately "better serve Canada's evolving economy, society and polity than nostalgia for a universalist welfare state that never worked all that well."

The implications for leisure policy are initially that in order to achieve minimum universal levels of park, recreation, and leisure provision, basic normative standards have to be applied and sustained through redistributive taxation policies. This would address the growing income gap that acts as a major barrier to recreation and leisure participation by low-income people. In addition, specific disadvantaged communities require targeted policies and programs that are flexible and adaptable.

Non-market access (i.e., not determined by the individual's ability to pay) is key to reducing social exclusion, addressing the needs of disadvantaged communities, and extending the benefits of recreation and leisure to the poor and other marginalized groups.

Governments may look to the private sector for advantageous partnerships in leisure provision, but over the long run not-for-profit agencies and professional recreation associations may prove to be more useful allies in achieving the goals and objectives of social inclusion. While it is unlikely that a unifying broad consensus on leisure policy can be achieved, given the contemporary social and economic context, the local state or municipality would appear to be the most active and effective of public institutions in the leisure domain. Leisure policy, then, should favour local action on a case-by-case, community-by-community approach in order to promote social inclusion. This "incremental" approach, which works to bring the disadvantaged and marginalized up to community social standards, would appear to be the policy wave of the future for social development through leisure.

REFERENCES

Battle, K. 2001. "Relentless incrementalism: Deconstructing and reconstructing Canadian income security policy." *Review of Economic Performance and Social Progress* September: 183–229.

Battle, K., M. Mendelson, and S. Torjman. 2005. "The modernization mantra: Toward a new architecture for Canada's adult benefits." *Canadian Public Policy* 31(4):431–37.

Borsay, P. 2006. *A History of Leisure: The British Experience since 1500.* London: Palgrave-Macmillan.

Bramham, P., I. Henry, H. Mommaas, and H. van der Poel. 1989. *Leisure and Urban Processes: Critical Studies of Leisure Policy in Western European Cities.* London: Routledge.

Bramham, P., I. Henry, H. Mommaas, and H. van der Poel. 1993. *Leisure Policies in Europe.* London: Cab International.

Canadian Council on Social Development. 2001a. *Four Hypotheses about the Public Policy Significance of Youth Recreation.* Ottawa: Canadian Council on Social Development.

Canadian Council on Social Development. 2001b. *Recreation: Not Just Fun and Games.* Canadian Council on Social Development. http://www.ccsd.ca/pubs/2001/ccsd-cprn/nr.htm (accessed April 3, 2007).

Canadian Council on Social Development. 2001c. *Growing Together: Priorities for the 2001 Federal Budget.* Canadian Council on Social Development. Section Two. http://www.ccsd.ca/pr/bud01/bud01pt2.htm (accessed April 3, 2007).

Canadian Council on Social Development. 2001d. *Growing Together: Priorities for the 2001 Federal Budget.* Canadian Council on Social Development. Section One. http://www.ccsd.ca/pr/bud01/bud01pt1.htm (accessed April 3, 2007).

Canadian Council on Social Development. 2003. *Imagining a Future of Inclusion.* Ottawa: Canadian Council on Social Development.

Canadian Council on Social Development. 2004. *What Kind of Canada? A Call for a National Debate on the Canada Social Transfer.* Canadian Council on Social Development. http://www.ccsd.ca/pr/2004/social_transfer/st.htm (accessed April 3, 2007).

Canadian Parks and Recreation Association. 2001. *Everybody Gets to Play – Recreation without Barriers.* Ottawa: CPRA.

Canadian Parks and Recreation Association. 2005. *The Recreation and Parks Community Endorses a National Recreation and Sport Infrastructure Program.* Ottawa: CPRA.

Coalter, F. 1988. *Recreational Welfare: The Rationale for Public Leisure Policy.* Aldershot, UK: Avebury.

Dawson, D., C. Andrew, and J. Harvey. 1991. "Leisure, the local state and the welfare state: A theoretical overview." *Society and Leisure* 14(1): 191–217.

de Bettignies, J.-E., and T. W. Ross. 2004. "The economics of public-private partnerships." *Canadian Public Policy* 30(2): 135–54.

Donnelly, P., and J. Coakley. 2007. "The role of recreation in promoting social inclusion." Canadian Council on Social Development. http://www.ccsd.ca/subsites/inclusion/bp/pd.htm (accessed April 3, 2007).

Dunleavy, P. 1980. *Urban Political Analysis*. London: Macmillan.

Freiler, C. 2003. *From Risk to Human Development: Social Inclusion as a Focus of Individual and Collective Well-Being*. Canadian Council on Social Development. http://www.ccsd.ca/perception/2612/risk.htm (accessed April 3, 2007).

Freysinger, V., and J. Kelly. 2004. *21st Century Leisure: Current Issues*. 2nd ed. State College, PA: Venture Publishing.

Government of Canada. 2006. *The Budget Plan 2006: Focusing on Priorities*. Ottawa: Department of Finance Canada.

Gratton, C. and P. Taylor. 2000. *The Economics of Sport and Recreation*. London: Taylor and Francis.

Harvey, J., C. Andrew, and D. Dawson. 1990. "Le loisir municipal et l'état-providence." *Recherches Sociographiques* 31(1): 25–44.

Henry, I. 2001. *The Politics of Leisure Policy*, 2nd ed. London: Palgrave.

Johnson, A. 2002. "Whatever happened to social development?" Canadian Council on Social Development. http://www.ccsd.ca/pubs/2002/finance.htm (accessed April 3, 2007).

Kapstein, E. 1999. "A global third way: Social justice and the world economy." *World Policy Journal* 15(4): 1–14.

Mackenzie, M., B. Sheldrick, and J. Silver. 2005. *State Policies to Enhance the New Economy: A Comparative Analysis*. Winnipeg: Centre for Policy Alternatives-MB.

Levitas, R. 1996. "The concept of social exclusion and the new Durkheimian hegemony." *Critical Social Policy* 16(1):5–20.

Miller, H. 2003. *Postmodern Public Policy*. Albany: State University of New York Press.

Mirecki, G. 1992. "Shaping Canada's future ... The essential benefits of recreation." *Recreation Canada*. October: 8–9.

Myles, J. 2005. *Postponed Adulthood: Dealing with the New Economic Inequality*. Ottawa: Canadian Council on Social Development.

Painter, M., and J. Pierre. 2005. *Challenges to State Policy Capacity: Global Trends and Comparative Perspectives*. London: Palgrave-Macmillan.

Richmond, T. 2004. "Social inclusion as policy: Challenges and opportunities." *Horizons* 7(2): 75–77.

Robert Gordon University Center for Public Policy and Management. 2007. *An Introduction to Social Policy.* http://www2.rgu.ac.uk/publicpolicy/introduction/policy.htm (accessed April 3, 2007).

Schram, S. 2000. *After Welfare: The Culture of Postindustrial Social Policy.* New York: New York University Press.

Scott, K. 2006. *The World We Have: Towards a New Social Architecture.* Ottawa: Canadian Council on Social Development.

Searle, M., and R. Brayley. 2000. *Leisure Services in Canada: An Introduction,* 2nd ed. State College, PA: Venture Publishing.

Smale, B., and D. Reid. 2001. "Public policy on recreation and leisure in urban Canada." In *Urban Policy Issues: Canadian Perspectives,* ed. Fowler, E. and D. Siegel. Toronto: Oxford University Press.

Social Planning and Research Council of British Columbia. 2006. *Everybody's Welcome: A Social Inclusion Approach to Program Planning and Development for Recreation and Parks Services.* Vancouver: SPARC-BC.

2

Addressing Inadequate Leisure Access Policies through Citizen Engagement

Janna Taylor and Wendy Frisby

... to make effective use of public and political spaces ... a more deliberative process is needed: one that engages policy actors in critical reflections on pervasive policy discourses and the accepted wisdom of prevailing policy narratives, rather than simply in finding out about poor people's perceived needs. (Cornwall 2001, 64)

INTRODUCTION

As we and others have argued, although there have been numerous critiques of the public recreation system, it remains one of the few places for potential democratization of participation, especially for the one in six families living below the poverty line in Canada who cannot afford to participate in organized recreation offered by the private sector (Frisby, Alexander and Taylor 2010; National Council of Welfare 2004; Tirone 2003/2004). In this chapter, we begin by discussing how neo-liberalism and traditional approaches to policy development exclude poor citizens from public recreation. We then present our findings from a web-based analysis of the leisure access policies of thirty-three different communities in Canada. This analysis reveals three main leisure access policy types, all of which are problematic. Drawing on social inclusion theory and the growing body of literature on citizen engagement, we then outline the advantages, challenges, and strategies for involving marginalized citizens to develop new and more relevant policy alternatives. We conclude by offering future research directions, as leisure policy analysis remains an important but relatively unexplored area requiring further attention (Harvey 2001; Henry 2001).

Many urban and rural communities across the country have mandates and the infrastructures to provide public recreation for all citizens (Reid 1995; Searle and Brayley 2000), but existing leisure access policies are woefully inadequate. As a result, citizens living on low income are systematically excluded from participating in activities in their own communities by the very public institutions that have mandates for including them (Frisby, Reid, and Ponic 2007; Labonte 2004). The consequences of this irony are significant, as those with the lowest incomes have the poorest health status (Anderson 2000; Raphael 2003) and research has shown that recreation can contribute to health and well-being in a number of important ways (Ponic 2007; Reid 2004). We contend that the continuing erasure of those living in poverty from public recreation policy agendas is partly due to two interrelated factors: one, the rise of neo-liberalism in local government, and two, a top-down non-participatory approach to leisure access policy development.

Brodie (2005) provides a cogent explanation of how poor citizens do not fit with the market model that underpins the neo-liberal logic of governance that took hold in the 1980s and continues to drive policy-making in Canada today. For her, when the poor are seen as inadequate or dysfunctional market players, equity agendas have less policy relevance because those living in poverty have no market value. As a result, those who are most likely to live below the poverty line, including families headed by single mothers, Aboriginal people, immigrants, persons with disabilities, older women living alone, and visible minorities, are becoming increasingly marginalized as the gap between the rich and the poor widens (Anderson 2000; National Council of Welfare 2004). This is occurring because the neo-liberal governance paradigm, with its policy imperatives reflecting individualization, privatization, economic efficiencies, and a market orientation have effectively usurped the post-war welfare state that emphasized social rights, equality, and democracy (Arai and Reid 2003; Finkel 2006). This moves poverty and other equity issues off the public policy agenda because citizenship becomes associated with consumption and economic production (Anderson 2000; Kershaw 2005). In these ways, neo-liberalism blinds us to:

> the daily realities of living in gendered, raced and classed bodies and to the fact that these bodies are treated differently and unequally across the entire spectrum of social relations … providing little discursive or institutional space to make claims on the state on the basis of morality, fairness, collective difference, or structural inequality (Brodie 2005, 91).

For Foucault (1997), "governmentality" refers to the complex pressures that cause individuals and institutions to conform to oppressive policies by relying on uniform rather than multifaceted understandings of certain groups. Thus, those who have benefited from the new economic and political order are increasingly likely to interpret both their prosperity and other's poverty as measures of individual achievements, rather than as resulting from structural inequalities that are institutionally embedded in public policy (Brodie 2005; Houlihan 2005). Tokenism, being ignored, being stereotyped, having policies and programs designed for them with no input, assuming that middle class professionals know what is best for them, and that wealthier citizens naturally deserve or want more are just some of the ways that people experiencing poverty feel excluded (Reid 2004; Swanson 2001). According to Swanson (2001, 22), this results in poor-bashing and "policies that take hope from people."

To counter class-based social inequalities, there is a growing body of literature calling for citizen engagement in policy development. Such "bottom-up" approaches are being used in other fields to open up spaces for the representation of the perspectives of people experiencing poverty on policy that addresses, not only the content, but also the structure of the policy process, along with the attitudes and behaviours of policy-makers (Brock and McGee 2002). This requires attention to subaltern voices to interrupt taken-for-granted structures inscribed through unbalanced power relations (Anderson 2000), and leisure researchers have a role to play in surfacing silenced perspectives (Frisby, Reid, Millar, and Hoeber 2005; Frisby 2006).

A participatory approach to policy development aligns with contemporary theorizing about health promotion because one's health is thought to be tied to the amount of control that people have over their daily lives (WHO 1986). Ruzek, Clarke, and Olsen (1997) argue that community is the ideal site for health promotion because it is the fulcrum between individuals and the structural factors affecting their health. When applied to the leisure field, the perspectives of people experiencing poverty on the benefits of public recreation and the pitfalls of current policies can reveal improvements and new alternatives (Frisby, Alexander, Taylor, Tirone, Watson, Harvey, and Laplante 2005). This is important because we will show that current leisure access policies are more focused on ensuring healthy fiscal bottom lines for recreation departments in a neo-liberal era than on fostering the meaningful participation of marginalized citizens in community recreation to promote health, social development, and other goals.

This schism between neo-liberalism and social inequality became very evident when we conducted a web-based analysis of leisure access policies in Canada. Due to numerous problems with current policies and application procedures, it is highly likely that the policies themselves are yet another deterrent to participation.

A WEB-BASED ANALYSIS OF SELECTED LEISURE ACCESS POLICIES IN CANADA

Leisure access policies are increasingly being made available to the public through information and communication technologies (ICTs) on the web. While citizens living on low income are the least likely to have access to such technologies in their homes, raising concerns about who controls and has access to the information, ICTs are being seen as tools that can create public space for deliberative citizen engagement (Gurstein 2007). As a starting point for learning more about leisure access policies, Janna Taylor conducted a web-based policy search of three communities that varied in population and geographic region in each of the ten provinces and the Yukon/Territories in Canada, for a total of thirty-three communities. Janna was well qualified to undertake this task because she is a former Director of a Recreation and Parks Department, a former President of the British Columbia Recreation and Parks Association (BCRPA), and has worked as a consultant and teacher in the field for several years. As a result, she is highly familiar with recreation department websites and the language associated with leisure access policies.

The web-based analysis was not meant to be comprehensive because it is possible that leisure access policies are embedded in programs for specific user groups that were not searched (e.g., for seniors and persons with disabilities) and the policies may have been advertised in other ways (e.g., in print material like leisure program guides or upon request at various venues). In addition, there may be policy alternatives in Canada other than those revealed in this search. None-the-less, the analysis does provide a snapshot of the difficulties that anyone would have locating them on the web, along with some of the dominant policy types and problems associated with the leisure access application process.

Given Janna's familiarity with public recreation, it was arguably easier for her to locate leisure access policies on the web than it would be for most citizens. However, she encountered considerable difficulty after locating the official home page for each municipality or regional district. Her troubles first began when there were a variety of different names for public recreation departments because terms like Community Services, Culture, Leisure, Recreation, Parks, Public Relations, and Sport appeared in different combinations as shown in Table 2.1.

Table 2.1: Different Names for Regional or Municipal Government Departments Offering Recreation

- Community Services
- Leisure and Parks
- Leisure Services
- Recreation
- Recreation and Culture
- Recreation and Leisure Services
- Recreation and Parks
- Recreation, Parks and Culture
- Recreation and Public Relations
- Parks and Community Services
- Parks and Recreation
- Parks, Recreation and Culture
- Sport and Recreation

This lack of consistency could create confusion for citizens attempting to find out what is available in their communities, especially for those who are transient and encounter different department and policy names each time they move. In smaller communities, reference was often only made to stand-alone facilities such as arenas and pools, rather than to specific departments. We chose not to reveal the names of the thirty-three communities because our goal was to provide an aggregate snapshot of policy alternatives, not to criticize specific departments or local governments. However, we do hope that our analysis will be informative to local policy-makers and that changes in the ways policies are developed and communicated to the public will be considered.

DEPARTMENT MISSION STATEMENTS

To situate the web-based leisure access policy analysis, department mission statements were first analyzed and the main themes appear in Table 2.2. Interestingly, no two mission statements were the same and only 45 per cent of the departments even provided one on their web site. The lack of mission statements was surprising, given that they are thought to provide a basis for internal strategic planning while communicating to the public what recreation programs and services are intended to accomplish (Searle and Brayley 2000). Only two mission statements referred to "respecting diversity" and only one expressed a commitment to providing "affordable recreation," although several did make reference to "accessibility," which could be interpreted in a number of different ways (e.g., wheel-chair accessible or affordable). Only one website emphasized "including all ages and sexes," and none referred specifically to the need to provide programs for residents regardless of class, race, ethnicity, religion, (dis)ability, or sexuality. Several of the mission statements included reference to personal, social, economic, and environmental benefits, presumably from the Canadian Parks and Recreation Benefits Catalogue (1997) that was developed to help communities justify public recreation services.

For those communities with mission statements on their web sites (55%), promoting health, quality of life and well-being; celebrating heritage; respecting the environment; promoting active lifestyles; and building community capacity were emphasized. However, these themes were not mentioned consistently across communities, suggesting that these departments have different visions of what their mandates are. In a further example, some mission statements did not mention citizen benefits or outcomes, as reference was only made to functional operations such as "developing, managing and preserving facilities, parks and open spaces."

Table 2.2: Themes Appearing in Departmental Mission Statements.

- Providing high quality, accessible opportunities for all residents.
- Providing enjoyable leisure opportunities to citizens and visitors to contribute positively to civic pride and the economy.
- Providing services that are accessible and affordable.
- Providing programs to meet the needs of a diverse and changing population.
- Promoting health and well-being, recognizing and respecting diversity, celebrating heritage and respecting the environment.
- Providing supervised recreational opportunities for all (including all ages and both sexes) in a safe, clean, and friendly environment and in a fiscally responsible manner.
- Providing activities that encourage active, healthy lifestyles and quality of life.
- Building community capacity.
- Empowering citizens to participate in positive community development.
- Developing, managing, and preserving facilities, parks, and open spaces.
- Managing and maintaining assets for shareholders.
- Recommending actions and policy to Council.
- Providing personal, social, economic, and environmental benefits.

A neo-liberal logic was very apparent in some of the language used in the mission statements and was particularly evident in the following quote taken directly from one of the web sites: "Department staff are challenged to commit to the belief that the assets they manage and maintain are, in reality, assets of the shareholders of our business – the citizens of this City." Referring to public recreation as a "business," to citizens as "shareholders," and to facilities and programs as "assets," reflects a business or market-oriented model, rather than one based on values of inclusion, accessibility, and social equality. Other evidence of neo-liberalism appeared in efficiency-oriented statements about providing recreation opportunities "in a fiscally responsible way" or to "contribute positively to the economy." Accountability, another key feature of a business approach to service delivery (Thibault, Kikulis, and Frisby 2004), was reflected in statements about departmental roles of "recommending actions and policy to Council."

LEISURE ACCESS POLICIES

The web-based search was also complicated because there was no consistency in what leisure access policies were called across the country, and in many communities, especially smaller ones, such policies were unavailable on the web. Examples of the labels found (sometimes couched as programs instead of policies) appear in Table 2.3. The inconsistency in policy labels makes it extremely difficult for citizens to locate and interpret them. In addition, most of the policies only emphasized financial assistance, even though there are numerous other barriers to participation encountered by poor citizens (e.g., child care, transportation, unfamiliarity with the public recreation system, racism and other forms of discrimination; Frisby, Alexander et al. 2005; Paraschak 2007; Tirone 1999/2000; Tirone 2003/04). Potentially distasteful names like the "Charity Policy" will be insulting to those who see participation as a right of citizenship, rather than as a form of charity to be doled out by local government (Harvey 2001). Cute names like *P.R.O. Kids, H.R.M. Kids, P.E.A.R.L.,* and *R.E.A.L.* may contain positive messages that counteract stereotypes associated with poverty, but they largely disguise the policy intent, making them difficult to find, especially as most citizens will not know what these acronyms stand for when conducting web searches. The *P.R.O. Kids* policy statement used in three of the communities outlined a number of benefits to participation, fund-raising had been done to supplement the program, and it was acknowledged that "fees are only one of the barriers to participation." As a result, assistance was available to cover the costs of supplies, equipment, and transportation to and from activities. This is important because initiatives that attempt to increase access to recreation without taking the overall living conditions of the target population into account are unlikely to be successful (Donnelly and Coakley 2002).

Table 2.3: Different Labels for Leisure Access Policies in Thirty-three Regional or Municipal Government Departments.

- Affordable Fun Program
- Care Program
- Charity Policy
- Fee Assistance Program
- Financial Assistance Program
- Free Programs
- H.R.M. Kids (stands for Healthy Recreation Motivates Kids)
- Kids Recreation Fund
- Jump Start Program
- Leisure Access Card
- Leisure Access Policy
- Leisure Access Program
- Leisure for Less
- P.E.A.R.L. (stands for Participation for Everyone in Active Recreation and Leisure)
- P.R.O. Kids (stands for Positive Recreation Opportunities for Kids)
- R.E.A.L. (stands for Recreation Experience and Leisure)
- Recreation for All
- Recreation Subsidies Available for People Living on Low Income

Some policy labels were problematic because they targeted only certain segments of the population (e.g., mostly children and youth), which excludes others who also live on low incomes, such as the mothers of these children who are often single parents. In addition, teens will not likely find the label "*Kids*" appealing. Multilingual web site information was noticeably lacking, as thirty of the web sites were in English only and three were in French only. This was surprising given Canada's official bilingual status and because of the growing immigrant population who do not speak either English or French as their first language. None of the web sites were interactive. Communication was one-way originating from the department and there was no space for citizens to ask questions, voice complaints, or offer alternatives to existing leisure access policies and procedures.

Some departments partnered with corporate sponsors to offer programs for free or at reduced fees. While this might be viewed as positive corporate social responsibility, it begs the question as to whether it is appropriate to be marketing products through this form of privatization to citizens who are the least able to pay (Thibault, Kikulis, and Frisby 2004). Several other departments partnered only with other public and non-profit organizations to provide free programs, and this could be an effective marketing strategy if the clients of these partner organizations are on low income and if recreation opportunities are adequately communicated to them.

What is not known is whether families living on low income had any input into free recreation program offerings or if they find any of them appealing. Our previous research demonstrated that male and female youth and parents from low income families saw numerous benefits to participation that were tied to health and social development and expressed interest in providing input into recreation policy-making and programming (Frisby, Alexander et al. 2005). However, none of them had ever been consulted and they were not optimistic that change would occur even if they were. The youth and parents largely found existing direct delivery offerings unappealing, were unaware of leisure access policies, and pointed to a number of barriers in addition to costly program fees. For example, they talked about experiences with racism, sexism, and ageism in addition to identifying other class-based constraints like being unable to afford transportation costs because recreation facilities were seldom available in their low income neighbourhoods (Frisby, Alexander et al. 2005). When the leisure access policies in their communities were read to them as part of the previous study, most of the youth and parents indicated they would not apply for a fee subsidy because the application procedures were cumbersome and dehumanizing.

Policy Types

Three main leisure access policy types were uncovered in the web-based search that we label as: i) the invisible or hard-to-find policy, ii) the prove poverty policy, and iii) the offer free programs policy. On only 31 per cent of the web sites was it possible to locate a specific leisure access policy, although some did refer to offering free programs. Of the few policies that provided clear instructions (30%), residents were referred to program guides, were notified that application forms could be downloaded or picked up at any facility, and were provided with the name of a specific contact person. Testimonials of how parents and youth had accessed the policy and benefited from participation were provided (e.g., increased self-esteem, healthy active living, personal growth, increased knowledge and skill development) and a listing of free activities and programs was usually available. However, as the following discussion of the policy types reveals, all three policy types were problematic, even when the application process was clearly stated, which was seldom the case.

The invisible or hard-to-find policy. In 60 per cent of the communities, Janna was either unable to find the equivalent of a leisure access policy or it took her more than thirty minutes to locate it. Although no specific policy was found in some cases, there was evidence that free or very low cost programs are being offered, so these were categorized as reflecting the "offer free programs" policy type (27%), rather than the "invisible or hard-to-find policy" (33%). Typically no details were provided about how one qualified or applied for the "hard-to-find policy."

Those interested in applying were asked to phone or drop by to inquire about a subsidy.

Leisure access policies were more difficult to find in smaller communities, perhaps because they rely less on web-based communications or because there is an assumption that residents will come in and inquire if they want one. In these instances, little evidence was found of public policy intervention to offset market imperfections that make it difficult or impossible for the poor to participate in commercialized forms of organized recreation (Henry 2001). This finding raises questions about whether these departments of local government simply do not have leisure access policies or whether they have inadequate ICT technology to advertise them. In either case, it would appear that reducing inequalities associated with access is not a major priority.

The offer free programs policy. Some communities do not have an explicit leisure access policy posted on the web but nevertheless offer a number of free programs (e.g., youth centres, play groups, after school programs, public swimming and skating), some of which are co-sponsored by commercial and non-profit organizations. Some of the free offerings were extensive and well advertised, even though no explicit policy was provided. In a small rural region involving a partnership between a number of districts and towns, a publication was put together to "showcase activities under $2 offered within regional recreation facilities and extends to cover parks, trails, community events, teen centers, transit information, plus valuable community contact information." On other web sites, there was considerable rhetoric about providing free programs, but restrictions like the following were found in some cases: "Due to increased demand for this service and the limited funding available, opportunities are restricted to one free program per registration season." This statement acknowledges that demand for free programs is increasing but once again uses an economic rationale for not making them more widely available.

The prove poverty policy. Of the communities that did have policies, the prove poverty policy type was the most common (40%) and was usually found in larger cities. It was characterized by "providing proof of financial need" by having provincial ministry officials or recreation staff confirm that total family incomes from all sources was below low income guidelines as stipulated on the application forms. Other forms of surveillance associated with this policy included having a Photo ID card, birth certificates, or medical cards, but it was not always clear if this differed from what other patrons are required to provide. Some of these policies were more exclusionary as only Canadian citizens or permanent residents could apply, suggesting that recent immigrants were not eligible.

There was considerable variety in what applicants received, ranging from some free programs to fee reductions ranging from 20 to 75 per cent, to small discounts (e.g., $2 off) for some admissions. In other cases, residents were allowed only one subsidized program per season. In one case, the subsidy was paid directly to the partnering organization offering the program. In another case, applicants were asked what they could contribute financially and whether they could "work off" the subsidy by volunteering, although this did not appear to be required. This stipulation ignores the disadvantages associated with poverty that would make volunteering very difficult (Arai and Reid 2003) and reflects an economic efficiency discourse whereby one must contribute their labour in order to receive something for free or at a reduced rate. In other communities, residents were simply asked to visit their local recreation centre to obtain more information, raising questions about how well trained staff were to answer questions, if approached. It is quite conceivable that having to travel to the centre to ask for the subsidy from an unspecified person could deter many from doing so.

Another variation on this policy type was found on two web sites that indicated financial assistance could be obtained as long as funding was available. In both cases, assistance was based on a first-come basis and applicants were required to have someone other than a relative verify their financial situation (e.g., a social worker, clergy, coach, or teacher). This language reinforces that those on low income are 'suspected cheats or freeloaders' who may be trying to abuse the system, so they must have a reputable person vouch that they are indeed poor. Reid (2004) describes this as a form of institutional exclusion whereby policies deter people from getting involved. Budget shortfalls were also being used as a rationale for not having to provide financial assistance for everyone who may be eligible, once again reflecting an economic imperative.

In sum, this web-based policy analysis reveals several inadequacies in leisure access policies that will likely deter most citizens living on low income from applying for them. This raises the questions about how sincere recreation departments are in catering to all citizens when they are increasingly under pressure to operate from a business-like mindset (Thibault, Kikulis, and Frisby 2004). Yet in a recent national survey (National Council of Welfare 2007), 97 per cent of respondents agreed or strongly agreed that governments should put a higher priority on fighting poverty in Canada, and reducing the isolation associated with not being able to afford social activities was rated as being of high importance. This confirms Donnelly and Coakley's (2002) argument that there is widespread concern for human rights, including the right to participate in recreation, that counter the dominant neo-liberal ideological climate characterized by user fees, privatization, and the ongoing reduction of opportunities, especially for the most vulnerable of citizens. This suggests that class-based exclusion represent a potential moment of resistance to neo-liberal logics that heighten hierarchies of inequality (Labonte 2004). Phillips (2006) argues that to address such exclusions, new collaborative relationships between government, civil society organizations, and citizens must to be forged.

CITIZEN ENGAGEMENT IN POLICY DEVELOPMENT

Little is known in the academic arena about how leisure access policies are developed, but given the findings presented above and the rational technical approach to policy development that has been mainstream in public administration since the 1950s (Brock and McGee 2002), we may be safe in assuming that policy is largely designed and implemented in a top-down fashion. In a neo-liberal era, this is because policy-makers are assuming that citizens living on low income are unable or unwilling to participate in the development of policy alternatives (Arai and Reid 2003) and are a drain on scarce resources, making it financially imprudent to encourage their widespread participation.

In contrast, the main assumption underlying participatory approaches that arose in the 1990s are that the intended beneficiaries of policy deliberations have important information to share that can result in imaginative and cost-effective policy alternatives (Berner and Phillips 2005). Rather than "offloading" or adopting a "do it yourself" strategy that leaves people experiencing poverty to fend for themselves, collaboration is crucial. This is because citizens can more readily interpret problems affecting their lives and consider relevant ways of addressing them, but active government involvement is required because they control resources and are ultimately responsible for public policy. Building on Freire's (1970) notion of *conscientization* where people begin to connect their personal situations to the larger structures surrounding them, social learning is integral to dismantling existing power relations when distant policy-makers have direct exposure to situations of poverty and when citizens learn more about how policy-making is conducted. According to Brock and McGee (2002, 10), it is this type of exposure and mutual learning that can provoke changes in vision, policy, and practice.

Involving citizens lies at the core of discussions about modernizing government by bringing new and more varied forms of knowledge into the policy-making arena. Phillips and Orsini (2002, 8) outline a number of steps that are necessary for this to occur, which would certainly require a radical shift in how public recreation in Canada currently operates. These steps include:

1. mobilizing interest by creating a public space for debate;

2. claims making – allowing individuals and organizations to express claims, positions, and values on public policy issues;

3. knowledge acquisition – sharing expert and experiential knowledge;

4. spanning and bridging – across networks and communities;

5. convening and deliberating – exercising citizenship skills and forming horizontal bonds of affiliation;

6. community capacity building – creating social capital through the emergence of leaders and through collective action that helps communities attract financial, human, and technical resources;

7. analysis and synthesis – reporting results of citizen involvement for policy-making; and

8. transparency and feedback – demonstrating how public input was used and whether it made a difference.

Leading local governments are at the forefront of developing innovative methods for citizen engagement, including interactive websites, citizen juries and panels, community development, and task forces (Lowndes, Pratchett, and Stoker 2001). However, while we see potential for the revitalization of public recreation using citizen engagement, we are not naïve to the significant challenges that arise when we consider who might participate and how. The process of "decontextualizing local people's knowledge" has brought about concerns about representation and filtering (Cornwall 2001). Apathy caused by previous exclusions, negative attitudes towards local authorities, a lack of awareness of opportunities, and gaps between consultation and policy approval are just some of the challenges to evoking meaningful and representative citizen engagement (Lowndes et al. 2001). It is also idealistic to assume that all citizens on low income will be willing and able to participate in policy development given the significant demands in their daily lives or that a unitary view of how to proceed will arise (Berner and Phillips 2005).

According to Chalip (1996), policy development processes that engage citizens should improve the human condition by empowering people to ameliorate difficult or oppressive social circumstances. However, the links between policy input and policy change are complex and there are no guarantees that information elicited from citizens will actually be considered by policy-makers (Anderson 2000). Rather than viewing the policy process in a rational or systemic way, the challenge is negotiating competing ideologies and unequal power relations amongst diverse collaborators, while considering how structural factors impede or enhance the process (Bryant 2002; Donnelly and Coakley 2002). In Bryant's (2002) framework, four policy outcomes are possible when citizens and policy-makers engage in policy development. These include: i) no policy change (e.g., when conflicting ideologies cannot be successfully negotiated or satisfactory alternatives are not identified), ii) normal policy change (e.g., when only minor adjustments to existing policies are made), iii) gradual or incremental paradigmatic change that result in major shifts in policy over time (e.g., when an alternative policy is implemented in stages), and iv) radical policy change (e.g., when there is a relatively swift and complete shift to a new policy model). In a public recreation context, incremental paradigmatic change or radical policy change is what is needed. Despite the challenges involved, citizen engagement offers a new way for reconfiguring relations with local government and for developing leisure access policies that offset some of the problems identified.

Concluding Thoughts

Finkel (2006, 3) defines social policy as "the set of non-market decisions, public and private, that determine the distribution of wealth to individuals and families and the degree of availability of human services to all members of society." Since the rise of neo-liberalism, social policy has increasingly become a means for avoiding the redistribution of resources in favour of the disadvantaged. Therefore, it becomes easy to dismiss all state actions as detrimental to those living in poverty, but we counter that grassroots participation can lead to improved social policy.

The three dominant leisure access policy types uncovered through our web-based analysis revealed the values and assumptions that influence policy choice and administrative practice. There was little mention of social inclusion, as concerns about policy being "abused" by wealthier citizens are reflected in the invisible or hard-to-find and requiring proof of poverty approaches. The classist nature of existing policies only marginally dealt with material inequalities and did not account for other material, cultural, and institutional forms of exclusion (Reid 2004). Because more women than men and more persons of colour than whites live in poverty, these policies are also gendered and racialized. Ageism is also very evident, as many of the policies targeted only children and youth, which ignores the fact that many parents and older citizens in Canada also live in poverty.

It was surprising that so few recreation departments provided mission statements and that there was considerable variability in how they publicly convey their mandates and leisure access policies. Given the confusion resulting from the different department names, mission statements, and policy labels, citizen engagement could, at the very least, provide input on terms and procedures that would be relevant to them. Input from citizens would not only reduce confusion but would likely uncover new approaches to encouraging meaningful participation and policy development. Additional research is required on whether interactive ICTs are an effective way to foster dialogue with citizens living on low income and what supports would need to be in place to foster this.

While academic interest in poverty policy analysis has grown in other fields because of both perceived failures and successes of government initiatives (Brock and McGee 2002; Cornwall 2001; Grindle and Thomas 1991), we were surprised that so little research has been done in the public recreation field. As others have argued, this may be in part due to the centrality of work rather than leisure as a policy imperative for dealing with poverty (Reid 1995; Reid and Golden 2005). Furthering this line of research could increase our theoretical understanding of the contemporary roles of government in leisure access policy-making, the relationships between the state and civil society, along with the contextual factors and dominant ideologies shaping policy debates. Additional research is also needed on the strengths and weaknesses of different policy-making processes, how policy is tied to resource distribution, and the impact of policy on citizens living below the poverty line. However, we agree with Houlihan (2005, 166), who argues that if policy development and implementation are to be evaluated, research should not "become preoccupied with strengthening neo-positivist approaches by attempting to identify ever more precise quantitative measures of impact and prescriptions." Rather, it must take politics, power relations, structure, agency, and subjectivities into account. As Cornwall (2001) notes, the challenge that lies ahead is in recognizing that poverty and exclusion cannot be tackled by simply enlisting participants in projects or programs. Active citizen engagement offers the potential for a new social order that can heighten the role of public recreation in social inclusion.

References

Anderson, J. M. 2000. "Gender, race, poverty, health and discourses of health reform in the context of globalization: A postcolonial feminist perspective in policy research." *Nursing Inquiry* 7: 220–29.

Arai, S. M., and D. G. Reid. 2003. "Impacts of a neo-liberal policy shift on citizenship and the voluntary sector." *Canadian Review of Social Policy* 52: 67–91.

Berner, E. and B. Phillips. 2005. "Left to their own devices? Community self-help between alternative development and neo-liberalism." *Community Development Journal* 40(1): 17–29.

Bryant, T. 2002. "Role of knowledge in public health and health promotion policy change." *Health Promotion International* 17(1): 89–98.

Brock, K., and R. McGee. 2002. *Knowing Poverty: Critical Reflections on Participatory Research and Policy.* London: Earthscan.

Brodie, J. 2005. The great undoing: State formation, gender politics, and social policy in Canada. In *Open Boundaries: A Canadian Women's Studies Reader,* ed. B.A. Crow and L. Gotell. 87-96, Toronto: Prentice Hall.

Chalip, L. 1996. "Critical policy analysis: The illustrative case of New Zealand sport policy development." *Journal of Sport Management* 10: 310–24.

Cornwall, A. 2001. *Beneficiary, Consumer, Citizen: Perspectives on Participation for Poverty Reduction.* Sida Studies No. 2. Stockholm: Sida.

Canadian Parks and Recreation Benefits Catalogue. 1997. Ottawa: Canadian Parks and Recreation Association.

Dawson, D. 1985. "On the analysis of class and leisure." *Loisir et Société/ Society and Leisure* 8(2): 563–72.

Donnelly, P., and J. Coakley. 2002. "The role of recreation in promoting social inclusion." Toronto: Laidlaw Foundation.

Finkel, A. 2006. *Social Policy and Practice in Canada.* Waterloo: Wilfrid Laurier University Press.

Foucault, M. 1997. *Discipline and Punish: The Birth of the Prison.* London: Pantheon.

Freire, P. 1970. *Pedagogy of the Oppressed.* New York: Herder and Herder.

Frisby, W. 2006. "Rethinking researcher roles, responsibilities and relationships in community development research." *Leisure/Loisir* 30(2): 437–45.

Frisby, W., T. Alexander, and J. Taylor. 2010. "Play is not a frill: Poor youth facing the past, present, and future of public recreation in Canada." In *Lost Kids: Vulnerable Children and Youth in Canada, the U.S., and Australia, 1900 to the Present,* ed. M. Gleason, T. Myers, L. Paris, and V. Strong-Boag. 215-229, Vancouver: UBC Press.

Frisby, W., T. Alexander, J. Taylor, S. Tirone, C. Watson, J. Harvey, and D. Laplante. 2005. *Bridging the Recreation Divide: Listening to Youth and Parents from Low-Income Families across Canada.* Ottawa: Canadian Parks and Recreation Association.

Frisby, W., C. J. Reid, S. Millar, and L. Hoeber. 2005. "Putting 'participatory' into participatory forms of action research." *Journal of Sport Management* 19: 367–86.

Frisby, W., C. Reid, and P. Ponic. 2007. "Levelling the playing field: Promoting the health of poor women through a community development approach to recreation." In *Sport and Gender in Canada,* ed. P. White and K. Young, 120–36. Don Mills, ON: Oxford University Press.

Grindle, M., and J. Thomas. 1991. *Public Choices and Policy Change.* Baltimore: Johns Hopkins University Press.

Gurstein, P. 2007. "Creating digital public space: Implications for deliberative engagement." In *Learning Civil Societies: Shifting Context for*

Democratic Planning and Governance, ed. P. Gurstein and L. Angeles, 89–117. Toronto: University of Toronto Press.

Harvey, J. 2001. "The role of sport and recreation policy in fostering citizenship: The Canadian experience." In Building Citizenship: Government and Service Provision in Canada, ed. J. Jenson, J. Harvey, W. Kimlicka, A. Maoni, E. Schragge, P. Greafe, and J.M. Fontan, 23–46. Ottawa: Canadian Policy Research Networks.

Henry, I. 2001. The Politics of Leisure Policy. London: Palgrave.

Houlihan, B. 2005. "Public sector sport policy: Developing a framework for analysis." International Review for the Sociology of Sport 40(2): 163–85.

Kershaw, P. 2005. Carefair: Rethinking the Responsibilities and Rights of Citizenship. Vancouver: UBC Press.

Labonte, R. 2004. "Social inclusion/exclusion: Dancing the dialectic." International Health Promotion 19(1): 115–21.

Lowndes, V., L. Pratchett, and G. Stoker. 2001. "Trends in public participation: Part 2 – citizens' perspectives." Public Administration 79(2): 445–55.

National Council of Welfare. 2004. Poverty Profile 2001. Ottawa: National Council of Welfare.

National Council of Welfare. 2007. Report on Responses to the Poverty and Income Security Questionnaire. Ottawa: Minister of Public Works and Government Services Canada.

Paraschak, V. 2007. "Doing race, doing gender: First Nations, 'sport,' and gender relations." In Sport and Gender in Canada, ed. K. Young and P. White, 137–54. Don Mills, ON: Oxford University Press.

Phillips, S. D. 2006. "The intersection of governance and citizenship in Canada: Not quite the third way," IRPP Policy Matters 7(4): 1–32.

Phillips, S. D., and M. Orsini. 2002. Mapping the Links: Citizen Involvement in Policy Processes. CPRN Discussion Paper. Ottawa: Canadian Policy Research Networks.

Ponic, P. 2007. Embracing complexity in community-based health promotion: Inclusion, power and poor women's health. PhD diss., University of British Columbia.

Reid, D. 1995. *Work and Leisure in the 21st Century: From Production to Citizenship*. Toronto: Wall & Emerson.

Reid, Donald G., and B. Leigh Golden. 2005. "Non-work and leisure activity and socially marginalized women: The issue of integration." *Canadian Review of Social Policy* 55: 39–65.

Raphael, D. 2003. "When social policy is health policy: Why increasing poverty and low income threatens Canadians' health and health care system." *Canadian Review of Social Policy* 51: 9–29.

Reid, C. 2004. *The Wounds of Exclusion: Poverty, Women's Health and Social Justice*. Edmonton, AB: Qualitative Institute Press.

Robb, C. 1999. *Can the Poor Influence Policy? Participatory Poverty Assessments in the Developing World*. Washington: World Bank.

Ruzek, S. B., A. E. Clarke, and V. L. Olsen. 1997. "Social, biomedical, and feminist models of women's health." In *Women's Health: Complexities and Differences*, ed. S. B. Ruzek, A. E. Clarke, and V. L. Olesen, 11–28. Columbus: Ohio State University Press.

Searle, M. S., and R. E. Brayley. 2000. *Leisure Services in Canada*. State College, PA: Venture Publishing.

Swanson, J. 2001. *Poor-bashing: The Politics of Exclusion*. Toronto: Between the Lines.

Thibault, L., L. Kikulis, and W. Frisby. 2004. "Partnerships between local government sport and leisure departments and the commercial sector: Changes, complexities, and consequences." In *The Commercialisation of Sport*, ed. T. Slack, 119–40. London: Frank Cass.

Tirone, S. 1999/2000. "Racism, indifference and the leisure experiences of South Asian Canadian teens." *Leisure/Loisir* 24(1): 89–114.

Tirone, S. 2003/2004. "Evening the playing field: Recreation in a low-income Canadian community." *Leisure/Loisir* 28(1–2): 155–74.

WHO (World Health Organization). 1986. *Ottawa Charter for Health Promotion*. Ottawa.

NOTES

1   Public recreation policies de-
     signed to include citizens living
     on low income have a variety
     of labels. We use "leisure access
     policy" because: i) it suggests
     that reduced fees alone will not
     reduce all the barriers to partici-
     pation, ii) it is not limited to a
     particular group (e.g., children
     and youth), and iii) this termin-
     ology is commonly used in pub-
     lic recreation.

Part Two:
Leisure and Alternative
Policy Frameworks
for Health and Social
Development

The chapters in this section offer alternative ways of conceptualizing social policy. In these chapters, the authors speak to the ways in which current social policy and approaches further exclude people who are already marginalized in Canadian society. Offering three alternative policy frameworks, these chapters challenge us to understand what are often deemed to be personal issues as social issues, to reconsider the situation of leisure within policy, and to understand individuals in the broader relational and community contexts in which they live.

Chapter 3 examines the role of leisure policy in poverty reduction. Reid, Golden, and Katerberg describe the consequences of poverty in Canada, suggesting policy options that move beyond viewing poverty as an economic problem with an economic solution. Instead, they argue the need to consider issues of human development, self-worth and dignity – accomplishment over accumulation – in poverty reduction strategies. Considering the complicating factors at the roots of poverty, they present a transformational model for social policy, emphasizing social and psychological aspects of human development through both work and leisure. With an emphasis on social cohesion and social solidarity, the authors discuss the value of "serious leisure" and recommend a shift in emphasis to "worthfare" rather than welfare to move us beyond a work-dominated society. The authors of this chapter suggest that leisure's role in the social policy arena has been underestimated in the past and needs to be made more central for those who are marginalized in society.

In Chapter 4, Sherry Dupuis focuses on improving the lives of persons with dementia and their families through enhanced social policy, leisure policy, and practice. Dupuis challenges traditional models that defined Canada's care for persons with Alzheimer's disease or a related dementia (ADRD) with a planning framework emphasizing active personal and community engagement of persons with dementia and their families. Principles such as respect for relationships, diversity and inclusiveness, fairness, and individual and community rights provide the foundation for three interdependent planning pillars – creation of an informed society; enabling and supportive environments; personal, social, and system connectedness – deemed central to the life experiences of the person with ADRD. The framework involves recreation and leisure professionals in challenging current perceptions and approaches to deinstitutionalization, with the aim of the framework to help those involved in dementia care to enhance effective support for people with ADRD and their families and to promote strong partnerships in dementia care.

Chapter 5 examines poverty and leisure as social determinants of health. It focuses on the politics of oppression and transformation in social policy. As part of this examination, Susan Arai and Rishia Burke examine life concerns of women living in poverty. They argue that, despite systemic issues of discrimination, lack of supports, experiences of social exclusion, and lower health status, social policies aimed at job skills and employment prevail as the dominant approach to addressing poverty in Canada. Using a framework built on critical race and feminist theory, Arai and Burke challenge the individualization of poverty and explore how new definitions of social policy may move us beyond a culture of blame, employment numbers, and welfare statistics. Examining poverty from a relational and community perspective, they examine leisure as a social determinant of health and, importantly, question how we respond to difference in community and provide critical reflections on the notion of social inclusion.

3

Removing the Scar: Social Solidarity and Leisure Policy

Donald G. Reid, B. Leigh Golden, and Leah Katerberg

INTRODUCTION

There are a number of critical issues facing modern society, not the least of which are the rising levels of poverty and income inequality that continue to plague Canada and other developed nations. Not only does poverty affect the health of individuals and society negatively, but it also marginalizes individuals from their community, producing alienation and a weakening of the social contract. Social exclusion and inclusion are major issues in society that demand serious attention.

Society often views inadequate income as the sole criterion for explaining poverty, but it is exceedingly more complex than that single variable. Details for some of these components are sketched out throughout this book and some will be expanded upon later in the chapter. What is important to state here is that many people who are marginalized in society, for whatever reason (be it health or social or psychological impairment), are also likely to suffer from poverty as well. So the issue of poverty is omnipresent when examining marginalization in society.

In order to speak to the issue of poverty adequately, new approaches and instruments need to be created and applied in the eradication of poverty throughout society. Specific to this chapter is the potential role for leisure in this matter. Leisure may be an overlooked instrument in the process of integrating people experiencing poverty into mainstream society and in creating and maintaining social solidarity among all citizens of the state. The effectiveness of leisure in that role depends on some fundamental structural changes to social values, social organization, and a drastic reconceptualization of the social contract.

Engaging marginalized individuals in mainstream society demands some basic but long-needed changes to the capitalist structure and present social organization of society. This transformation should not be thought of as simply incorporating people experiencing poverty into the *status quo*. Change, thus, should be based in a critical analytical perspective following the critical theories of Habermas and the Frankfurt School (Kellner 1989). As Geuss (1981, 55) instructs, "(c)ritical theories aim at emancipation and enlightenment, at making agents aware of hidden coercion, thereby freeing them from that coercion and putting them in a position to determine where their true interests lie."

Perhaps the major challenge in achieving the goal of the social integration of those in poverty, and in realizing solidarity among all citizens in the system, is in designing a satisfactory approach to its implementation. Fundamentally, this would involve creating parity among all actors in the system, which starts with appropriate language. As Thomassen (2006, 6) is quick to point out when analyzing Derrida's work, "language is not a transparent medium but itself a site of political struggle, because it matters which concepts and distinctions we use, how we describe things, and so on." How society defines poverty and social assistance at the moment precludes other definitions. Capitalist society associates poverty and social assistance with dependence and as negative or even anti-social. This long-standing classical view precludes innovative ways of understanding (and perhaps dealing more effectively with) the problem of poverty and its true eradication.

The goal then is to collectively come to consensus on what constitutes poverty and how society should eradicate it. While this may seem a daunting challenge, social integration of people who become marginalized is not just a matter of facilitating access into the *status quo* but of creating a truly pluralistic society that accommodates multiple lifestyles and distributes resources justly, thus supporting alternative ways of life. This transition would result in a new social contract and not just in assimilating those experiencing poverty to the present system. The pluralistic society embraces manifold forms for achieving the integrative and productive life that we all seek. In present society, the elite and owners of capital have defined the condition of poverty and society's approach to dealing with it and with those subjected to that state. There need to be alternatives to that singular view.

This chapter discusses the subjects outlined above in some detail. It approaches this discussion through defining the important concepts, particularly poverty and marginalization. Furthermore, it outlines what constitutes the *status quo* when it comes to how society views poverty and its eradication. It proceeds by providing insight into the predominant worldview that guides and constructs present approaches to poverty and individuals who are dispossessed. Presently, the chapter delineates an alternative social contract that would transform society particularly in terms of how it describes and deals with individuals experiencing poverty and social marginalization. The new social contract encourages a pluralistic society that accommodates various approaches to life. It supports and reveres accomplishment over accumulation and consumption as the social markers in society. Leisure, particularly "serious leisure" (Stebbins 1982), is seen to play a legitimate role in defining the new social contract.

DEFINING POVERTY AND MARGINALIZATION

The prevailing notion in North American society and Western European nations is that our social organization strategy is exclusively capitalist. However, this may be a misrepresentation of how society actually works. When we examine the complex structures and processes that constitute many of the components of society, we find a much more pragmatic organization in everyday life. Certainly, the economic system can be described as mostly capitalist, but when we examine society's approach to solving other social problems, we discover a more pragmatic approach to social construction. For instance, in the Marsh Report (1975), the foundation for Canada's social welfare state, social welfare is constructed as an insurance program for those who find themselves out of work for short periods of time, but it has also made provision for those amongst us who may be dependent on the public wage for extended periods, and perhaps with little hope of engaging in paid employment in the future. It is unfortunate that modern Canadian society has reinterpreted that sentiment to mean that social assistance programs are a poor substitute for work and that the goal of government is to get as many recipients off the welfare rolls as quickly as possible.

Modern society has been modelling those on social assistance and experiencing poverty on the design of the worker. This has narrowed the potential solutions to the problem considerably. As a result, the focus for government involvement has been on managing the process and not on determining the outcome. Of course, the goal of getting people off the welfare roll is quite different from eradicating poverty. Yet many of our fellow citizens have erroneously assumed that the two potential goals are not only related but one and the same.

It can be argued that modern society, certainly since the days of the Marsh Report, has become much more complex, requiring a reconsideration of what conditions are important for driving the social welfare system. When considering such enterprises as social development and social policy, what is required is a mixed approach to institution building, including social democratic values in addition to pure capitalist ideas. Poverty in the developed world is not just a matter of attaining and consuming a designated amount of income, but it is also an issue of perception and how the notion of citizenship is constructed. It is about one's station in society as measured by the expectations held by all members of that society. As Reid (2006, 5) suggested when testifying about rural poverty before the Senate Standing Committee on Agriculture and Forestry:

I started [my research] with trying to define rural poverty and that too I found to be somewhat of a frustrating experience. I have come to the conclusion that individuals evaluate their station within the social order in which they live and whether or not they command sufficient resources to meet the minimum requirements of life based on their society's set of social standards and values. Poverty is a contested concept, and it is not an absolute variable from my point of view. It is something that is society-defined and society-driven.

In addition to satisfying the basic needs required for achieving subsistence, those of us who live in the developed world also have need to maintain solidarity with all other members of society. The notions expressed above are aimed at achieving what Rousseau was concerned with when he wrote *The Social Contract* in 1762. As Rousseau (1968, 50) stated then, "the social order is a sacred right which serves as a basis for all other rights. And as it is not a natural right, it must be one founded on covenants." Implied in this notion of the social contract is the goal of encouraging people to live in social harmony. Again, as Rousseau (49) suggests, "(M)an [sic] was born free, and he [sic] is everywhere in chains. Those who think of themselves the masters of others are indeed greater slaves than they." Of course modern society in the developed world does not countenance slavery, yet perhaps our society's equivalent to the slaves in Rousseau's time are those who are denied access to resources which would allow them to live in a state consistent with the goals of the society in which they maintain citizenship. This harmony can only be achieved through equal access to social institutions like justice and economic security and through the reaping and sharing of benefits brought about by collective action (i.e., economic activity).

If social solidarity is to be maintained, then all members of the collective must have access to civic institutions and be able to achieve the basic life-style expected by the general population. This has been the promise of capitalism, allowing some citizens to be left out of achieving those amenities jeopardizes social solidarity and the system itself over the long term.

Today, the greatest deterrent to achieving solidarity is the alarming differentiation between the classes and the increasing separation between the rich and the poor. As Judith Maxwell (2002, iii) reminds us, "over the past quarter century, disparities in earnings from employment have widened. The well paid have experienced earnings gains, while market incomes at the low end of the spectrum have stagnated or even declined." Using Statistics Canada 2001 census data, Morissette and Zhang (2006, 3) suggest:

> After increasing between 1984 and 1999, the gap between families in the top and bottom 20% of wealth distribution continued to widen between 1999 and 2005. The wealthiest 20% of families held 75% of total household wealth in 2005, compared with 73% in 1999 and 69% in 1984.

Poverty is particularly difficult for young families. Again, as Morissette and Zhang (3) remind us:

> While the median wealth of families overall rose 26% between 1984 and 2005, it fell substantially among those in which the major income recipient was aged 25 to 34. In 2005, these families had a median wealth of $13,000 (in 2005 dollars), much lower than the $27,000 and $17,000 registered in 1984 and 1999 respectively. The decrease in wealth among young families occurred mainly because the cumulative earnings of young men – the sum they received over several years – fell substantially between the 1970's and the 1990's. Over the 1994-to-2004 period, their cumulative earnings averaged roughly $267,000 much less than the $300,000 for the 1973-to-1983 period.

If the gap in wealth continues to widen, social solidarity will eventually be eroded and possibly threatened. Taking Rousseau's position, everyone in the population has a right to expect a certain level of existence beyond mere survival, simply by being a member of the social order in which they are attached. What has constrained the dialogue leading to agreement on what elements and organizational strategies are required to constitute the social contract is present society's dogmatic focus on the market system as the sole arbiter of one's station in life and the singular mechanism for achieving inclusion. The market system portrays the "ladder of success" as the image by which individuals are to be valued. Those on the top are deserving of the society's highest payouts because they are seen as contributing the most to the system. Those on the bottom rungs contribute less and thus deserve less from society. This may seem fair in the context of the market system, but the ladder of success is merely a manufactured representation of the goals inherent in the system. If instead a wheel is used as a metaphor to represent citizens' involvement, with spokes of equal length supporting the structure, then each member of society contributes based on each one's own capacity and station in life. The adoption of this image moves social inclusion further from a charity-based solution to poverty, towards mutual respect and a socially based equality model.

Definitions of poverty emanate from a philosophical position and a way of viewing the world. Those oriented to emphasizing market solutions to poverty reduction are likely to favour a definition of poverty that provides sustenance but not comfort to those without work. These approaches feature incentives that, theoretically at least, motivate those without work to re-engage in employment. The basic assumption for those who hold this view is that there is paid employment available for everyone, therefore unemployment is temporary and will last only until the unemployed person can be matched up with an existing job. The focus of problem-resolution is on eliminating the individual's deficit.

Those on the other end of the spectrum would view poverty as a condition that is not engineered by the individual but the result of severe and inadequate conditions produced by society. Furthermore, these conditions may be a result of circumstances beyond simply the lack of work. While paid work may be desirable even to those suffering from poverty, there may be constraints, either on the part of the individual or in society, that prevent engagement in the market economy and an individual's ability to rise above a given state of poverty. Most recently, there is a growing segment of people experiencing poverty in society who are actively engaged in employment yet still cannot manage to climb out of the poverty trap because of low and deteriorating wages. The "working poor," like the proliferation of food banks, has become a large and persistent institution in modern society. In some ways the need for food banks define us as a social order. The focus of the problem from this point of view is on the system deficit rather than the individual.

As a few authors in this volume have already made clear, there are many ways that poverty is *officially* defined. The standard definitions of poverty that provide the basis on which poverty may be tackled in the future are outlined below. Implied in each of these approaches to under-standing and dealing with poverty is the world view on which they are constructed. That is, listed from most conservative and market-oriented to a social development approach: the basic needs method; the market basket approach; the low income cut-off concept; and the low income measure calculation.

Christopher Sarlo (2001) has championed the basic needs approach to defining poverty. He defines poverty thresholds by measuring the min-imum consumption (as opposed to income) necessary to sustain physical well-being. The basic needs approach focuses on estimating the cost of basic shelter (low-cost apartments), clothing, and dietary needs (enough calories to avoid hunger). In Sarlo's view, a family is poor if its before-tax income is insufficient to pay for a basket of "basic needs" items.

The market basket measure of poverty is said to have been developed by Human Resources Development Canada to measure or define pov-erty (Human Resources and Social Development Canada 2006). This measure of poverty is based on the estimated cost of purchasing a basket of goods and services deemed to represent the standard of consump-tion for a typical family of two adults and two children. This basket of goods includes the costs of food, clothing, shelter, transportation, and other goods and services that are determined for different regions across Canada.

The low-income cut-off (LICO) has been developed by Statistics Canada as a surrogate measure for poverty (Canadian Council on Social

Table 3.1: Incidence of Low Income in Canada by Province, Low Income Measure (LIM).[1]

Name	Low-income (economic families)	Incidence of low-income in 2000 % (economic families)	Low income (population in private households)	Incidence of low income in 2000 % (population in private households)
Newfoundland and Labrador	24,800	16.3	95,275	18.8
Prince Edward Island	3,745	9.8	16,735	12.6
Nova Scotia	34,845	13.4	147,020	16.6
New Brunswick	27,765	13.1	111,365	15.7
Quebec	295,950	14.7	1,345,490	19.1
Ontario	364,320	11.7	1,611,505	14.4
Manitoba	38,565	13.3	180,975	17.5
Saskatchewan	30,280	11.8	144,435	15.8
Alberta	83,635	10.5	395,650	13.8
British Columbia	144,835	13.9	672,045	17.8
CANADA	1,048,740	12.85	4,720,495	16.21

Source: Statistics Canada 2001.

Development 1994). Under the LICO approach, Statistics Canada sets its low-income threshold at 20 percentage points above the average proportion of income spent by families on food, shelter, and clothing. If the family's income falls below this threshold, Statistics Canada classifies the family as "low-income." In 1992, for example, the average family of four spent 43 per cent of its after-tax income on food, shelter, and clothing. Adding 20 percentage points implies a LICO after-tax threshold equal to 63 per cent of after-tax income devoted to food, shelter, and clothing.

The low-income measure (LIM) identifies low-income Canadians as those living in families that have an after-tax income lower than 50 per cent of the median income for all Canadian families in a given year

(Senate Standing Committee on Agriculture and Forestry 2006). Using the low income measure from the 2001 census data, Statistics Canada provides a calculation of those in poverty in Canada (Table 3.1).

If solidarity is to be considered a societal goal, then a relative, rather than absolute, measure of poverty is most useful in that quest. The absolute basic needs approach, for example, may ensure that every member of society does not starve but does not address the issue of marginalization. In a developed world context, those who are without property and possessions are cast to the margin.[2] For those experiencing poverty, their dearth of personal possessions occurs within a consumer society where consumption of material goods is the force that we are told gives meaning to and defines social life.

In this context, poverty also extends to disposable income that enables individuals to participate in community life at least to a minimum level. Even when public agencies wave fees for participation in recreational events, for example, there are usually expenditures that occur around the actual event that limit participation by those who lack income (see Taylor and Frisby in this volume). Expenditures associated with equipment, transportation to and from the event, and the socializing that occurs before or after the occasion often represent insurmountable barriers and constraints to participation by those experiencing poverty.

A Critical Examination of the Conceptualization of Poverty in a Capitalist System

Employing Korpi and Palme's models of social policy (1993), Veli-Mutti Ritakallio (2002) completed a comparative study examining poverty and income equality among several countries in the world, specifically from the Nordic region, Central Europe, and North America. In addition to analyzing data that identifies the countries where poverty has grown more rapidly than others, they are also able to demonstrate to what extent the different types of social systems are able to slow down or reduce the impact of poverty and the various pressures in the economy for widening the gap in income inequality. The basic category models are: means testing, basic security, corporatist and institutional. Their analysis is presented in Table 3.2.

Table 3.2: Characteristic Features of Various Models of Social Policy.

	MODEL, REPRESENTATIVE COUNTRY AND CHARACTERISTIC FEATURE			
Dimension	Means Testing (UK, Canada, USA)	Basic Security (–)	Corporatist (Netherlands, France, Germany)	Institutional (Norway, Sweden, Finland)
Coverage of social policy	The poor	The entire population	Linked to employment	The entire population
Level of basic security	Low	Sufficient	Low	Sufficient
Means testing	Key feature	Not essential	Not essential	Not essential
Earnings related benefits	Based on private insurance	Based on private insurance	The unemployed are covered	The unemployed are covered
States role in social policy	Limited	Moderate	Moderate	Extensive
Universal public services	None	Some	None	Day care, education, health services, old people, etc.

Source: V. M. Ritakallio, *Trends of Poverty and Income Inequality in Cross-national Comparison* (2002).

Interestingly, Canada is perceived by the researchers to be in the same category as the United States and the UK. While this placement may be contentious, it does signify that while Canada has done better than its category partners in some areas, it still produces double-digit poverty rates, whereas the Nordic countries and most of Central Europe exhibit much lower poverty levels. Notwithstanding the poverty rates in Canada, it is arguable that Canada embraces programs and features from several of the other categories in addition to the means-testing category, particularly the programs found in the institutional group. While it is true that social assistance is means-tested, such programs as Medicare and education are universally distributed to all Canadian citizens. Certainly the absence of a universal day care program places Canada outside the Nordic countries and, hence, the most liberal of the categories in the typology.

As in many other spheres in modern society, poverty and marginalization take on differing characteristics. While poverty is quite visible in the urban centres in Canada, it is less so in rural areas. Because of its stigma, rural people tend to keep poverty hidden as much as possible, thereby reinforcing the notion that to be in poverty is to be deviant and less than a full and contributing citizen. As the Senate Standing Committee on Agriculture and Forestry studying rural poverty (2006, v) concluded:

> The rural poor are, in many ways, invisible. They don't beg for change. They don't congregate in downtown cores. They rarely line up at homeless shelters because, with few exceptions, there are none. They rarely go to the local employment insurance office because the local employment insurance office is not so local anymore. They rarely complain about their plight because that is just not the way things are done in rural Canada. The rural poor are also underresearched. With few exceptions, the academic and activist communities have been preoccupied with studying and highlighting the plight of the urban poor.... Some argue the rural poor are invisible because despite what some of the statistics say, the rural poor are not really that poor: very few go hungry, fewer still are homeless, and many enjoy easy access to nature and its abundance while benefiting from the tightly-knit social fabric that many rural settings provide.

A recent study conducted by Reid and Katerberg (2007) concluded that this apparent lack of visibility should not be interpreted to mean that rural areas in Canada are without people in poverty. Traditional rural culture, at least in the Canadian context, demands that families, including people experiencing poverty, deal with those difficulties within the family and independently from society, and accepting charity is considered as a personal failing that runs deep. In Canada, hard times have been dismissed or at the least gone unnoticed in many rural areas in Canada and it is often left up to individual families to deal with poverty, and usually on their own. Rural citizens experiencing poverty, particularly single people, often migrate to urban centres to escape the stigma of poverty, where services for the poor are usually much better developed, and where anonymity can be achieved as well. These features are often found attractive by the rural poor, causing them to migrate reluctantly to urban centres when options for staying in the rural area run out (Cloke, Milbourne, and Widdowfield 2003). All of these revelations about the distinctiveness of rural poverty dictate that much more research on the dynamics of rural poverty is needed.

Regardless of whether one resides in urban or rural areas, it is time for society to identify the most appropriate vehicles for eradicating poverty and the marginalization of people experiencing poverty. If society is to progress to the next level of development, several shifts in traditional social welfare practices will be required. In addition to establishing new and innovative approaches to social policy development, the overarching subject of this book, there also need to be lifestyle changes that positively affect the environment, including the reduction of greenhouse gasses and climate change.

While on the surface there may not appear to be a relation between social and environmental policy, on closer examination it seems that they may share a common solution. That solution is the fundamental shift in societal values from one of accumulation and consumption to one of accomplishment (Reid 1995). No longer will the familiar bumper sticker espousing, "he who dies with the most toys wins" be viewed with the same amusement in the future as it has been in the past. The long-held value of accumulation and consumption as the method for marking oneself off in society is no longer practical or desirable. This value must be replaced with one that stresses value to self and contribution to society as the social marker of the future.

In order to make this transition possible, two fundamental alterations to the social contract are needed. The first is to focus on the economic sphere and move from a society that favours growth to one that embraces distribution as its defining characteristic. There are a growing number of economists and academics (see, for example, Costanza 2000; Coombs 1990; Daley and Cobb 1989) trumpeting the idea that the goal of infinite growth in the modern economy is now detrimental to human existence rather than the positive outcome it was traditionally thought to be. Recent country studies have shown that social contracts that attempt to provide some measure of equality in society result in a reduced poverty rate compared to those where social policy is weak. As Ritakallio (2002, 151) tells us:

> The differences in poverty among the countries studied correspond with the respective models of social policy more clearly in the mid-1990's than they did 15 years earlier. Generally speaking, the poverty rate is slightly under 5 per cent in the Nordic countries, around 7.5 per cent in Central Europe, 10 per cent in Canada, 12.5 per cent in the UK, and as high as 17.5 per cent in the USA. The analysis of income inequality produced a similar picture. In comparison to poverty, however, the change is rather less extensive. The Nordic countries, in particular, have been able to respond to the rise in market income differences so that the income inequality for disposable incomes has hardly increased at all. Canada shows a parallel trend. The USA and, in particular, the UK reflect a movement in the opposite direction.

Capitalism has been good at producing growth in the economy but not good at distributing the results of that growth. As the above quotation demonstrates, as growth in profit in the private sector rises, the separation between the rich and poor also increases in countries that have a weak social welfare system.

This transition from growth to distribution may provide a new challenge but a possible solution to the major problems with which present society is confronted. It can be argued that in this new reality where environmental issues are more critical than ever, those living in poverty and the unemployed are not the drain on society as it was once thought. In fact, they are arguably the segment of society that consumes the fewest resources and therefore are the greatest conservers. It is the wealthy among us who extravagantly squander the earth's resources in pursuit of greater profit and luxury at the expense of the planet.

Second, we need to consider the monoculture created by the orthodoxy of classical economics. As a result of relatively recent neo-liberal thinking, society has had a singular approach to reducing poverty. It has been thought that through growth there will be "a rising tide to lift all boats" and eventually propelling all citizens out of poverty. This has not been the case as evidenced by the growing number of the working poor in society at a time when growth has been fast-paced throughout much of the developing world and in more developed countries such as Canada. Consequently, we as a society have witnessed the failed policies of welfare and workfare. As Reid and Golden (2005:63) have argued, it is now time for a new approach to the problem of poverty eradication; an approach they describe as "worthfare":

> As we progress into the 21st century what is crucial is the realization that poverty rates have not been positively affected by the workfare model and what is now essential is to conceptualize the problem differently. A Worthfare (developmental policy) approach would take us forward to a holistic conceptualization of the individual with unique and distinct needs and abilities that are directly related to the capacity of that individual to be of value to themselves and the community in which they live. The worthfare model includes a guaranteed annual income (Reid 1995) as the method of tackling the poverty issue. As conceived here, the Worthfare model recognizes that all individuals will not find a place in the market economy but that through non-work and leisure activity each can make a contribution to themselves and their community that will, in the long run, be of great value to them personally and benefit society generally. What may be needed most to make this approach work is some encouragement and social engagement skills in the form of poverty reduction and life-long learning.

The goal of this model for development rests on the vision of establishing a personal sense of self-worth and dignity through poverty reduction and engagement in community activity and service, and not solely dependent on entry into the market economy as ultimately desirable as that eventuality may be.

The essence of the worthfare model will be expounded upon further in the remainder of this chapter.

The two fundamental changes that will allow society to advance beyond the barriers that we now face are: shifting the focus from economic growth to distribution as the major economic problem to be solved, and moving from a singular approach to lifestyle creation (i.e., accumulation) to a pluralistic model, which includes various approaches to life construction mainly relying on accomplishment to create achievement in life. This transition would move us away from our current modelling of the welfare state after the corporatist capitalist organization where we model welfare recipients on the model of the worker. As was noted earlier, this narrows the potential solutions to the problem. The focus has been on managing the process, not the outcome, and this focus needs to be reversed.

A rethinking of the path humanity has tread during the last millennium is in order at this critical point in time. As Costanza (2000, 1) instructs:

> The world is at a critical turning point. There is significant uncertainty about how things will go in the next few years, but there is growing consensus that the decisions we make as a society, at this critical point, will determine the course of the future for quite some time to come. There is a tendency in thinking about the future to simply extrapolate past trends. If we have been getting materially richer in the past, then the future will be more of the same. If the environment has been deteriorating, then it will continue to do so. But one of the lessons we can learn from history

is that trends do not continue smoothly. There are turning points and discontinuities that were impossible to predict from past trends. The most critical task facing humanity today is the creation of a shared vision of a sustainable and desirable society, one that can provide permanent prosperity within the biophysical constraints of the real world in a way that is fair and equitable to all of humanity, to other species, and to future generations.

The major question to be addressed then is: how do we construct a new social contract? The fundamental answer to that question must start with Habermas's notion of communicative action; that is "action oriented towards mutual understanding" (as noted in Thomassen 2006, 3–4). In this case, we think about mutual understandings between society and the sub-culture of people living in poverty. Thomassen (13) in his critique suggests that Habermas's work emphasizes the "distinctiveness of everyday communicative practices and their contribution to social integration." Take for example the rhetoric expressed everyday by our governments and business leaders that denounce those on social assistance as being dependent. How is it that someone is considered dependent when on welfare but not so when they are employed by General Motors? Both are constrained for their livelihood and dependent on an external organizer; one on government and the other on the corporation, but it is the latter in the common wisdom generated by the hegemonic forces in society that is not considered to create dependence. In any case the use of the word "dependent" is highly emotive and follows on Derrida's discussion of the use and misuse of language presented earlier in this chapter.

How we understand poverty and social marginalization is a matter of perception or how each of us views the world generally. For the most part, this perception is overwhelmingly shaped by hegemonic forces that dominate the social discourse in society (Geuss 1981). What most of us have come to accept as the natural order of the universe may not represent everyone's reality, however. A classic work by R. D. Laing (1967) provides a framework for these ideas. Laing (17) suggests "[w]e can see other people's behaviour but not their experience. The task … is to relate my experience of the other's behaviour to the other's experience to my behaviour." We interpret this to mean that people often run the risk of interpreting the behaviour of others based on their own perceptions of how they experience the world or are told how the world should be ordered.

How we experience the world is also shaped by the hegemonic forces supporting those who wish to develop the social order in accordance with what they view as the "good society." This has resulted in defining poverty and marginalization largely from the point of view of those who are not experiencing that condition but are likely situated on the opposite end of the wealth continuum. Additionally, those shaping the societal view stand to benefit the most from the order they create. This systemic malfunction has caused our society to see poverty and marginalization as solely an economic problem resulting from the lack of work (not to be confused with the lack of income). Furthermore, society has defined the social contract from a capitalist and work-oriented standpoint and has summarily dismissed the potential contributions of alternative lifestyles, like leisure, as a vehicle to achieve social solidarity and inclusiveness.

Of course, work in the market economy will continue to hold its psychological power over the majority of individuals in society; however, there may be a growing number of individuals among us that for numerous reasons will never be able to fit into that mainstream. Rather than continue to make work the only option for those individuals, society needs to present additional choices for achieving a fulfilling and satisfying lifestyle. It is contended here that leisure can act as both a positive vehicle for individual growth and development and as an instrument of resistance to social hegemony and the increasing alienation we see growing in society. This idea is contrary to the dominant view that life without work is a less-than-human existence and that leisure should be viewed as a reward for work. People who hold this view would contend that those not working should have no reasonable expectation for experiencing satisfying leisure. However, it is suggested here that leisure may, in fact, provide a legitimate vehicle for maintaining contact with others in society and for reducing the alienation and marginalization produced by poverty.

However, the legitimation of leisure as a vehicle for social integration and its organization are two formidable challenges to society. Not only will it challenge the present social organizational structure that our society has embraced, but it will also present a test to those who might benefit from such a new structure. Results from recent research by Golden (2008) suggests that many individuals who are living in poverty and are marginalized in society suffer in varying degrees from debilitating social, psychological, and emotional problems. Participants in Golden's sample displayed personal and social constraints, making participation in some leisure as difficult as it was for them to engage in work. Additionally, society would need to put more resources into reorganizing leisure institutions that are built on the workday timetable in order for them to become more adaptable and flexible in both their objectives and scheduling.

The Role of Leisure in Poverty Reduction

As the analysis of poverty above emphasizes, society generally focuses on income (or lack thereof) as the basic criteria or unit of measure of self-worth. Today however, contributing factors to poverty or "poverty risk" must be incorporated into the model to broaden the analysis. Thus, when discussing poverty in the twenty-first century, we need to include such variables as education, well-being, personal security, engagement with the larger society, and meaningful, psychologically engaging activity, whether produced through work or leisure. In the information age, the lack of these elements in one's life should be viewed as indicators of and contributors to poverty. In addition to poverty of income, we need to conceptualize poverty as a social and psychological deficit as well.

During the period when the fisheries in Atlantic Canada were being exhausted due to over-harvesting and the government invoked the cod moratorium, fishers who found themselves suddenly out of work were faced with two fundamental questions. The first was: "how am I going to put food on the table to feed my family?", an economic question to be sure. The second question was: "what will I do when I get out of bed tomorrow morning?", a life-meaning and lifestyle question. Similar questions have been faced by many other workers who suddenly find themselves without paid employment. While the first issue demands an economic solution, the second is not so simple to categorize. What is certain is that it is not solely an economic question; in fact, a potential solution to that difficulty for many may lie outside the economic realm completely. Constructing a satisfactory lifestyle under these conditions may have more to do with leisure in the final analysis than with work.

There have been numerous attempts at defining leisure. All of these attempts focus on a single attribute of leisure but a truly comprehensive definition has been elusive. Additionally, these definitions reflect a social attitude about the major preoccupation of a particular society and how it views the world. Thorstein Veblen (1953) defined leisure as a function of social class. Veblen originated the term "conspicuous consumption" and applied it to the privileged class. In present society, it has been mainly characterized as a form of activity or recreation (Veblen 1953), denoting the consumptive nature of the phenomenon. Sebastian De Grazia (1962) sees it as a time-bound concept, where time is fragmented into sectors rather than being seamless and integrated. Aristotle provided the classical view that sees leisure as *aschola* or a matter of education (Bammel and Burrus-Bammel 1992). John Farina (1985) views leisure not as a commodity but as the freedom from the necessity of being occupied, or a mental and emotional state. Joseph Pieper (1963) conceptualized leisure as a state of mind. Robert Stebbins (1982) added the notion of "serious leisure" to the discussion. This suggests that leisure might be a bridge between our present concept of work and consumption and casual leisure (which is also often consumptive). This new concept may provide the transition from the accumulation aspect of work within the market concept to the idea of accomplishment that is more a notion of process and meaning than outcome. It is Stebbins's ideas about serious leisure that form the foundations for this section of the chapter and, hence, the new social contract. Serious leisure has great potential to be a legitimate contributor to the success of humanity in dealing with the many social and environmental problems with which it is confronted.

Stebbins (1982) sets out six qualities that distinguish serious from casual or "unserious" leisure. Serious leisure occasionally necessitates the need to persevere; it often fills the role of a career as it may sometimes demand significant personal effort based on special knowledge; it may provide some durable benefit to the individual and society; it may possess a unique ethos where participants operate in their own social worlds; and its participants identify strongly with their chosen pursuit. Stebbins stresses the social and psychological motivations found in hobbies, volunteering, and being an amateur as the essence of serious leisure. In these activities, people can find their passion in life ("following your bliss" as Joseph Campbell [1988] described it) that result in the accomplishment of Stebbins's six qualities. What is most important is the motivation that drives an individual to take up the pursuit. It is not done for financial incentive but for the intrinsic and the extrinsic social rewards that emanate from the involvement. While some endeavours have the potential to develop into remunerating activity, the starting point for these involvements is dependent on the interest in the activity itself and not with the drive for recompense.

Human society, particularly in developed countries, is at a crossroads. The socio-economic system, particularly with regard to how we produce and distribute wealth, is in trouble, as are our efforts to react to recently identified environmental concerns. It quite conceivably may be that our society is in the midst of a transition from the industrial society with all of its exploitative trappings to a new social order that is based on values other than those embedded in the growth and accumulation economy. Stebbins's idea of serious leisure may play a predominant role in that transition and new social contract. Figure 3.1 sets out that transition in diagrammatic form.

While serious leisure may not play a large role in poverty reduction or its eradication directly through income generation, it can speak to issues of marginalization, particularly exclusion and inclusion leading to social solidarity. Stebbins's introduction of "serious leisure" into the Leisure Studies literature provides an alternative to the work imperative in the post-industrial era. Until now, leisure has been seen as an add-on to the main focus of life, which has devoted itself to production and

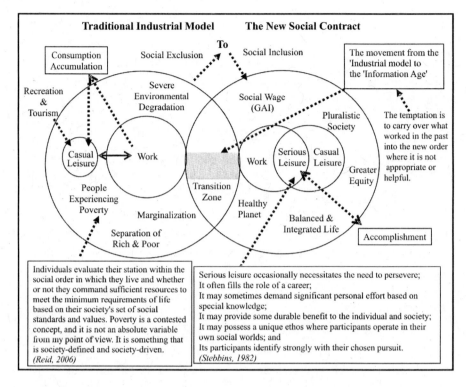

Traditional Industrial Model   **The New Social Contract**

To

Consumption Accumulation

Social Exclusion   Social Inclusion

The movement from the 'Industrial model to the 'Information Age'

Recreation & Tourism

Severe Environmental Degradation

Social Wage (GAI)

Pluralistic Society

The temptation is to carry over what worked in the past into the new order where it is not appropriate or helpful.

Casual Leisure ← → Work

Work   Serious Leisure   Casual Leisure

Greater Equity

People Experiencing Poverty

Transition Zone

Marginalization

Healthy Planet

Balanced & Integrated Life

Separation of Rich & Poor

Accomplishment

Individuals evaluate their station within the social order in which they live and whether or not they command sufficient resources to meet the minimum requirements of life based on their society's set of social standards and values. Poverty is a contested concept, and it is not an absolute variable from my point of view. It is something that is society-defined and society-driven. *(Reid, 2006)*

Serious leisure occasionally necessitates the need to persevere;
It often fills the role of a career;
It may sometimes demand significant personal effort based on special knowledge;
It may provide some durable benefit to the individual and society;
It may possess a unique ethos where participants operate in their own social worlds; and
Its participants identify strongly with their chosen pursuit.
(Stebbins, 1982)

Figure 3.1: Transition from the Status Quo to a New Social Contract

consumption. Given those ideas may have outlived their usefulness and penultimate place in human affairs, there is need for society to construct an alternative *raison d'être*. Certainly an additional choice for those among us who understand that humanity cannot be sustainable over the long-term if it continues to be devoted to increasing consumption at the same or at a faster rate than it did during the industrial revolution, is urgently needed.

Undoubtedly, the understanding of the consequences of such environmental concerns as global warming and climate change has altered the basis for decision-making in society. Unfettered consumption of resources in the pursuit of the nobility of traditional forms of work, as it was once considered, is now understood to be unacceptable if the planet is to survive this most recent crisis. The question of whether or not we can shake off the long-time tradition and rhetoric about the psychological attractions of work and find substitutes for gaining those rewards in less consumptive ways is yet to be determined.

Work has become so ingrained in the human enterprise that it may now hold the status of being a Jungian archetype (Reid 1995) and perhaps has become part of the collective unconscious. That said, Stebbins's notions of serious leisure maintain some of the intrinsic psychological components that paid work has provided the worker since the industrial revolution and possibly even earlier. However, some of those psychological rewards seem to have been lost to the pervasive drive to accumulate and consume wealth as the sole driving force of the work paradigm. Personal satisfaction seems to play a declining role in the work paradigm as the later stages of the industrial society unfolds. Such popular sayings as "shop till you drop" and "work, spend, work" are meant to define who we are in life's modern struggle. No longer is work the measurement for defining human development but has given way to the "size" of the income one can command as the demarcation point. For more and more of us, work is now instrumental and only a means to consumption. A transition from this dehumanizing state of affairs to one that is devoted to self-discovery and service to community makes sense in a society that is attempting to come to grips with a potential catastrophic environmental event, increasing violence, alienation in society through the increasing separation of the rich and poor, and a search for meaning through such experiences as fundamentalist religions.

Individual and social development could become the demarcation measurement for the new social contract. While some will find it in work, many may seek it elsewhere. In this new system, social assistance case workers (traditionally the mediators in the system) would need to concern themselves with the progression of the individual in life construction, not with reducing the size of the welfare roll or in monitoring the individual for violations of the system rules. To follow Habermas's concept (1987), case workers would be motivated and guided by the *life world* and not the *system world*. Mair and Reid (2007) utilize Habermas's ideas of the life world and the system world in the following way, as they argue that the life world is "an intimate, familiar, knowable world of tradition, known through commonly interpreted and understood meanings and communication. In contrast, the notion of the system world identifies a world driven by formalized and institutionalized knowledge systems that are technical and externally imposed. This is a world dominated by systems of capital and power and is increasingly de-coupled from the world of shared social and cultural understandings" (513).

A change in system motivation would necessitate a change in professional practice. Case workers would become life skills coaches and mentors and would not assume responsibility for the overseer and enforcer role. Other such instruments that could be considered in the paradigm change are a transition from means-tested social welfare programs to a universal social wage (guaranteed annual income). However, this is a subject worthy of a chapter unto itself and will not be discussed any further here. That said, these suggested changes to the present system seem to be a much more humane and productive method for engaging all those left out of the market system and, consequently, marginalized from society. Our track record as a society in eradicating poverty by tying it directly to the market mechanism in a coercive way has not produced the desired effect. Unemployment and, consequently, poverty remain high and by all accounts are getting higher. Also, there is an increasing number of individuals and families who are engaged in paid work that suffer from poverty as well. It can be argued that we have carried over a social welfare system that was produced for an industrial structure inappropriately into the information age. It is time for development of a new social contract that is more representative of and useful to the new reality. That new social contract needs to incorporate serious leisure as a major instrument in achieving the goal of social solidarity and in combating social alienation.

REFERENCES

Bammel, G., and L. Burrus-Bammel. 1992. *Leisure and Human Behaviour* (2nd ed.). Dubuque, IA: Wm. C. Brown.

Campbell, J. 1988. *The Power of Myth: Program 2. The Message of the Myth* (video recording, with Bill Moyers). New York: Mystic Fire Video.

Canadian Council on Social Development. 1994. *A Working Definition of Statistics Canada Low Income Cut-Offs.* http://www.ccsd.ca/pubs/archive/fb94/fs_povnk.htm.

Coombs, H. 1990. *The Return of Scarcity: Strategies for an Economic Future.* Cambridge: Cambridge University Press.

Daley, H., and J. Cobb, Jr. 1989. *For the Common Good.* Boston: Beacon Press.

Cloke, P., P. Milbourne, and R. Widdowfield. 2003. "The complex mobilities of homeless people in rural England." *Geoform* 34: 21–35.

Costanza. R. 2000. *Visions of Alternative (Unpredictable) Futures and Their Use in Policy Analysis.* http://www/ecologyandsociety.org/vol4/.

De Grazia, S. 1962. *Of Time, Work, and Leisure.* New York: Twentieth Century Fund.

Farina, J. 1985. *Psycho Social Dynamics of Leisure.* Toronto: Georgian College of Applied Arts and Technology, Publication No. 118.

Geuss, R. 1981. *The Idea of Critical Theory: Habermas and the Frankfurt School.* Cambridge: Cambridge University Press.

Golden, B. L. 2008. Rural poverty, serious leisure, and social integration. Ph.D. Diss., University of Guelph.

Habermas, J. 1987. *The Theory of Communicative Action: A Critique of Functionalist Reason,* vol. 2; trans. T. McCarthy. London: Polity Press.

Human Resources and Social Development Canada. 2006. *Low Income in Canada: 2000–2002 Using the Market Basket Measure.* Ottawa: Human Resources and Social Development Canada.

Kellner, D. 1989. *Critical Theory, Marxism and Modernity.* Baltimore: Johns Hopkins University Press.

Korpi, W., and J. Palme. 1993. "Social policy, crisis and reforms: Sweden in international comparison." In *Ekonomikomessionens Forslag, Bilagedel 2. Statens Offentliga,* 16 (*Report of the Government's Commission on Economic Policy,* 16) ed. Nya Villkor for Ekonomi och Ploitik (New Conditions for Economics and Politics), 135–70. Stockholm: Finansdepartementet.

Laing, D. R. 1967. *The Politics of Experience.* Toronto: Random House.

Mair, H., and D. G. Reid. 2007. "Leisure research and social change: A millennial state of the art." *Leisure/Loisir* 31(2): 501–22.

Marsh, L. 1975. *Report on Social Security for Canada* (revised edition). Toronto: University of Toronto Press.

Maxwell, J. 2002. *Smart Social Policy: Making Work Pay*. Ottawa: Canadian Policy Research Networks.

Morissette, R., and X. Zhang. 2006. *Revisiting Wealth Inequality*. Ottawa: Perspectives, Statistics Canada.

Pieper, J. 1963. *Leisure the Basis of Culture*. New York: New American Library.

Ritakallio, V. 2002. "Trends of poverty and income inequality in cross-national comparison." *European Journal of Social Security* 4(2): 151–77.

Reid, D. 1995. *Work and Leisure in the 21st Century: From Production to Citizenship*. Toronto: Wall & Emerson.

Reid, D., and B. Golden. 2005. "Non-work and leisure activity and socially marginalized women: The issue of integration." *Canadian Review of Social Policy* 55: 39–65.

Reid, D., and L. Katerberg. 2007. Homelessness in the countryside: Report on rural homelessness. Waterloo: Unpublished research report for the Regional Municipality of Waterloo Social Services. *School of Environmental Design and Rural Development*, University of Guelph.

Rousseau, J. J. 1968. *The Social Contract*, ed. M. Cranston. New York: Viking Penguin.

Sarlo, C. 2001. *Measuring Poverty in Canada*. Toronto: Fraser Institute.

Senate Standing Committee on Agriculture and Forestry. 2006. *Understanding Freefall: The Challenge of the Rural Poor (Interim Report)*. Ottawa: Queen's Printer.

Statistics Canada. 2001. *Incidents of Low Income among the Population Living in Private Households, by Province (1996–2001 Census)*. http://www40.statcan.ca/l01/cst01/famil60a.htm.

Stebbins, R. 1982. "Serious leisure: A conceptual statement." *Pacific Sociological Review* 25: 251–72.

Thomassen, L., ed. 2006. *The Derrida-Habermas Reader*. Chicago: University of Chicago Press.

Veblen, T. 1953. *Theory of the Leisure Class: An Economic Study of Institutions*. New York: Macmillan.

NOTES

1   This table presents the statistics for all the provinces and for Canada as a whole. It does not present statistics for the territories in Canada. Poverty in the territories is quite different because of geographic regional affects, ethnicity, and the traditional practices of the inhabitants.

2   While it is recognized that other factors (e.g., disability, race, religion) are instrumental in marginalizing individuals, for the purpose of this discussion we focus on economic status.

4

Improving the Lives of Persons with Dementia and Their Families through Enhanced Social Policy, Leisure Policy, and Practice

Sherry L. Dupuis

I'm still the same person,
Still loving and caring,
Still want to hear
All that you're sharing.

I may not understand
All that you say,
But I do want inclusion
In your life every day.

Please help me to be
All that I can be,
And I will respond
Just you wait and see.

(Poem written by Shirley Garnett; in Mitchell et al. 2006)

In 2009, an estimated 500,000 Canadians, or one in eleven older adults, were living with Alzheimer's disease (AD) or a related dementia (ADRD) (Alzheimer Society of Canada 2009), of which over 64 per cent had Alzheimer's disease, the leading cause of dementia (Johnson, Davis, and Bosanquet 2000). Although ADRD is often associated with aging, over 70,000 persons with dementia are under the age of 65 (ASC 2009). With the rapidly increasing older adult population, the numbers of persons with dementia in Canada is projected to increase dramatically over the next several decades. In fact, an estimated 50 per cent more Canadian families will be facing ADRD by 2014, and by 2034, over one million Canadians will have an illness causing dementia (ASC 2009). Similar increases have been predicted for other developing countries, including the United States, the UK, and Sweden (Aevarsson and Skoog 1996; Ferri et al. 2005). These increases have significant implications, both for those diagnosed and their families, but also create a range of additional challenges for the provision of care due to the related communication, behavioural, and functional issues associated with dementia (Sachs, Shega, and Cox-Hayley 2004). Given these projections and the potential implications, Alzheimer associations in Canada, the United States, and other countries around the world have identified dementia as an international health priority and have advocated for governments to understand the broad implications of the changing demographic landscape and begin to plan for how to address the needs of persons with ADRD and their families. They have urged governments and communities to consider whether they are truly ready to address this situation.

At the same time, long-term care (LTC) organizations in Canada, both in community and in LTC settings, are undergoing dramatic changes and pressures including: a move towards aging-in-place initiatives; workforce crises such as high staff turnover and absenteeism, low staff morale, and difficulties recruiting and retaining skilled professionals; rising expectations of families of what community services and LTC homes should provide; and calls for alternative social models of care, beyond the traditional medical model, that allow for increased citizen choice and provide programs and services that are needs-based and humanistic in their approaches (Gibson and Barsade 2003; Gold 2002;

Stevens 2001). In fact, there is growing consensus that the way LTC is currently delivered, regulated, and financed is neither adequate to meet the needs of the growing numbers of older adults we will witness over the next several decades, and particularly those who are and will be diagnosed with an illness causing dementia, nor an acceptable approach to ensuring the highest quality of life (Miller, Booth, and Mor 2008). Given these pressures and concerns, many have emphasized the urgent need for culture change in community planning, generally, and LTC approaches, more specifically, moving away from the current provider-driven approaches to more person, family, and relationship-centred models (Hall and McWilliam 2006; McWilliam et al. 2001). Culture change is the process of re-examining the values, beliefs, attitudes, behaviours, and approaches embedded within an organization and involves the development and implementation of a comprehensive set of fundamental reforms in order to "create caring communities where both empowered front-line staff and [LTC clients and families] can flourish" (Rahman and Schnelle 2008, 142–43). Culture change and planning will ensure that organizations and communities are proactive in addressing the needs of older adults, families, and staff working in LTC and beyond and that the necessary resources, approaches, and supports are in place so that quality of life can be maintained and enhanced (Rahman and Schnelle 2008).

Until very recently, dementia and dementia care have received very little attention in the political arena and, therefore, there has been little government policy focused specifically on persons living with dementia and their families (Sassi and McDaid 1999). An exception is Ontario's five year, comprehensive strategy focussed on ADRD, which culminated in the convening of the *Roundtable on Future Planning for People Affected by Alzheimer's Disease and Related Dementias* and its development of a planning framework that would address the impact of ADRD on government programs, communities, and Ontario as a whole. The Roundtable included researchers, health care, social services and other professionals, policy-makers, family partners in care, and persons living with dementia all working together to improve the quality of life of persons with dementia and their families. The Roundtable embodied a coming together of a passionate group of individuals representing all key stakeholder groups relevant to dementia care who were committed to changing the way communities care for and support persons living with dementia and their family members.

The resulting framework not only challenges our assumptions about persons with dementia but challenges communities to think differently about how persons with dementia are supported in their communities. The outcome of the approach proposed in the planning framework is the ability of all persons with dementia to live *meaningful lives* (as defined by persons with dementia and their families themselves) no matter what stage one is at in the dementia journey, through continued and *active personal and community engagement.* Achieving this outcome will require significant culture change. It will necessitate redressing the way we currently support persons with dementia and their families through the abandonment of current paternalistic and deficit-focused models, such as those embedded in the traditional paradigm of the biomedical model. Policies and programs from this perspective focus on servicing the illness and fixing people rather than on "getting on with life" (Robinson 1993). These models would be replaced by those that recognize the self-determination and capabilities of persons with dementia and that emphasize their continued full citizenship focusing on meaningful participation, engagement, inclusion, social connectedness, reasonable accommodation, and respect (Stainton 2005). Again, opportunities to continue to live in meaningful ways and for full participation in community become the outcomes. From this perspective there is a need for opportunities, programs, and services, both in community and in long-term care settings, which support a life of meaningful activity and engagement *beyond* work and notions of productivity (Stainton 2005). As in the equality of well-being model for people with intellectual disabilities proposed by Rioux (1994), the basis for distributive justice shifts "away from economic contribution as the primary factor of entitlement and recognises other forms of participation as valuable – including those non-market, non-productivity contributions that people ... can make" (174). Leisure in its various forms becomes a necessary vehicle in communities for meaningful activity and engagement for persons with dementia and their families. Perhaps more importantly though, leisure provides a space for coming together, for developing, fostering, and enabling supportive communities, a space where strong social ties and trust can be developed and nurtured (Arai and Pedlar 2003; Coalter 2006; Pedlar and Haworth 2006). Such communities are essential if we hope to achieve the outcome of living meaningful lives through personal and community engagement for all persons with dementia and their families.

This chapter introduces the planning framework and discusses the framework's implications for social policy, leisure policy, and practice. The framework moves beyond a biomedical and social psychological approach and adopts a social model and socio-cultural approach. It incorporates a vision, a set of six guiding principles, three planning pillars, and five enabling mechanisms that should guide all research, policy, and practice in dementia care. In serving as a guide for practice, the overall goals of the framework are to: 1) help those involved in dementia care enhance their ability to support people with ADRD and their families in humanistic ways; 2) promote strong linkages across sectors in the creation of supportive dementia communities; and 3) mobilize authentic dementia care partnerships.

TOWARDS A SOCIO-CULTURAL APPROACH TO DEMENTIA AND DEMENTIA CARE

If we view dementia only as a 'disease' then we are tempted to abdicate our fundamental responsibility as human beings for the welfare of our fellows, and leave it to scientists in laboratories to discover the pill, potion, gene or magic bullet that will 'treat' or even 'cure' dementia. But if we see dementia as a condition of which organic degenerative brain disorder is only one part, but which is also fuelled by fear, anxiety, shame, and incomprehension of both the person concerned, those with whom they are in contact, and the wider society in which we all have our being – then we can begin to see that we have a role to play ourselves. The consequences of such a view of dementia is empowering for all concerned; we all have the possibility to feel better about ourselves.... In expanding our model of dementia we return humanity and self-respect both to those 'with' dementia and those 'without' it. (Barnett 2000, 24)

Dementia and dementia care have been dominated by biomedical and psychological models that have defined dementia within a disease or sickness framework (Gilliard, Means, Beattie, and Daker-White 2005). Any "problems" experienced by the "patient" are attributed to physical changes in the brain; that is, to individual neuropathology (Downs 2000). Individuals diagnosed with dementia are described in objectified ways – as "demented" – and as "victims" and "sufferers." The discourse around families who provide care focuses on the "burden" of caring for someone with dementia (Downs 2000; Robertson 1991). As Henderson (1995) and Bond (1992) note, the biomedical conceptualization of de- mentia has had enormous implications, including:

- the setting of research priorities focused on diagnosis, medical treatment, and finding a cure;

- the structure of professions and occupations, with health care professionals having the authority to determine what is most important to consider for individuals with dementia and their families;

- dementia care practices with a focus at the individual level, that is, on clinical assessment and treatment, physical maintenance, and task-based approaches to care; and

- the public policy agenda focused on deficiency-oriented policies and programs.

An over-reliance on the physical/biological aspects of dementia has meant that the wider social context in which people with dementia live their lives has been relatively ignored. As a result, the behaviours of *per-sons* with dementia are too often understood without reference to their context such as psychosocial aspects, environmental conditions, or other traumatic life events. Individuals are often defined by misunderstood behaviours, and, even though behaviours may be appropriate, they are labelled deviant because the individual has a diagnosis of dementia. Focusing on deterioration and the negative outlook on ageing can lead to increased stereotyping, labelling, and stigma and can act to restrict opportunities available for continued growth and even accelerate a person's decline (Bender and Cheston 1997).

In the late 1980s – early 1990s, Kitwood proposed an alternative framework for understanding dementia, which focused more on the expression of the illness rather than the disease progression and highlighted the dialectical interplay between neuropathology and the social-psychological context of the individual (Kitwood 1989, 1990). From this perspective, changes in the brain are viewed as only one factor in dementia. Other factors such as the characteristics of the physical and social environment, labelling, the life history of the person and personal loss, and the support network around the person can all have an impact on the person with dementia and the progression of the disease. Person-centred care grew out of this conceptualization of dementia and focused on enhancing the "personhood" of individuals with dementia (Kitwood and Bredin 1992; Kitwood 1997). The key feature of this care philosophy is that it places the person at the centre of all care decisions, not the disease. It implies that choices are offered and decisions are made in keeping with the person's wishes and desires and focusing on the continued capabilities of the person rather than an emphasis on what the person is no longer able to do.

People with dementia are an extremely heterogeneous group and differ in terms of the availability of personal, social, and institutional resources necessary to cope with the changes experienced throughout the dementia journey. Although Kitwood's framework helped to reframe dementia and dementia care away from a deficit approach, his psychosocial model fails to fully account for how these different "lived" circumstances influence how individuals think about and experience dementia, how it is embodied, and how they and others respond to it (Adams 1998; Downs 2000; Pollitt 1996). It focuses primarily on the person with dementia and neglects the experience of the family as a unit (Adams 1998, 2005) and fails to take into consideration the socio-political and socio-cultural factors that greatly influence the experience of dementia and may limit how one cares (Adams 1998, 2005; Gilleard and Higgs 2000). This is important because the socio-cultural "context in which care is provided will influence who cares and whether services are used" (Downs 2000, 372).

A social model of disability and a social-cultural approach to dementia and dementia care considers how the social, political, and built environment can serve to either enable or disable persons with dementia and their families (e.g., Gwilliam and Gilliard 1996; Marshall 1994). It moves from a micro and individualistic lens to a more macro and systemic lens. "A social model makes us confront the ways in which we discriminate against people with dementia and marginalize all people with dementia in the way services are designed and delivered. It asks uncomfortable questions about whether or not the dementia care 'industry' works to the advantage of persons with dementia [and their families]" (Gilliard et al. 2005, 582). As Barnett (2000, 35) emphasizes: if we place "the person, rather than society, at the heart of any plan for change, environmental and social barriers to empowerment will ultimately be overlooked or undermined in favour of individualised interventions." What is needed is an alternative approach that challenges us to think about how "community" can change so as to enable those living with dementia to transcend the disease and get on with living life. It also requires moving beyond working *for* persons with dementia and their families to actively working *with* them to determine what needs to be changed and how best to do that.

A PLANNING FRAMEWORK FOR ENABLING PERSONS WITH DEMENTIA AND THEIR FAMILIES

> The best community ... is one in which all kinds of methods create all kinds of situations in which each of us finds relationships where our gifts are recognized and magnified. (McKnight 2005, 117)

Framework Vision

The aim of the planning framework is to realize a society where all persons with ADRD and their family partners in care live meaningful lives across the progression of the illness through active personal and community engagement. The primary objective is to create supportive, inclusive communities that enable families as caring units to live in meaningful ways and to continue to be engaged in their communities. The goal of communities should be to assist families to continue to live in "normalized" ways, to live "ordinary" lives despite dementia, which means supporting a life of meaningful activity without work for those with ADRD (Priestley 2000; Rimmer et al. 2005; Robinson 1993). As McKnight (1992) emphasized: "[The] goal should be clear. We are seeking nothing less than a life surrounded by the richness and diversity of community. A collective life. A common life. An everyday life." (62). When this is realized, the family, rather than embracing an orientation toward *servicing the illness*, can focus on "getting on with life" (Robinson 1993).

Guiding Principles

The framework has at its core six principles reflecting fundamental values that should serve as the foundation for all planning for persons with ADRD and their families. Most fundamental is the principle of a *relationship-based or partnership approach* to care. A relationship-based or "partnership" approach recognizes *all* those involved in dementia care and acknowledges that care is affected by the dynamics and interactions of all those involved in care, including persons with dementia, their family partners in care and those formal providers working to support them. Such an approach recognizes and respects the multiple and equally valuable knowledge-bases needed for quality dementia care and support (Adams and Clarke 1999; Dupuis et al. in press). Therefore, it advocates for the mobilization of true partnerships in care that allow for active involvement in decision-making by persons with dementia, families, and formal service providers at all levels. This requires the development of strong, trusting relationships or networks based on a sense of security, continuity, belonging, purpose, fulfillment, and significance experienced by all in the relationship (Nolan et al. 2003, 2004). It moves beyond merely asking persons with dementia and their family members about their experiences and needs, to actively including them in decision-making about how to address those needs and develop solutions.

The Roundtable recognized that special attention needed to be given to *the ethical principle of "do no harm"* by considering the various ways in which our care practices and approaches may cause unnecessary suffering and the ways in which persons with ADRD might be harmed. Unnecessary and inappropriate assessments, being silenced or dismissed, being excluded, not recognizing continued abilities and contributions, and using deception can all cause unnecessary suffering for persons with ADRD (Mitchell, Jonas-Simpson, and Dupuis 2006). Neglect, undue restraint, prescribed-drug abuse, and paternalistic approaches are other ways in which persons with ADRD might be harmed and suffer un-necessarily. All members of society need to be well informed about the potential for harm, and practitioners need to have the courage and open-ness to take a critical look at themselves, their practices, and the impact of these on persons with dementia and their families (Mitchell et al. 2006; Schön 1983, 1987).

Adopting a rights–based approach, the framework recognizes a num-ber of fundamental *individual and community rights* of persons with demen-tia as valued "citizens" in our communities. These include the right: to choice, citizenship, and self-determination (i.e., having the right to live as they choose and to retain control over their lives as much as possible); to interdependent relationships with others (i.e., committed and recipro-cal relationships of mutual support); to full engagement in life and in community throughout the progression of the illness; and to respect and dignity (e.g., to be treated as valued, whole persons of worth with the right to continue to speak for oneself). These rights acknowledge the continued potential of all persons with dementia and challenges no-tions of the loss of self so prevalent in dementia discourse. This approach forces us to embrace the fact that all persons with dementia have a future despite the fact that they are often "written off" after a diagnosis. It requires understanding the person's hopes, goals, and aspirations and assisting him or her to achieve them and to continue to grow and develop. It requires access to meaningful interactions and activities and ensuring that all persons with dementia continue engaging with their community through participation and involvement. It requires a service culture that is open to possibilities, willing to take risks, and creative in their abilities to think outside traditional models (Dowling et al. 2007).

Persons with dementia are a heterogeneous group, differing in numerous ways in terms of their biographies of life experiences and circumstances. Such diversity in our communities means that a "one size fits all" approach will not work and that a range of responses to ADRD that *respects diversity and inclusiveness* will be needed in order to meet the specific and changing needs of *all* persons with dementia throughout the disease process. For example, marginalized populations, such as the homeless or under-housed and others who may be financially disadvantaged, face significant challenges when living with ADRD that need to be considered. Furthermore, the needs of persons with Down Syndrome, who are at higher risks for subsequently developing AD, and their often older partners in care, will be different and thus will require alternative approaches. The planning framework embraces an inclusive approach and recognizes that diverse and culturally appropriate responses to care and support are required across the life course of ADRD in order to ensure continued full engagement in life. Individual attributes should not create barriers to care and support as a result of systemic inequities.

Respect of diversity and inclusiveness goes hand in hand with the guiding principle of *fairness in eligibility and accessibility*. Limitations to current policies and regulations around eligibility criteria for services and programs, the amount and type of services provided, and what volunteers and home support workers are allowed to do in their jobs make it difficult to meet the unique and changing needs of persons with dementia and their families (Dupuis and Smale 2004). Addressing fairness issues in eligibility and accessibility is critical to ensuring that all persons with dementia continue to live meaningful lives and has been identified as a core value that should underlie all planning for ADRD (Cox et al. 1998). In his theory of justice, Rawls (1971) describes fairness "as the product of policies and institutions that promote equality of opportunity and tolerate inequalities in receipt of social goods only to the extent that they benefit the least well off among us" (Capitman 2003, 130). Capitman notes that, from an equal opportunity perspective, public health and social policies "are fair to the extent that all individuals have equal access to whatever services maximize their potential to enjoy as much age-appropriate normal functioning as possible under reasonable resource constraints." (130). This approach requires minimizing those factors, such as inequitable access to economic and social capital or physical environments, which might threaten opportunities for age-appropriate "normal" functioning no matter what the health or disability status of the individual. For equality to happen there must be a recognition of difference to ensure that those who are most marginalized have access to full participation and citizenship (Rawls 1971; Stainton 2005).

Accountability, the final principle, has to do with "the procedures and processes by which one party justifies and takes responsibility for its activities" (Emanuel and Emanuel 1996). Accountability includes notions of transparency (Did the party reveal the facts of its performance?), liability (Did the party face consequences for its performance?), controllability (Did the party do what was desired?), responsibility (Did the party follow the rules?), and responsiveness (Did the party fulfill its expectations for demand/need?) (Koppel 2003, 181). The overall goal of planning for ADRD is to optimize the quality of life for people living with ADRD and their partners in care. This requires: (1) a collective accountability by citizens to the vision expressed in the framework, including the use of performance indicators linked to the framework's principles and values; (2) accountability by the government to provide adequate resources and support to persons with dementia, their family partners in care, all service providers, and communities; (3) accountability by health care professionals, other service providers and the broader community to use their skills and resources to the greatest effect for the benefit of those living with ADRD and their partners in care; and (4) accountability of individuals and their families to participate, to the extent possible, in collaborative planning activities with service providers and the community. Quite simply, it is important to be able to demonstrate that strategies and initiatives developed for persons with dementia and their partners in care make a positive difference in their lives.

Planning Pillars for Recognizing the Vision

Critical components of the planning framework are the three planning pillars or foundational building blocks. These pillars encompass the essential life experiences that affect the well-being of the person seeking to *live* with dementia and those who partner with them in their care. These pillars are interdependent and are relevant at the individual, community, and systems levels. When used in planning, they address promoting and sustaining: an informed society; enabling and supportive environments; and personal, social, and system connectedness (see Table 4.1).

An informed society is one in which all citizens have adequate and accurate information about dementia – information that is based, not only on scientific and clinical knowledge, what is sometimes referred to as "expert" knowledge, but also on a "living" or "experiential" knowledge of dementia (Gaventa and Cornwall 2006) only those with dementia can possess. When a society is informed, the individual citizen is knowledgeable about his or her own health, including prevention strategies and strategies for living well with ADRD, as well as about situations that affect others in the community. An informed society requires ready access to the resources and opportunities that support such a degree of awareness. When ADRD-related information is effectively distributed at the individual, school, service, and broader community levels, then the preconditions for an informed society about ADRD are assured and the stigma surrounding dementia can be reduced, if not eliminated.

Table 4.1: Planning Pillars for Recognizing the Vision.

An Informed Society	Enabling and Supportive Environments	Personal, Social, and System Connectedness
• individual and public awareness	• functional, accessible physical environment	• continued community engagement and participation
• education for persons with ADRD and their families	• supportive social environment	• citizen input in planning, delivery and evaluation
• education and training for service providers	• safety and security	• collaboration and partnership among service providers
• learning opportunities for the broader community	• flexible and fluid, needs-based access to services and support across the continuum of care	• linkages between formal and informal support sectors
• discovery and translation of knowledge, and use of best practice at all levels	• options in self- and facilitated-care and income security and support for family partners in care	
	• equitable approaches to rural/urban and other diversity issues	

People with ADRD and their family partners in care are too often and too easily marginalized as they gradually lose friends, see important informal support systems shrink, and are forced to withdraw from participation in the wider community. Obstacles to community participation, however, are preventable through the development of *enabling and supportive environments*, those in which the physical and psychological, social, spiritual, and financial needs of all those with dementia are met and full community participation is possible – environments that are based on the ideals central to communitarianism. Pedlar and Haworth (2006) described the key features of democratic communitarianism:

- individuals flourish only in and through communities;

- healthy communities are a prerequisite for strong, healthy and vigorous individuals;

- solidarity is a central value for we become who we are through our relationships wherein we find reciprocity, loyalty, and a shared commitment to the good; and

- participation is a right and a duty and communities are positive goods only when they provide the opportunity and support to participate in them. (524)

A communitarian perspective recognizes individual human dignity but also the social embeddedness of all humans.

> A communitarian perspective recognizes that the preservation of individual liberty depends on the active maintenance of the institutions of civil society where citizens learn respect for others as well as self-respect; where we acquire a lively sense of our personal and civic responsibilities, along with an appreciation of our own rights and the rights of others; where we develop the skills of self-government as well as the habit of governing ourselves, and learn to serve others – not just self. (Etzioni, Volmert, and Rothschild 2004, 13)

Being able to access normal activities and patterns of life require enabling and supportive environments for persons with dementia, environments that: provide functional and more accessible physical environments, foster supportive environments that are rich in human capital; ensure safety and security in our communities; provide flexible and fluid local services, supports and programs that better meet the needs of families with dementia across the continuum of care and support; include work place policies that enable persons with dementia to stay in their jobs for longer periods of time and support family members in providing ongoing care; provide options for self- and facilitated-care and income security of family care partners; and ensure these programs and services are available to all persons with dementia no matter where they live.

Individuals cannot be viewed in isolation. A relationship-based approach conceives of the person diagnosed with ADRD and his or her family partners in care as being actively connected with each other, with their community, and with needed health care and community social support providers and professionals. Thus, *personal, social,* and *system connectedness* dictates a deliberate planning approach that supports community engagement and participation by the person with dementia; provides opportunities for citizen input in planning, delivery, and evaluation of programs and supports; ensures collaboration and partnerships among service providers both within and between different community sectors; and promotes linkages between formal and informal support sectors. Essentially, the goal is the facilitation of meaningful relationships at the individual, service, and broader community levels.

THE IMPLICATIONS OF THE PLANNING FRAMEWORK FOR SOCIAL POLICY, LEISURE POLICY, AND PRACTICE

So what does all this mean for communities and for policy? It means that a *coordinated and integrated system* of health care and *expanded* supportive community services is needed, one that has *leisure and recreation* at the *centre* of the system. Such an integrated system would necessitate the breaking down of the silos between ministries and between local organizations, institutions, and services that currently exist. In partnership with others working in health, community support, and other services, the goal of the public recreation and leisure sector would be to help the family experiencing dementia as a unit adjust and adapt to the changing circumstances, to support its members in functioning well, and to assist them in continuing to live in "normalized" ways despite dementia (Dupuis and Smale 2005; Robinson 1993). The means by which to do this is to create an environment that provides opportunities for choice, self-determination, and the development of interdependent relationships – an environment that enhances the coping capacities of families. It also means that recreation and leisure practitioners need to play a more direct role in addressing the systemic issues that may threaten the well-being of dementia families and may limit their abilities to live meaningful lives and continue to be engaged in their communities. This approach of course will necessitate the recognition by government, policy-makers, planners, and others in the system of the unique and important contributions that recreation and leisure can make in helping families get on with their lives.

This approach also will require an *inclusive system built on strong partnerships* that value and respect the multiple and equally valuable knowledge bases needed for enabling dementia families and developing strong supportive communities (Adams and Clarke 1999). Such partnerships must allow for the direct involvement in decision-making by persons with dementia, family partners in care, and professionals at all levels and from a range of agencies and services working in both community and long-term care (LTC) settings. It would require the creation of what Stainton (2005) refers to as a "partnership board" or an adapted version of what McKnight (1992, 1997) calls an "associational community." Such a board or community would be made up of local citizens, including people with dementia, family partners in care, leisure and recreation professionals, health and social service providers, and other persons from the community identified as being important to the group. The purpose of this partnership would be to come together and collectively make decisions about policy and planning needed to ensure continued engagement of persons with dementia and their families in their communities. In guiding the new coordinated and integrated system, they would be responsible for: identifying the strengths in the community as well as the barriers to meaningful and engaged lives; deciding how best to use the strengths and resources in the community to address the barriers and other issues identified; building relationships between and among local citizens, local organizations, and local institutions; and finding innovative and creative solutions and mobilizing the support needed to address needs, implement changes, and strengthen communities (Toqueville 1945). This approach to care and support allows for the development of a system of dementia care that is proactive rather than reactive and is better able to anticipate issues and challenges rather than simply responding when crises arise (Zarb and Oliver 1993).

There are multiple realities in dementia care and these realities change over the progression of the disease. Consequently, each dementia family will face many different demands and have many different needs, and these needs will change over the course of the disease. No one service or program working on its own can meet the individualized needs of dementia families. What is needed is a collaborative, seamless network of *flexible options and programs* responsive to the unique, changing, and individualized needs (e.g., physical, emotional, social, cultural) of dementia families (Smale and Dupuis 2004). There is an urgent need to improve the quality and the range of options and services available to dementia families (MacCourt 2006; Smale and Dupuis 2004), including opportunities for meaningful leisure and recreation and engagement in communities. Critical to family empowerment is the availability of user-directed or self-managed services and programs offering a range of service delivery options that respect the choices of dementia families and allows them to respond more quickly and effectively to their own changing demands and needs (Pedlar et al. 1999; Zarb and Oliver 1993).

Although a much broader range of housing options is needed for persons with dementia in our communities, including independent living homes, some persons with dementia and their families benefit greatly from *quality* support and care in larger residential facilities, particularly those persons who are at greater risk of isolation in their communities (Oldman and Quilgars 1999). In Canada, 50 per cent of all persons with dementia live in LTC homes (Canadian Study of Health and Aging 1994). Once a person with dementia moves to a LTC home, they are often cut off from their communities. This is because many LTC homes continue to operate as "total institutions" (Goffman 1961) with the assumption that they can meet all resident needs within the confines of the home. With the complex needs of persons living in these settings, this is simply not possible. If we hope to achieve the outcomes of the framework, "what is [greatly] needed is the elimination of the imaginary lines that demarcate the life within LTC settings from life outside those walls. This will require more positive discourses on old age and nursing homes/homes for the aged and a move towards an understanding of LTC facilities as valued, integrated components of our communities" (Dupuis, Smale, and Wiersma 2005). Rowles et al. (1996), for example, described an ethnographic case study of a rural nursing home that challenged the stereotype of LTC facilities as separate entities from the community. This rural nursing home established an integral place within the local community, where residents continued their involvement in the community and community members actively participated within the facility. This case study highlights the exciting "possibility of community integration as an underlying institutional ethos and aspiration" (199), as the authors conclude:

> By translating such an ethos in practical terms, it is possible to envisage nursing homes that play an expanded role in the community by providing day care, respite care, health clinics, hospice programs, health fairs for local residents, and a setting for community recreational, social, and civic activities. (Rowles et al. 1996, 199)

Here, recreation and leisure professionals play a pivotal role in creating an "institution without walls" and shifting the discourse on LTC settings by challenging current perceptions of these settings. Reframing our LTC settings as places of continued life and thriving and integral components of our communities, however, also will require the elimination of policies that restrict continued engagement of those who move to LTC settings in their communities. Examples of such policies are those that do not allow for participation in community day-away programs upon admission to a LTC facility. Furthermore, in order to ensure the fluidity of leisure services across the continuum of care, strong partnerships between recreation and leisure practitioners, and others, working in both community and LTC settings is critical.

Practising relationship-centred care takes time and hard work and strong partnerships are more likely to happen when there is continuity in those involved over time. However, there remains a critical shortage of human resources and high staff turnover rates in the current health care and community support service system (Dupuis and Smale 2004). Staff shortages are also evident in the recreation and leisure sector, resulting, for example, in very high resident-to-staff ratios in LTC settings (Dupuis et al. 2005). Investment is needed into developing an increased and stable workforce in dementia care, including those working in recreation and leisure. In order to do this, we must provide a fair, competitive, and uniform pay system, including better benefits and working conditions, for those who choose to work in dementia care. It might also require tax benefits in order to entice young people into dementia care. Unless the undervaluing of those who provide formal dementia care as indicated by the low wages and unmanageable workloads is addressed, "there will be an absence of action to lead to improvement in care provision experienced by persons with dementia" (Innes 2002, 486).

The planning framework depends on community and social networks that are strong and supportive. This means addressing the wider social issues such as the stigma attached to dementia and the misunderstanding of persons living with dementia through the investment in public awareness initiatives. Leisure and recreation professionals can partner with persons with dementia and play an important role in breaking down the stigma and fear associated with dementia by providing safe spaces for the voices of persons with dementia to be heard and for the demonstration to others of the continued potential of persons with ADRD. We also need to educate all those in our communities about the role that leisure and recreation can play in the promotion of cognitive function and health and the prevention of ADRD and in the maintenance and enhancement of family well-being across the dementia journey (Dupuis and Smale 2005).

CONCLUSION

The planning framework developed by the Roundtable has important implications for improving the quality of life of persons with dementia and their families living in our communities, but it may also be relevant to others in our communities, particularly others who are marginalized. If we hope for the framework to be adopted in practice, however, we need the commitment of government, local communities, and community organizations to the principles at the core of the framework. Government leadership and support, together with adequate funding and resources, including the realignment of resources to where they are most needed to support the individual choices of persons with dementia, are paramount if we hope to create a more responsive and collaborative system. Policy-led considerations on how to redesign the current system based on the partnership approach and reflective of the principles is necessary if we hope to achieve the outcome of meaningful lives through active personal and community engagement for all persons with dementia. Recreation and leisure must be at the centre of the new enabling network. Systemic changes that are necessary for this reframing of the way we support persons with dementia will also require the authority of legal mandates.

In accordance with the guiding principle of accountability, the intended outcomes and how they will be evaluated must be made explicit in any proposed plan(s) to address the needs of the ADRD community of interest. Doing so will ensure that all involved accept responsibility and are accountable. Incentives must be given to those communities, activities, and programs that support people *in* community life (McKnight 1992). Communities and community organizations must be able to demonstrate that they are achieving the vision and show evidence of how persons with dementia are being supported in living meaningful lives and maintaining continued engagement in their communities.

Finally, in keeping with a relationship-based approach, it is essential that the community in general and the ADRD community of interest in particular be actively and meaningfully engaged in the planning process. Instead of the well-being of those living with such illnesses being planned for by others, they need to be included as full partners at the planning table. Including them in meaningful ways in the development of and implementation of policies and programs is essential to arriving at plans that are responsive to the reality of their existence and respectful of their values. This will require a shift in professional attitudes and approaches and a change in how we view relationships with persons with dementia, moving from patient–professional expert relationships to citizen-facilitator relationships (Clarke 1999). In working together, we can better address the needs of persons with dementia and their families and ensure that all dementia families maintain quality of life and function well despite dementia.

REFERENCES

Adams, T. 1998. "The discursive construction of dementia care: Implications for mental health nursing." *Journal of Advanced Nursing* 28(3): 614–21.

Adams, T. 2005. "From person-centred to relationship-centred care." *Generations Review* 15(1): 4–7.

Adams, T., and C. L. Clarke. 1999. *Dementia Care: Developing Partnerships in Practice.* London: Baillière Tindall.

Aevarsson, O., and I. Skoog. 1996. "A population-based study on the incidence of dementia disorders between 85 and 88 years of age." *Journal of the American Geriatrics Society* 44: 1455–60.

Alzheimer Society of Canada (ASC). 2009. *Rising Tide: The Impact of Dementia on Canadian Society.* Toronto: Alzheimer Society of Canada.

Arai, S., and A. Pedlar. 2003. "Moving beyond individualism in leisure theory: A critical analysis of concepts of community and social engagement." *Leisure Studies* 22: 185–202.

Barnett, E. 2000. *Including the Person with Dementia in Designing and Delivering Care.* London: Jessica Kingsley.

Bender, M. P., and R. Cheston. 1997. "Inhabitants of a lost kingdom: A model of the subjective experiences of dementia." *Ageing & Society* 17: 513–32.

Bond, J. 1992. "The medicalization of dementia." *Journal of Aging Studies* 6(4): 397–403.

Canadian Study of Health and Aging (CSHA). 1994. "The Canadian study of health and aging: Study methods and prevalence of dementia." *Canadian Medical Association Journal* 150: 899–913.

Capitman, J. 2003. "Effective coordination of medical and supportive services." *Journal of Aging and Health* 15(1): 124–64.

Clarke, C. L. 1999. "Dementia care partnerships: Knowledge, ownership and exchange." In *Dementia Care: Developing Partnerships in Practice*, ed. T. Adams and C. Clarke, 5–35. London: Baillière Tindall.

Coalter, F. 2006. "The duality of leisure policy." In *A Handbook of Leisure Studies*, ed. C. Rojeck, S. Shaw, and A. J. Veal, 162–81. New York: Palgrave Macmillan.

Cox, S., I. Anderson, S. Dick, and H. Elgar. 1998. *The Person, the Community and Dementia: Developing a Value Framework*. Dementia Services Development Centre, Department of Applied Social Science, University of Stirling.

Dowling, S., J. Manthorpe, and S. Cowley. 2007. "Working on person-centred planning: From amber to green light?" *Journal of Intellectual Disabilities* 11(1): 65–82.

Downs, M. 2000. "Dementia in a socio-cultural context: An idea whose time has come." *Ageing & Society* 20: 369–75.

Dupuis, S. L., J. Gillies, J. Carson, C. Whyte, R. Genoe, L. Loiselle, and L. Sadler. In press. "Moving beyond patient and client approaches: Mobilizing authentic partnerships in dementia care."

Dupuis, S. L., and B.J.A. Smale. 2004. *In Their Own Voices: Dementia Caregivers Identify the Issues*. Final report prepared for the Ministry of Health and Long-term Care and the Ontario Senior's Secretariat as part of Initiative #6 of Ontario's Alzheimer Strategy. Waterloo, ON: Murray Alzheimer Research and Education Program.

Dupuis, S. L., and B.J.A. Smale. 2005. "The Dementia Supportive Environment Framework: Implications for recreation and leisure." In *The Two Solitudes: Isolation or Impact? Book of Abstracts, CCLR 11*, ed. T. Delamere, C. Randall, and D. Robinson, 148–55. Nanaimo, BC: Canadian Association for Leisure Studies.

Dupuis, S. L., B.J.A. Smale, and E. Wiersma. 2005. "Creating open environments in long-term care settings: An examination of influencing factors." *Therapeutic Recreation Journal* 39(4): 277–98.

Emanuel, E. J., and L. Emanuel. 1996. "What is accountability in health care?" *Annals of Internal Medicine* 124(2): 229–39.

Etzioni, A., Volmert, A., and Rothschild, E. 2004. *The Communitarian Reader: Beyond the Essentials*. Oxford: Rowman & Littlefield.

Ferri, C. P., M. Prince, C. Brayne, H. Brodaty, L. Fratiglioni, M. Ganguli, et al. 2005. "Global prevalence of dementia: A Delphi consensus study." *Lancet* 366: 2112–17.

Gaventa, J., and A. Cornwall. 2006. "Power and knowledge." In *Handbook of Action Research*, ed. P. Reason and H. Bradbury, 71–82. Thousand Oaks, CA: Sage.

Gibson, D. E., and S. G. Barsade. 2003. "Managing organizational culture change: The case of long-term care." *Journal of Social Work in Long-Term Care* 2(1/2): 11–34.

Gilleard, C., and P. Higgs. 2000. *Cultures of Ageing: Self, Citizen and the Body.* Harlow, UK: Prentice Hall.

Gilliard, J., R. Means, A. Beattie, and G. Daker-White. 2005. "Dementia care in England and the social model of disability: Lessons and issues." *Dementia* 4: 571–86.

Goffman, E. 1961. *Asylums.* New York: Doubleday.

Gold, M. F. 2002. "Freeing the human spirit." *Provider* (Jan.): 21–32.

Gwilliam, C., and J. Gilliard. 1996. "Dementia and the social model of disability." *Journal of Dementia Care* 4(1): 14–15.

Hall, J., and C. McWilliam. 2006. "About the culture of in-home nursing." *Home Health Care Services Quarterly* 25(3): 75–90.

Henderson, J. N. 1995. "The culture of care in a nursing home: Effects of a medicalized model of long-term care." In *The Culture of Long-Term Care: Nursing Home Ethnography*, ed. J. N. Henderson and M. D. Vesperi, 37–54. Westport, CT: Bergin & Garvey.

Innes, A. 2002. "The social and political context of formal dementia care provision." *Ageing & Society* 22: 483–99.

Johnson, N., T. Davis, and N. Bosanquet. 2000. "The epidemic of Alzheimer's disease: How can we manage the costs?" *Pharmacoeconomics* 18: 215–23.

Kitwood, T. 1989. "Brain, mind and dementia: With particular reference to Alzheimer's disease." *Ageing & Society* 9: 1–15.

Kitwood, T. 1990. "The dialectics of dementia: With particular reference to Alzheimer's disease." *Ageing & Society* 10: 177–96.

Kitwood, T. 1997. *Dementia Reconsidered: The Person Comes First*. Buckingham, UK: Open University Press.

Kitwood, T., and K. Bredin. 1992. "Towards a theory of dementia care: Personhood and well-being." *Ageing & Society* 12: 269–87.

Koppel, J. 2003. *The Politics of Quasi-Government: Hybrid Organizations and the Dynamics of Bureaucratic Control.* Cambridge: Cambridge University Press.

MacCourt, P. 2006. *Discussion Paper: Possibilities for Federal Government Action on Alzheimer Disease and Related Dementias.* Ottawa: Public Health Agency of Canada.

Marshall, M. 1994. Emerging trends in dementia care: Some thoughts on the next ten years. Concluding presentation at Alzheimer's Disease International conference, Edinburgh.

McKnight, J. 1992. "Redefining community." *Social Policy* 23/24: 56–62.

McKnight, J. 1997. "A 21st century map for healthy communities and families." *Families in Society* 78(2): 117–27.

McKnight, J. 2005. "Community and its counterfeits." In *Ideas: Brilliant Thinkers Speak Their Minds*, ed. B. Lucht, 112–28. Fredericton, NB: Goose Lane Editions.

McWilliam, C., C. Ward-Griffin, D. Sweetland, C. Sutherland, and L. O'Halloran. 2001. "The experience of empowerment in in-home services delivery." *Home Health Care Services Quarterly* 20(4): 49–71.

Miller, E. A., M. Booth, and V. Mor. 2008. "Assessing experts' views of the future of long-term care." *Research on Aging* 30(4): 450–73.

Mitchell, G J., C. Jonas-Simpson, and S. L. Dupuis. 2006. *'I'm Still Here' DVD and a Teaching-Learning Guide to Understanding Living with Dementia through the Medium of the Arts*. Waterloo: Murray Alzheimer Research and Education Program.

Nolan, M. R., U. Lundh, G. Grant, and J. Keady. 2003. *Partnerships in Family Care*. Buckingham: Open University Press.

Nolan, M. R., S. Davies, J. Brown, J. Keady, and J. Nolan. 2004. "Beyond 'person-centred' care: A new vision for gerontological nursing." *Journal of Clinical Nursing* 13(3a): 45–53.

Oldman, C., and D. Quilgars. 1999. "The last resort? Revisiting ideas about older people's living arrangements." *Ageing & Society* 19: 363–84.

Pedlar, A., and L. Haworth. 2006. "Community." In *A Handbook of Leisure Studies*, ed. C. Rojeck, S. M. Shaw, and A. J. Veal, 518–32. New York: Palgrave Macmillan.

Pedlar, A., L. Haworth, P. Hutchison, A. Taylor, and P. Dunn. 1999. *A Textured Life: Empowerment and Adults with Development Disabilities.* Waterloo: Wilfrid Laurier University Press.

Pollitt, P.A. 1996. "Dementia in old age: An anthropological perspective." *Psychological Medicine* 26: 1061–74.

Priestley, M. 2000. "Adults only: Disabilty, social policy and the life course." *Journal of Social Policy* 29(3): 421–39.

Rahman, A. N., and J. F. Schnelle. 2008. "The nursing home culture-change movement: Recent past, present and future directions for research." *The Gerontologist* 48(2): 142–48.

Rawls, J. 1971. *A Theory of Justice.* Cambridge, MA: Belknap Press of Harvard University Press.

Rimmer, E., C. Stave, A. Sganga, and B. O'Connell. 2005. "Implications of the Facing Dementia Survey for policy makers and third-party organisations across Europe." *International Journal of Clinical Practice* 59: 34–38.

Rioux, M. H. 1994. "Towards a concept of equality of well-being: Overcoming the social and legal construction of inequality." *Canadian Journal of Law and Jurisprudence* 7(1): 127–41.

Robertson, A. 1991. "The politics of Alzheimer's disease: A case study in apocalyptic demography." *International Journal of Health Services* 20(3): 429–442.

Robinson, C.A. 1993. "Managing life with a chronic condition: The story of normalization." *Qualitative Health Research* 3(1): 6–28.

Rowles, G. D., J. A. Concotelli, and D. M. High. 1996. "Community integration of a rural nursing home." *Journal of Applied Gerontology* 15(2): 188–201.

Sachs, G. A., J. W. Shega, and D. Cox-Hayley. 2004. "Barriers to excellent end-of-life care for patients with dementia." *Journal of Nursing Scholarship* 32: 251–58.

Sassi, F., and D. McDaid, eds. 1999. *Transnational Analysis of Socio-Economic Aspects of Alzheimer's Disease in the European Union.* London: London School of Economics and Political Science.

Schön, D. A. 1983. *The Reflective Practitioner: How Professionals Think in Action.* New York: Basic Books.

Schön, D. A. 1987. *Educating the Reflective Practitioner.* San Francisco: Jossey-Bass.

Smale, B. J. A., and S. L. Dupuis. 2004. *In Their Own Voices: Guiding Principles and Strategies for Change by and for Dementia Caregivers in Ontario.* Final report prepared for the Ministry of Health and Long-term Care and the Ontario Senior's Secretariat as part of Initiative #6 of Ontario's Alzheimer Strategy. Waterloo, ON: Murray Alzheimer Research and Education Program.

Stainton, T. 2005. "Empowerment and the architecture of rights based social policy." *Journal of Intellectual Disabilities* 9(4): 289–98.

Stevens, C. H. 2001. "A timeless dream." *Balance* 7 (Nov./Dec.): 7–18.

Toqueville, A. de. 1945. *Democracy in America.* New York: Knopf.

Zarb, G., and M. Oliver. 1993. *Ageing with a Disability.* London: University of Greenwich.

5

Poverty and Leisure as Social Determinants of Health: The Politics of Oppression and Transformation in Social Policy

Susan M. Arai and Rishia Burke

INTRODUCTION

The gap between the rich and the poor is growing in Canada (Campaign 2000 2006a, 2006b; Robson-Haddow 2004). Even after the impact of government transfer payments and income taxes, the poorest 20 per cent of the population in Canada held only 5 per cent of the income in 2003, while the richest 20 per cent secured 43.7 per cent (National Council of Welfare 2006). The crisis-oriented and reactive measures we put into place to address poverty such as food banks, shelters, and welfare payments have not been enough to address the root causes of poverty, and they have also been whittled away in the cutbacks that local communities have experienced over the last decade. Furthermore, leisure studies has predominantly been absent from this discussion. This issue is addressed by many of the authors in this book. The idea for this chapter stems from a series of research projects that we have been engaged in with women living in poverty and a number of non-profit and municipal government organizations addressing poverty through community initiatives at the local level.

To address the issue of poverty, we must broaden social policy beyond an emphasis on job skills, employment connections, and social assistance to address the systemic issues of discrimination, lack of supports, social exclusion, and lower health status resulting from experiences of oppression. We must also ensure that the voices of the people most affected by the policy are heard in the policy arena. The poverty rate in Canada was 15.9 per cent in 2003 (National Council of Welfare 2006). In that year almost one in six Canadians lived below the poverty line. In reality, the rate of poverty is much higher, as this statistic does not include people living in institutions or people who are Aboriginal living on reserves. In addition, if we look at the poverty rate over the five-year period between 1996 and 2001, 30.7 per cent of Canadians fell into poverty for at least one year (National Council of Welfare). Some remained there for only one year, while 5.9 per cent or one million people lived in poverty for the entire five years (National Council of Welfare).

This chapter presents a rethinking of poverty and offers suggestions for transforming communities in an effort to better address it. We argue for the need to confront the oppressions and power inequalities that underlie poverty and to reconceptualize poverty as a relational and community issue in order to respond to the systemic nature of inequality in Canada. The *Ottawa Charter for Health Promotion* (World Health Organization 1986) identified the social determinants of health as "prerequisites for health," and where peace, shelter, education, food, income, a stable eco-system, social justice, and equity were identified as the fundamental conditions and resources for health. We argue here that leisure should be included among these prerequisites if we are going to address poverty in a meaningful way. This includes thinking about poverty in a dynamic and complex way, broadening our understanding of social policy and therefore our range of options for intervention and transformation. Furthermore, we argue that broadening our view of leisure helps to emphasize its relational aspects as a way to address poverty and that embodying a politics of difference is imperative for creating change.

Rethinking Our View of Poverty

As a society we have predominantly defined poverty as an individual issue, if not in word then in our practices. How society defines poverty significantly impacts our ability to understand who is affected and to develop necessary interventions for alleviation, as well as to determine who is involved in changing the conditions that create poverty. A national definition of poverty does not exist in Canada, and thus poverty alleviation has been left to a myriad of practices. Drawing broadly from the social science literature, poverty is defined in the following ways:

1. as a *measure*;

2. as the experience of *powerlessness, voicelessness and social exclusion*;

3. in terms of relationships and the impact on an individual's access to the *social determinants of health*; and

4. as a *community issue*.

We argue that society's emphasis on defining poverty as a measure narrows our focus to poverty being an individual issue, while the other three approaches frame poverty as a relational and social issue. Integrating these definitions of poverty results in a more comprehensive understanding of poverty from which we may then move forward to action for change and transformation. Each of these ways of defining poverty is described further in the sections that follow.

Poverty as a Measure

Measures of poverty such as low income cut-offs (LICOs)[1] and market basket measures (MBMs)[2] provide us with an indication of the number of people living in poverty and the depth of the poverty experienced. Although Statistics Canada is careful to say the LICO is not a "poverty line," it is commonly used as such (Canadian Council on Social Development 2001) to define the individuals who live in poverty and those who do not. In 2005 the before-tax LICO for a community with a population of 100,000 to 499,999 ranged from $17,895 for one person to $33,251 for a family of four (National Council of Welfare 2006).

The issue with monetized definitions, or measures of poverty, is that they are highly individualized and they leave inequality and access to prevailing standards of life unaddressed. The missing piece in this analysis is a cultural understanding of what it means to live in poverty, or the understanding that poverty is extremely harsh for those living below the average standard in society. The obvious issue, with arbitrary lines drawn in the sand is: if you find yourself just above the LICO or just barely able to afford the market basket of goods, are you really no longer poor?

POVERTY AS POWERLESSNESS, VOICELESSNESS AND SOCIAL EXCLUSION

Poverty is gendered and racialized. Acting on poverty requires understanding who actually lives in poverty and the differences experienced. If we, as a society, wish to move beyond victim-blaming and victimizing, we must recognize the multiple oppressions that people experience and that poverty, and the stigma of poverty, is not independent of other kinds of oppression. Defining poverty as the experience of powerlessness, voicelessness, and social exclusion considers issues of power and the multiple layers of oppression and stress associated with living in poverty that must be addressed if we are to assist individuals to move out of poverty and experience social inclusion.

Poverty is often associated with those who are homeless and living on the streets, but it is important to realize that many living in poverty are also invisible in our society. While the poverty rate in Canada in 2003 was at 15.9 per cent, the poverty rate is considerably higher among some groups (Statistics Canada 2006). There is greater poverty among women than men, and poverty is on the rise among young adults. There is also a significant portion of the population known as the "working

Table 5.1: Comparison of average income and poverty rates among marginalized groups in Canada.[b]

	Women		Men	
	Poverty rate (% living below LICO)	Average Income	Poverty rate (% living below LICO)	Average Income
All Canadians	17.1	$24,400	14.7	$39,300
Foreign-born	23.0	$22,400	20.0	$48,000[c]
People with disabilities	26.0	$17,200	20.0	$26,900
Visible minority	29.0	$20,000	28.0	$29,000
New immigrant	35.0	$16,700	35.0	$38,000[c]
Aboriginal	44.0[a]	$12,300	–	$15,500
Single parents	48.9	–	20.0	–

Notes: [a] For women living off-reserve (CRIAW, 2006). [b] Source: Statistics Canada (2006). [c] Approximation based on chart information.

poor." The experience of poverty in Canada is greatest among women, lone-parent families, visible minorities and immigrants, people with disabilities and mental health concerns, survivors of abuse and trauma, and children (Breitkreuz 2005; Lee 2000; Lindsay and Almey 2006; Séguin and Divay 2002; Wilton 2004) as reflected in the poverty rates and income levels noted in Table 5.1.

The gendered nature of poverty speaks to the number of women who live in poverty and also the depth of poverty. The poverty rate among women was 17.1 per cent compared to a poverty rate of 14.7 per cent among men (National Council of Welfare 2006). When we look across different subgroups, the picture clearly reveals the intersection of other forces of oppression that heighten the experience of poverty among women (see Table 5.1). Across all categories of women, average income levels continue to be lower than those of men. Across all professions and occupations, women's earnings are, on average, 61 per cent of that of men. Poverty strategies that focus only on gaining access to employment ignore the systemic inequities that women experience in the system of wages and employment in Canada. There are clear structural reasons for women's lower incomes: the presence of children, lower wages, cuts to social assistance, and having inadequate pensions and contributions to RRSPs (Canadian Research Institute for the Advancement of Women [CRIAW] 2006). Almost one in every two single-parent mothers will live in poverty (Statistics Canada 2006; see Table 5.1). Women earn less than men even if they work in the same sectors in the same jobs. There are no occupations where women's average earnings exceed that of men's (Pay Equity Task Force 2004), not even in female-dominated areas such as clerical work and teaching (CRIAW 2006). The majority of women are employed in retail services, education, health industries, and in small firms (Drolet 2002). In addition, women are over-represented in part-time, seasonal, and precarious work.

If we are going to alleviate poverty we must do more than just focus on getting people into jobs; we must concern ourselves with the type and quality of jobs. Women contribute to 68 per cent of the part-time work force and only 42 per cent of the full-time work force in Canada (Statistics Canada 2006). The result is that many women often do not have protection under labour codes or collective bargaining agreements. Most jobs do not include flexibility, autonomy, or benefits necessary for women.

Table 5.1 also reveals the racialized nature of poverty. Almost one in three (29%) of women who are visible minorities (whether Canadian or foreign-born) will live below the LICO, and if you are a new immigrant (arriving since 1995) the chance of living in poverty is increased (35%). In 2000, approximately one in every four immigrant women and women with disabilities had incomes below the LICO, in contrast to

Canadian-born women and men. Almost one in every two Aboriginal women will live in poverty (Statistics Canada 2006; see Table 5.1). For women living on reserves the situation is much worse as 47 per cent of the population makes less than $10,000 per year (CRIAW 2006). Aboriginal women face numerous challenges, including discrimination, difficulty in speaking English or French, a history of abuse or violence, isolation, and a lack of resources. In part, as a result of the continuing impacts of the Indian Act, they face insecurities related to housing as well as access to services both on and off reserve (CRIAW 2006).

There is a need to proceed with caution in how we approach difference. Among those who live in poverty, continued oppression makes some people invisible, and it holds others up to become the target of judgment and blame. Often, where marginalized people are made more visible, they are held up as targets of judgment. Or we drive people out of sight and out of our consciousness, and in many ways we remain unaffected by poverty. There is an *othering* that happens with poverty. The idea is to not make the people more visible (as in quota policies) but to make the experience of oppression, the systemic causes of that oppression, and the similarities in experiences of all people more visible.

What is not revealed in Table 5.1, but is closely related to the statistics that we see is the issue of violence against women[3] and children and the connection to poverty. Among adults who have experienced abuse-related trauma in childhood, the average income is lower than those who did not (Alisen 2003). Individuals who have experienced sexual assault were found to have an income deficit of about $6,000 per year (MacMillan 1999). Abuse-related trauma may have prolonged and lasting impacts on an individual's work, career, and personal and social relationships (Centre for Addiction and Mental Health 2004; Mosher, Evans and Little 2004; Russell 1999).

Thus, there is a need to understand poverty as the result of power relationships and issues of violence and abuse, patriarchy, and racism must be confronted directly.

Poverty as Relational Access to the Social Determinants of Health

Poverty is relational and based in power. We can no longer afford to think in terms of categories that divide us – rich–poor, sick–healthy, oppressed–privileged – if we are to address poverty. The focus of change must be on building stronger relationships between people and to build a greater consciousness about our interrelatedness. Poverty is not an individual issue. As Burman (1996) describes it, poverty is "relational and an integral part of the workings of mainstream society. It is not fundamentally about the attributes of a person facing economic hardship but about the wrenchings and realignment of personal projects, relationships and exchanges following hardship" (17).

When we understand poverty as relational, addressing it also means addressing patriarchy, racism, and violence against women and children. As described in the previous section, the persons at greatest risk of living in poverty are those who experience multiple factors of socially constructed oppression, including violence against women, tightly bound gender norms in relation to work, active discrimination based on (dis) ability and mental illness, and racism. These forms of oppression lead to social isolation and social exclusion. Each of these oppressions often results in isolation from social networks and social capital, and an internalized oppression that leads to a diminished sense of self. This makes options limited and individual choices difficult to make.

A social determinants of health framework is useful in that it enables us to understand the impact of prolonged experiences of poverty. Poverty is often identified as the most important determinant of health, as it is highly associated with diminished access to the other determinants of health (e.g., housing, education, social supports, health care). Diminished access is not only the result of minimal financial resources but also diminished relationships and social supports. While the determinants of health identify *what* people need in order to be healthy (e.g., income, housing) and quality of life examines *how* these aspects contribute to health and well-being through a process of unfolding and becoming, social inclusion emphasizes a proactive human development approach calling for more than the removal of barriers and risks (Richmond and Saloojee 2005). In a policy context, social inclusion emphasizes opportunities for citizen participation, capacity, and agency and encourages the tools (economic, social, health, educational and legal) that make autonomy possible (Mitchell and Shillington 2005).

Where social inclusion and the centrality of relationships are not considered, access to the determinants of health is experienced by people living in poverty like an encounter with a brick wall. Each of the relational oppressions experienced adds a layer of bricks to a wall which must be scaled in order to fully experience the things that determine health. Poverty is a wall of relational oppression. Layers of this wall include relational oppressions related to:

the community economy- lack of jobs available in rural communities, safety of work available to women

racism - being a new immigrant with unrecognized qualifications, racism related to language and accent

ableism- having a disability and a welfare system that makes it challenging to move off of ODSP, inflexibility in the workplace, stigma experienced in relation to disability

stigma of having a mental illness- experiencing challenges of moving off of ODSP, inflexibility in the workplace, stigma of having a mental illness

violence- having a history of abuse or trauma (financial losses, lower health status, diminished choice and self esteem)

being a lone parent- unstable housing, lack of access to affordable child care when working shifts

ageism- being an older woman returning to the workforce (perceptions about work experience and education in relation to age)

patriarchy- being a woman receiving 67% the wages of men, more experiences of part-time and seasonal work and consequently a lack of health benefits, gaps in employment and the challenges of re-training and making connections to employment

When an individual is woven into the fabric of society, the determinants of health are assumed aspects of daily living. While access to education, employment, housing, and health care are experienced by people who are wealthy, for a woman, living in poverty accessing the determinants of health is like scaling a brick wall. There develops an expectation that the individual must secure these determinants of health to be deemed a worthy citizen. Supports become institutionalized and create multiple barriers for a woman to negotiate. Several authors describe the experiences of stigma and oppression among people who receive social assistance (Burman 1996; Mosher, Evans and Little 2004; Polakoff and Gregory 2002) and the challenges people experience in trying to access supports including social assistance, employment supports, education, housing, child care, health, and mental health services (Breitkreuz 2005; McMullin, Davies and Cassidy 2002; Williamson and Reutter 1999). Women living in poverty speak about feeling ashamed when their children's friends see the apartments or homes they live in, or when neighbours see them going into a food bank, or "feeling like nothing" because they are receiving Ontario Works. These statements help us to understand how women living in poverty experience the determinants of health and the need for relational supports. As one woman we spoke to described, "when you have support it's amazing what you can do. Every resource can be out there, but if you don't have somebody to say it's okay, or maybe somebody to give you that gentle nudge in the right direction, all those resources don't mean anything" (Christine).

POVERTY AS A COMMUNITY ISSUE

> It doesn't take much to shatter a comfortable middle class existence. Unless your job is rock solid, your marriage is impregnable, your investments are risk proof, and you are certain that your health will never fail, you can't rule out the chance that you or your children might some day need help. (Carol Goar, columnist from the *Toronto Star*, May 18, 2007, A24)

Poverty affects us all. When we focus on poverty as an individual issue, we neglect the impact of poverty on our collective health and well-being. We are all at risk of experiencing poverty and if we do not fall into that pit of poverty then we are going to be affected in other ways. Poverty has wide-sweeping effects on the quality of life and health of not only individuals and families but also communities (Canadian Council on Social Development 2000; National Council of Welfare 2001–02; Williamson and Reutter 1999). Understanding poverty as a community condition considers the ways continued cycles of poverty begin to erode community. When we turn a blind eye to poverty, or leave root causes and their impacts to be unaddressed, there are five main ways that continued cycles of poverty begin to erode community.

First, poverty affects community health. Common impacts of poverty on women include acute and chronic health, being susceptible to infectious and other diseases, increased heart disease, clinical depression, stress, vulnerability to mental illness and self-destructive coping behaviours. Groups experiencing social exclusion tend to sustain higher health risks and lower health status (Galabuzi 2004). People living in poverty experience high levels of stigma and discrimination and related to this is a high degree of stress. Single parents are more likely to report having fair to poor mental health and describe challenges in terms of their ability to handle day-to-day demands or unexpected problems (Government of Canada 2006; McCain, Mustard and Shanker 2007). Researchers such as Freiler, Rothman and Barata (2004) point to the destructive emotional effect of poverty on children and adults. Children who live in poverty often experience poor health, social and emotional difficulties, difficulties in academic achievement, decreased access to opportunities for skill-building, and limited outlets for creativity and play. The experience of overcrowding also leads to the re-emergence of diseases such as tuberculosis.

Second, poverty leads to constant moves that break down the social fabric of a community. The urban poor tend to be more transient and their lives are disrupted by constantly moving (CRIAW 2006). Nearly 30 per cent of children have changed schools three times before the age of 11, in contrast to 10 per cent of higher-income children (Campaign 2000

2006a; 2006b). Poverty traps and limits people's choices and "hidden homelessness" makes people transient, temporarily staying with family, friends or a man or woman. This increases vulnerability to conflict or violence, especially for women (CRIAW 2006).

Third, as a community we have the knowledge and awareness of the complex causes of poverty, and yet we enable a culture of blame and judgment to continue to place limits on our own future. When people are blamed for being poor, it erodes their spirit and self-esteem and becomes internalized, turning into self-abuse; it robs people of the very spirit that they require to move out of poverty (CRIAW 2006). When individuals are blamed for being poor, it takes attention away from the state of the economy, social policy, unemployment, and the impact of poverty on our children. When we limit our vision, we limit our future potential for improving our own communities.

Fourth, chronically limiting people's choices may lead to crime. Only a minority of people turn to crime to supplement their income. However, a long-term study has shown that the most frequent criminal offenders came from the poorest families with the worst housing (CRI-AW 2006). Studies have revealed that most female offenders are women with low levels of education, few job skills, no economic resources, living alone in poor conditions, and unable to support themselves (Chunn and Gavigan 1995).

Fifth, the participatory nature of democracy is eroded when so many people living in poverty are excluded from decision-making structures in our communities. Viewing poverty as a community issue requires a strong social inclusion discourse that includes a concern with rights, citizenship, and restructured relations between marginalized and excluded communities and the institutions of the dominant society. As Richmond and Saloojee (2005) describe, social inclusion focuses on valued recognition and valued participation by those excluded from full participation in society and from the benefits of society. One of the strengths of our communities is the diversity within them. When women, new immigrants, single-parents, Aboriginal, working poor, and/or people with disabilities are excluded from decision-making structures, we lose valued assets and our strength as a community. The result is an erosion of participatory democracy. When we allow people to continue to live in poverty, we all suffer.

Moving to Transformation

At the heart of this chapter is a focus on reconceptualizing poverty and addressing the role of leisure studies in addressing this social issue. What can we do about poverty? Here we make four suggestions in response to this question. We can start by thinking about poverty in a dynamic and complex way. We can broaden our view of social policy and therefore our range of options for intervention and transformation. We can broaden our view of leisure from that of an individual pursuit to emphasizing the relational aspects of leisure and the role that it may play in addressing poverty. And in our understanding and approaches to creating change, it is imperative that we embody a politics of difference or else we risk perpetuating the oppressions connected to poverty.

Starting with the Dynamics and Complexities of Poverty: The Hourglass of Poverty

Drawing on the four ways that poverty can be defined – as a measure; as powerlessness, voicelessness, and social exclusion; as relational access to the social determinants of health; and as a community issue – we need to think in terms of dynamic and complex solutions to address poverty. To hold all of these definitions in our imagination as we attempt to confront poverty, we may think about the inner workings of poverty as an hourglass. The sand in the hourglass is a symbol of the oppression and social exclusion that trickles down from society and institutions to individuals and families and weighs down upon the foundations of community over time. Every time the hourglass is turned, each solitary grain of sand resettles itself representing the repeated breaking of relationships and the isolation of individuals from each other. As a society we have tended to keep turning over that hourglass, re-creating institutions of oppression that perpetuate cycles of poverty. As evidence of this, in 1989 the federal government declared an end to child poverty by the year 2000. That year our child poverty rate was at 16.2 per cent and by 2003 it had risen to 17.6 per cent. The question we might ask then is: how can we keep that hourglass from continually turning?

Thinking in terms of the hourglass of poverty, we need to keep these four definitions of poverty in mind if we are going to address poverty in a comprehensive and meaningful way. We also need to do more than that. The next time we allow that oppression to trickle down and lead to the experience of poverty, the next time that we turn that hourglass over, can we think about actions for change and transformation? And if we are going to think about transformation, we need to think about more than fiscal policy, about more than just employment strategies. There is a much larger role for recreation and leisure studies to play in the lives of individuals, families, and communities living with poverty. In addition, there is a need to also consider the power and potential for transformation and the opportunities for hope and healing among the people who live in poverty and all members of the community. These aspects are addressed in the following sections.

BROADENING OUR UNDERSTANDING OF SOCIAL POLICY OPTIONS TO ADDRESS POVERTY

There is a need to look at a more comprehensive social policy approach to addressing poverty. We need an approach that includes a broad definition of social policy that incorporates leisure in the vision alongside fiscal and economic policy. We also need policy that is proactive and focuses on building community capacity, building relationships of strength where oppression has worn away experiences of community and isolated individuals from each other.

Where poverty is defined broadly with a focus on social and cultural aspects of the experience, increasing access to the determinants of health, and promoting social inclusion, action requires that we take an equally broad approach to understanding the policy options that are required to address poverty. We need to move beyond narrow definitions of social policy, which focus solely on welfare and income security (social insurance, public assistance, health and welfare services, housing) and look to policy options included in broad definitions of social policy which include activities of government that affect social life (marriage and divorce legislation, arts and culture, economic policy, policies affecting families) including access to, and the delivery of leisure in the public and non-profit domains.

Another way to broaden our understanding of social policy is to consider the range of ways in which policy is developed and is played out in community. We need to consider not only the development of explicit social policies but also the implications of policies that happen by default, from our failure to act. Here three forms of policy can be considered:

- *policy by default* results when we do not have social policy that addresses poverty at the community level. When this happens the community is forced to devise impromptu approaches to meet basic needs (access to food, shelter, health care).

- Over time, these "stop gap" measures (e.g., shelters, foodbanks, clothing drives, Christmas baskets) become institutionalized in the community, resulting in *de facto policy* or policy that arises from what is done, however, the systemic issue remains unaddressed.

- *de jure* forms of policy are explicit statements of policy and include the reactive, preactive, and proactive policy options described in legislation and statutes or by-laws (Burch 1994).

- *Reactive policy* includes approaches that are regulatory and punitive (e.g., sentencing and fines) and include prohibition of activities such as loitering or sleeping in public places.

- *Preactive policy* focuses on preventing a condition, for example, increases in pricing or taxation to reduce consumption of alcohol or drugs.

- *Proactive policy* is focused on capacity building (e.g., focusing on the healthy development of children, youth and adults) and mandatory actions.

While many of our current interventions focus on fixing individuals (e.g., employment supports), which tend to be reactive (e.g., Ontario Works), there are a broader array of approaches needed to assist individuals and communities to disentangle from systemic oppressions and poverty. If we view the inner-workings of poverty using the hourglass model, we understand the necessity for a focus not only on individuals but also on communities, not only on reactive approaches to social policy but also more proactive approaches that contribute to transformation through relationships and community. In the transformation of poverty, the sand in the hourglass becomes the potentiality of individuals, families and communities for transformation; that is, for social engagement, for returning to paid work or some other contribution to society, for resisting patriarchal gender roles and other forms of oppression, for re-creating relationships of power and creating a different social and political system in community.

We cannot focus solely on reforming the system without considering the individuals and families who live in poverty. In their own voices, the people we have worked with describe the need to be considered as a whole person – persons with a voice and multiple challenges and strengths. There is a role here for preactive approaches focused on building resiliency among individuals and families. The hourglass model emphasizes the development of policies that allow children (and adults), to borrow a phrase from Mustard, McCain and Shanker (2007), to not only survive but to thrive. This will also invoke a stronger proactive policy role for leisure and communities and a more dominant emphasis on social inclusion and the role of leisure as a relational determinant of individual and community health. It is also important to remember that when a person stands up with resistance and mindfulness to transform themselves, this does not mean that society was not sick with oppression. Therefore our transformations must also address violence, racism, and patriarchy in community both directly and through preactive and proactive forms of policy.

LEISURE AS A RELATIONAL DETERMINANT OF HEALTH AND SOCIAL INCLUSION

Leisure is more than a vehicle for developing skills that increase employability. More fundamentally, leisure has the potential to enable an individual to experience a sense of self outside of the oppression created by unemployment and poverty, or the oppression or abuse experienced in the home. For an individual who has experienced poverty and other forms of oppression, there is a need to redevelop a sense of self and sense of social self beyond the oppression. Nancy describes the employment that would help her to overcome the gender-based oppression that she experiences in her home:

> my husband, I have always been there for him on the weekend.... If this was a job that really did something to me inside ... something I needed mentally and emotionally ... that I didn't get all of those years, and I could see this was something that meant something more to me than staying second place behind my husband ... and if it meant that I had to work the weekends then I could do it. (Nancy)

This can only be done through leisure in the context of community. This includes not only finding a job but also opportunities for volunteering or community organizing. If we broaden our understanding of leisure beyond diversionary activity and as something subservient to work, we may see the potential that leisure has for meaningful participation in community, including making a contribution through community organizing. In the case that the woman is not able to work (due to childcare needs or limitations created by mental illness or disability), social assistance levels must be in place to support the individual at a level that will still enable her to participate and make a contribution to her community without stigma. Reid, Golden, and Katerberg (this volume) speak about the new social contract and the need for an emphasis on "worthfare" rather than workfare. Against the isolation of people who have experienced abuse and trauma, addictions, mental illness, disability, and/or exclusion based on gender and race, we need to consider leisure not only as an individual pursuit but also a relational determinant of health. In our study when we asked the women what message they would like to send to decision-makers, they talked about the need for relationships: the desire to connect with other women and contribute to community using their knowledge that has been hard-won through experience.

While income has the most significant impact on a person's experience of health (World Health Organization 1997), it is not sufficient to help individuals to break out of the welfare cycle (Browne, Byrne, Roberts, Gafni, and Whittaker 2001). When we focus on poverty as a community condition, we must invoke a strong social inclusion element that focuses not only on rights and citizenship but also on restructured relationships between marginalized and excluded communities and the institutions of dominant society. Social inclusion emphasizes opportunities for participation, capacity, and agency (Mitchell and Shillington 2005). Many authors point to the importance of leisure activities for the health of people on social assistance (Reid and Golden 2004; Reid, Frisby, Millar, Pinnington, and Ponic 2000). Therefore, as Freiler, Rothman, and Barata (2004) note:

> all families must be a part of safe, vibrant communities with well-developed community infrastructure, such as public libraries, accessible recreation/cultural services and well-resourced public schools. It is in healthy, inclusive communities where parents can sustain environments in which their children can thrive, not merely survive. (14)

Here leisure is an important relational determinant of health, and an important proactive policy would be the emphasis on the inclusion of all children and youth in leisure opportunities in the community. We need equal access to programs and services in community regardless of income. As Gina Browne and colleagues describe, access to leisure can help children and youth to build resiliency to offset the negative developmental impacts of a life of poverty (cf. Browne et al., 1999; Browne et al. 2001). Browne et al. (2001) state that access to community services can positively impact childhood development and resiliency independently of socio-economic status.

In doing so, we need to create inclusive spaces for people to build relationships that support difference and people's expression of diversity and do not reproduce the oppressions that are so intimately intertwined with poverty. The question becomes: can we transform leisure opportunities so that we are not adding another layer of bricks in the wall for people living in poverty? This is addressed in the final section of this chapter.

ACKNOWLEDGING A POLITICS OF DIFFERENCE IN SOCIAL POLICY

There is an emerging literature on the importance of community approaches to crafting more humane and inclusive spaces for people to flourish (Arai and Pedlar 2003; Burman 1996; Frisby, Reid, Millar, and Hoeber 2005). These spaces may be women-only spaces, or spaces for women of colour or disability, or spaces specifically for one group, as long as the barriers between those spaces are permeable so that we all might move in and out freely and at will. A report from Canadian Municipalities indicates that for individuals to participate in the community, sustain good health, form a stable base, and access adequate food and shelter, it is important to have an adequate income. Poor access to community resources and low participation in community is the result of low income and results in isolation from the community (Arundel 2003). Therefore, overcoming the brick wall also requires access to relational experiences to connect to other economic capital and other determinants of health; steps on a ladder that may help an individual to get over a wall. In addition there is a need for what Don Dawson refers to in this volume as the new social architecture: moving beyond using social policy with the aim only to protect people from the market.

Whatever the option is that we wish to provide for supporting people as they move beyond poverty, whether it is employment strategies or access to recreation and leisure opportunities, some flexibility must be built into the system in terms of flexible hours and conditions, accessible child care, and appropriate accommodations. Else the supports become *another brick in the wall* and will oppress where the intention was to provide opportunities for transformation. At the heart of poverty is the issue of power, and therefore this approach also considers differences within categories of people and the need for individualized and flexible supports that do not dehumanize or diminish, but rather, further strengthen and support. In the words of the women who participated in our study, there is a need for consistent support and *to be treated as a whole human being*. Here women-centred approaches and mentors are important to support women on the path back to community: a person(s) to stay with the women and hold them through every step of the process. Holding does not mean doing for or holding one's hand. Rather it refers to a Buddhist concept of bearing witness to people's struggles and experiences, providing an opportunity for discourse about the challenges encountered on the path.

The movement toward transformation begins with understanding the unique paths travelled by different women (including women who are new immigrants, or living with a disability or mental illness, or women who have experienced trauma and abuse) and the multiplicity of their experiences. There is a need for women-centred supports and a specific understanding of the need for flexible, individualized supports, which help to build relationships and to overcome the barriers that divide and isolate individuals (rejecting, labelling).

Conclusions

Many of the ideas presented in this chapter are not new. What is new is the reconceptualization of poverty and leisure together, the bringing together of these ideas into our imagination to overcome the fragmentation in our thinking about poverty, individuals, leisure and community with an eye on the radical transformation that is needed if we are going to address not only the immediate individual experiences of poverty but also the underlying systemic issues intertwined with the creation of poverty in the first place. In this chapter we argued for the need to confront the oppression and power that underlies poverty and to reconceptualize poverty as a relational and community issue with the necessary inclusion of leisure as a community and social policy strategy for addressing poverty in a meaningful way. We identified the range of social policy options for intervention and transformation and the need to incorporate the politics of difference centrally in our attempts to create change and transformation. These ideas are only the beginning, and our road ahead is to refine and deepen our understanding of these ideas and their implications for research and practice in leisure studies.

REFERENCES

Alisen, P. 2003. *Finding Courage to Speak: Women's Survival of Child Abuse.* Boston: Northeastern University Press.

Arai, S., and A. Pedlar. 2003. "Moving beyond individualism in leisure theory: A critical analysis of concepts of community and social engagement." *Leisure Studies* 22: 185–202.

Arundel, C. 2003. *Falling Behind: Our Growing Income Gap.* Hemson Consulting Ltd. and Federation of Canadian Municipalities. http://www.fcm.ca/english/documents/falling.pdf. (accessed February 17, 2006).

Breitkreuz, R. 2005. "Engendering citizenship? A critical feminist analysis of Canadian welfare-to-work policies and the employment experiences of lone mothers." *Journal of Sociology and Social Welfare* 32(2): 147–65.

Browne, G., C. Bryne, J. Roberts, A. Gafni, S. Watt, S. Halane, I. Thomas, B. Ewart, M. Schuster, J. Underwood, S. Flynn Kingston, and K. Rennick. 1999. "Benefiting all the beneficiaries of social assistance: The 2-year effects and expense of subsidized versus nonsubsidized quality child care and recreation." *National Academies of Practice Forum* 1(2 April): 131–42.

Browne, G., C. Byrne, J. Roberts, A. Gafni, and S. Whittaker. 2001. "When the bough breaks: provider-initiated comprehensive care is more effective and less expensive for sole-support parents on social assistance." *Social Science & Medicine* 53(12): 1697–1710.

Burch, H. A. 1991. *The Why's of Social Policy: Perspectives on Policy Preferences.* New York: Praeger.

Burman, P. W. 1996. *Poverty's Bonds: Power and Agency in the Social Relations of Welfare*. Toronto: Thompson.

Campaign 2000. 2006a. "Child poverty in Ontario … promises to keep." Available from http://www.Campaign.2000.ca.

Campaign 2000. 2006b. *Oh Canada! Too Many Children in Poverty Too Long … 2006 Report Card on Child and Family Poverty in Canada*. Available from http://www.Campaign.2000.ca.

Canadian Council on Social Development (CCSD). 2000. *Urban Poverty in Canada Statistical Profile*. Canada. http://www.ccsd.ca/pubs/2000/up/b1-1.htm (accessed January 26, 2005).

Canadian Council on Social Development. 2001. *Recreation and Children's Youth Living in Poverty: Barriers, Benefits and Success Stories*. Produced for the Canadian Parks and Recreation Association, Ottawa. http://www.cpra.ca.

Canadian Research Institute for the Advancement of Women (CRIAW). 2006. *Women and Poverty*. Available from CRIAW, 151 Slater Street, Suite 408, Ottawa, Ontario, K1P 5H3. or http://www.criaw-icref.ca.

Centre for Addiction and Mental Health. 2004. *Women and Trauma: The Effects of Abuse Related Trauma*. http://www.camh.net/about_addiction_mental_health/abuse_trauma_effects.html (accessed February 28, 2005).

Chunn, D. and S Gavigan. 1995. "Women, crime and criminal justice in Canada." In *Canadian Criminology*, ed. M. Jackson and C. Griffiths, 275-314. Toronto: Harcourt Brace.

Drolet, M. 2002. "Can the workplace explain Canadian gender pay differences?" *Canadian Public Policy* 28 (Supplement 1): S41–S63.

Freiler,C., L. Rothman, and R. Barata. 2004. *Pathways to Progress: Structural Solutions to Address Child Poverty. Campaign 2000 Policy Perspectives*. Toronto: Campaign 2000.

Frisby, W., C. J. Reid, S. Millar, and L. Hoeber. 2005. "Putting 'participatory' into participatory forms of action research." *Journal of Sport Management* 19: 367–87.

Galabuzi, G. E. 2004. "Social exclusion." In *Social Determinants of Health: Canadian Perspectives*, ed. D. Raphael, 235–51. Toronto: Canadian Scholars Press.

Goar, C. 2007. "Poverty is everyone's business." *Toronto Star*, May 18, A24.

Government of Canada. 2006. *The Human Face of Mental Health and Mental Illness in Canada*. Ottawa: Minister of Public Works and Government Services Canada.

Hamilton, N., and T. Bhattie. 1996. *Population Health Promotion: An Integrated Model of Population Health and Health Promotion*. Ottawa: Health Canada.

Lee, K. 2000. *Urban Poverty in Canada: A Statistical Profile*. Ottawa: Canadian Council on Social Development (CCSD).

Lindsay, C., and M. Almey. 2006. "Immigrant women." In *Women in Canada 2005*. Ottawa: Statistics Canada.

MacMillan, R. 1999. "Adolescent victimization and income deficits in adulthood: Rethinking the costs of criminal violence from a life course perspective." *Criminology* 38(2): 553–87.

McCain, M. N, J. F. Mustard, and S. Shanker. 2007. *Early Years 2 Study, Putting Science into Action*. Toronto: Council for Early Child Development.

McMullin, J. A., L. Davies, and G. Cassidy. 2002. "Welfare reform in Ontario: Tough times in mother's lives." *Canadian Public Policy* 28(2): 297–314.

Mitchell, A., and R. Shillington. 2002. *Perspectives on Social Inclusion: Poverty, Inequality and Social Inclusion*. Toronto: Laidlaw Foundation.

Mosher, J., P. Evans, and M. Little. 2004. *Walking on Eggshells: Abused Women's Experiences of Ontario's Welfare System*. Toronto: York University.

National Council of Welfare (NCW). 2001–02. *The Cost of Poverty*. National Council of Welfare, 9th floor, 112 Kent Street, Ottawa, ON, K1A 0J9.

National Council of Welfare. 2006. Poverty Profile 2002 and 2003. Available from the National Council of Welfare, 9th Floor, 112 Kent Street, Place de Ville, Tower B, Ottawa, ON, K1A 0J9 or http://www.ncwcnbes.net.

National Forum on Health. 1997. *Canada Health Action: Building on the Legacy. The Final Report of the National Forum on Health*. Ottawa:Health Canada.

Pay Equity Task Force. 2004. Pay Equity: A New Approach to a Fundamental Right. Ottawa: Government of Canada. Pay Equity Task Force.

Polakoff, E., and D. Gregory. 2002. "Concepts of health: women's struggle for wholeness in the midst of poverty." *Health Care for Women International* 23(8): 835–45.

Reid, C., W. Frisby, S. Millar, B. Pinnington, and P. Ponic. 2000. *Women Organizing Activities for Women (WOAW): SSHRC Phase 2 Report on Community Partner Profiles and the Benefits and Barriers of Participation in Community Recreation*. Women Studies, University of British Columbia, Vancouver.

Reid, D. G., and L. B. Golden. 2004. *Non-Work Activity and the Socially Marginalized*. School of Environmental Design and Rural Development, University of Guelph.

Richmond A. Saloojee, eds. 2005. *Social Inclusion: Canadian Perspectives*. Halifax: Fernwood.

Robson-Haddow, J. 2004. *The Key to Tackling Child Poverty: Income Support for Immediate Needs and Assets for Their Future*. Caledon Institute of Social Policy. http://www.caledoninstitute.org.

Russell, E. H. D. 1999. *The Secret Trauma: Incest in the Lives of Girls and Women*. New York: Basic Books.

Séguin, A., and G. Divay. 2002. "Urban poverty: Fostering sustainable and supportive communities." In *The Federal Role in Canada's Cities: Four Policy Perspectives*, ed. F. L. Seidle. CPRN Discussion Paper No. F27. Ottawa: Canadian Policy Research Networks.

Statistics Canada. 1993. "The violence against women survey." *The Daily*. Ottawa: Ministry of Industry.

Statistics Canada. 2006. *Women in Canada: A Gender-Based Statistical Report*. Ottawa: Statistics Canada. http://www.statcan.ca/bsolc/english/bsolc?catno=75F0002MIE2006004.

Williamson, D. L., and L. Reutter. 1999. "Defining and measuring poverty: Implications for the health of Canadians." *Health Promotion International* 14(4): 355–64.

Wilton, R. 2004. "Putting policy into practice? Poverty and people with serious mental illness." *Social Science & Medicine* 58(1): 25–39.

World Health Organization. 1986. *Ottawa Charter for Health Promotion*. http://www.hc-sc.gc.ca/hppb/phdd/resources/subject_health_promotion.html (accessed August 27, 2004).

World Health Organization. 1997. *The Jakarta Declaration on Leading Health Promotion into the 21st Century*. http://www.who.int/hpr/NPH/docs/jakarta_declaration_en.pdf (accessed August 27, 2005).

NOTES

1   Low income cut-offs (LICOs) are income thresholds, determined by analyzing family expenditure data, below which families will devote a larger share of income to the necessities of food, shelter, and clothing than the average family would. To reflect differences in the costs of necessities among different community and family sizes, LICOs are defined for five categories of community size and seven of family size (Statistics Canada 2006).

2   The Market Basket Measure of poverty considers the cost of food, shelter, and clothing, and the prices of the necessities in the basket are adjusted for current pricing and location. The market basket includes specified quantities and qualities of goods and services related to food, clothing, and footwear, shelter, and transportation. It also contains other goods and services such as personal and household needs, furniture, telephone service, and modest levels of goods related to reading, recreation, and enter-

tainment (e.g., newspaper and magazine subscriptions, fees to participate in recreational activities or sports, video rentals, tickets to local sports events).

3   Women outnumber men nine to one in the experience of trauma (Statistics Canada 1993), and are considerably more likely to be victims of sexual assault and criminal harassment than men. In 2003, violent assaults against women included common assault (53%), sexual assault (13%), and assault with a weapon causing bodily harm (11%) (Statistics Canada 2006).

4   The social determinants of health include adequate income, social supports, educational attainment, employment supports, housing, safe living environments, food and nutrition (Hamilton and Bhattie 1996; National Forum on Health 1997). The understanding is that the more determinants an individual, family or child has the "healthier" they are or they have a higher quality of life.

PART THREE:
SOCIAL POLICY FROM
THE PERSPECTIVE OF
THE MARGINS

The chapters in this section shed light on issues of power in community and social policy and examine the experiences of people who are often placed on the margins of society. These chapters examine the challenges created within social policies targeting immigration and multicultural-ism, social housing, and federal prisons and explore leisure as a contested site where marginalization or social change may occur. In chapter 9, our assumptions about social inclusion are challenged with an exploration of urban Aboriginal hip-hop – maintaining the margins and the potential of leisure to challenge dominant production systems.

Chapter 6 examines multiculturalism and leisure policy. It is particularly concerned with enhancing the delivery of leisure servi-ces and supports for immigrants and minority Canadians. Through a neo-Marxist lens, Susan Tirone underscores the relationship between social policies focused on immigration, multiculturalism, and leisure and highlights the historical interplay of cultural pluralism, control, and capital accumulation throughout Canada's immigration policies. Tirone reviews contemporary theories guiding cultural and leisure policies and reveals the challenging relationship between them, providing examples such as: early immigration policy bringing newcomers to Canada to support the leisure of others; challenges to sport participation by people wearing hiijab exemplifying social exclusion and behavioural control in leisure policies; and the existence of racialized barriers preventing access to leisure and the creation of ethnic enclaves for leisure experiences. Tirone recommends improvements in recreation supports for newcomers and minorities through the generation of a deeper understanding of the intended and unintended impacts of multiculturalism policy.

Chapter 7 is concerned with leisure and social development in the context of women who "offend." Darla Fortune, Alison Pedlar, and Felice Yuen discuss the role of leisure in the lives of federally sentenced women. The authors consider the expectation of women's social inclusion upon release as well as policy shifts in federal corrections systems. To this end, they describe how these are often at odds with society's notion of the "offender" and the forces of oppression that characterize the lives of women who are incarcerated. Fortune, Pedlar and Yuen describe an innovative project that engages community volunteers in recreation activities alongside women serving their sentences. They argue leisure may be one area where women who are incarcerated can maintain dignity, respect, participation, and inclusion in society. Furthermore, the system of volunteerism underscoring the programs helps both groups to realize common interests and accomplishments and to celebrate difference.

Chapter 8 makes a plea for restoring our collective obligation for one another. In the context of exploring opportunities for addressing homelessness and social housing, Heather Mair and Dawn Trussell examine issues of homelessness and social housing in Canada. They challenge the reader to engage in broader debates about social policy and public responsibility for social welfare. Building on research undertaken with individuals who are, or are at risk of being, homeless, the authors unmask power relationships underlying the politics of poverty and homelessness. Within this critical framework, Mair and Trussell argue social policy discussions about access to safe, secure, and stable housing must be re-injected with a sense of our societal, collective obligation. The authors describe leisure as the context where issues of homelessness and reclaiming the revanchist city may be discussed, debated, confronted, and reconsidered and our societal collective obligation restored while respecting diversity, privacy, and control.

Chapter 9 presents an exploration of urban, Aboriginal-Canadian young people and hip-hop. Karen Fox and Brett Lashua critically explore the intersections of youth-centred "leisure's" offering a reconceptualization of social policy and social inclusion. Using the metaphor of musical rhythms to challenge our assumptions about marginalization and inclusion, and evoking the image of "holding gently," they reflect on their recent work with Aboriginal young people's exploration of hip-hop. They argue our uncritical acceptance of marginalization as "something to be fixed" is based on intentions to create one "normal" system rather than embracing issues of difference, multiplicity, and expressive diversity. For Fox and Lashua, margins can be both "safe havens" for difference and sites of oppression. They argue the expressive initiatives underpinning leisure by urban Aboriginal youth may create alternative resolutions and strategies necessary for dynamic diversity.

6

Multiculturalism and Leisure Policy: Enhancing the Delivery of Leisure Services and Supports for Immigrants and Minority Canadians

Susan Tirone

This chapter is about policy and the leisure experiences of ethnic minority groups and newcomers in Canada. I begin with an overview of Canada's immigration policies; the policies that have guided Canada's recruitment, reception, and treatment of immigrants over the past 120 years. Multiculturalism, a policy framework on which we base our notions of inclusion of racial and ethnic minorities and newcomers in society, is also discussed. The chapter then provides an overview of theoretical frameworks that inform the development of immigration policy and the leisure policy relevant in the lives of immigrants, especially those who identify with minority ethnic groups. I then present an overview of the historic association between leisure and newcomers and minority groups. This discussion includes how much of the leisure of dominant group Canadians is provided and facilitated by immigrants and minority ethnic Canadians; how leisure may become a control mechanism that serves to impose assimilation imperatives on minority groups; and how leisure associated with traditional cultural practices of minority groups is often the context in which both minority group and dominant group

Canadians experience richness and diverse life experiences. I also look at how some of the problematic aspects of leisure have endured to the present time. The chapter concludes with a series of recommendations for how leisure policy could further enhance leisure, social inclusion, and equitable service delivery for all Canadians. Before proceeding with the chapter, it is important to say something about the language I have used to describe people who have immigrated to Canada and whose ancestry is something other than white. Since people of colour are far more plentiful in the world than white people, it would seem erroneous to use the word "minority" to describe them. However in Canada, phrases used by the federal government are "ethnic minority" or "racial minority." For this reason, and since this chapter focuses on much of the policy discussion at the federal level, I will continue to use these phrases throughout this chapter.

CANADA'S IMMIGRATION POLICIES

Canadian policies regarding immigration and ethnic minorities have existed since the end of the nineteenth century. The federal government uses policy to determine who gets into Canada, and these policies often have had a bearing on how the lives of immigrants unfolded after immigration. Some of the history of Canada's immigration policy and legislation and the context in which it developed is reviewed here.

The first federal immigration legislation, the Immigration Act of 1896, was intended to stop the free entry of immigrants into Canada and to exert control over who would be allowed to immigrate (Elliott and Fleras 1990). Prior to that time, no legislation existed to regulate immigrants. Until the start of the First World War, the Canadian west experienced a period of cultural pluralism characterized by an influx of people of diverse religious, cultural, and linguistic backgrounds such as Mennonites, Icelanders, and Russian Doukobors, many of whom accepted the invitation of the government of Canada to settle the prairie provinces (Kordan 2002). Their peaceful coexistence and their interest in preserving some aspects of their heritage, such as language and religious practices, is considered to have been the model for later multi-culturalism polices of the 1960s (Elliott and Fleras 1990).

Things changed considerably at the outbreak of the First World War when immigration policy became much more restrictive, setting the tone for how immigration would happen for the next five decades (Elliott and Fleras 1990). At that time Canada began to exert control over who could enter the county. Although keenly interested in economic expansion, nation-building, and growth, immigration policies reflected the discrimination, fear, and ethnocentric beliefs of the ruling British and Northern European Canadians. Terms such as "absorptive capacity" and "enemy alien" began to appear within the text of immigration policy documents and discriminatory policies developed that encouraged immigration only from "preferred" countries where people were predominantly white (Elliott and Fleras 1990). In the years between the Immigration Act of 1910 and the Immigration Act of 1952, immigrants suffered from numerous atrocities resulting from these policies, including the internment of Ukrainians during the First World War, the internment of Japanese, Italian, and German immigrants during the Second World War, and the refusal by the Canadian government to accept a boatload of Jewish refugee children from Nazi Germany in 1939 (Abell and Troper 1982; Bella 1987; Elliott and Fleras 1990; Kordan 2002).

A More Humanitarian Immigration Policy

It is important to note that Canada's immigration policy has always been linked to capital accumulation as it has long been a tool to address labour shortages and to encourage economic expansion. In 1966, the Department of Manpower and Immigration was established in an attempt to dismantle the racism inherent in past practice and to become more humanitarian and universal in recruiting immigrants (Reitz and Banerjee 2007). This led to the development of a "points system" introduced in 1967 whereby a potential immigrant could earn points based upon education, occupation, and language, while country of origin, race, and ethnicity were eliminated from the selection criteria (Elliott and Fleras

1990). In 1976 a revised Immigration Act expanded the family class of immigrants to enhance family reunification, and the business class to attract entrepreneurs and investors. Elliott and Fleras note that, although Canada was awarded the 1987 United Nations Nansen medal for its refugee efforts, we failed to respond to the needs of Afghan refugees, which was "every bit as callous and unforgiving as our behaviour in the era before the points system" (58). Policies aimed at humanizing our approach to recruiting and receiving immigrants did not soften our stance when responding to injustices occurring outside of Canada.

The 1960s saw Canada's first shift from east-west migration to north-south migration and the arrival of large numbers of immigrants from non-European, non-white countries (Chiswick and Miller 2002). These more recent newcomers have enhanced the availability of ethnically diverse goods in Canada, including a vast array of food and restaurants, music, clothing, and other products that not only are important for the leisure and social well-being of minority Canadians but also have enhanced the leisure of dominant groups. However, the new north-south pattern of migration means that new immigrants in the last ten to fifteen years look and sound different from the immigrants we have known in the past. They are more likely to wear different clothing and to practice religious and cultural traditions that are unfamiliar to most Canadians. In addition, they are likely to be among the most visible in society because of their unique appearance and languages.

In 1971 Prime Minister Trudeau announced Canada's multiculturalism strategy, emphasizing values associated with freedom and the rights of all members of society to share and preserve their cultural heritage. The Multicultural Act was declared in 1988, providing a legislative foundation for this philosophy of social diversity and inclusion (Elliott and Fleras 1990). The philosophy and government legislation associated with multiculturalism were meant to ensure equality and a vibrant society where people of all races and ethnicities would participate together. However, as a policy framework it has been criticized for focusing on negative freedoms or efforts to prevent injustices from occurring (Roberts and Clifton 1990). For example, multiculturalism has led to the creation of policies that address wrongs such as unfair employment practices or lack of access to services such as education and health care. Alternatively policies could focus on positive freedoms that would enable people to pursue their interests and the traditional cultural practices they prefer (Roberts and Clifton 1990). Others criticize multi-culturalism for being highly idealistic, describing a country in which communities declare their diversity, social exclusivity, and harmony, but where these ideals are not in fact realized by all minority groups, and for providing little direction for how it can be implemented (Reitz and Banerjee 2007).

The Canadian Charter of Rights and Freedoms was created in 1985 to address and protect individual rights, including the rights of individuals to their multicultural heritage. The Charter is the legal *bottom line* or last resort when injustice has occurred preventing individuals from experiencing their traditional cultural practices. To ensure the quality of life of immigrants and ethnic minority Canadians and to ensure their leisure reflects their diversity and their desire for inclusion, we would benefit from something that creates a middle ground between the ideals of the multiculturalism framework and the Charter. As is discussed in more depth below, policies informed by these ideals and by the law may be of use.

THEORETICAL FRAMEWORKS

Several theoretical perspectives have informed immigration studies and policy initiatives and leisure relevant to immigrants and minority ethnic Canadians. Leisure in this discussion is conceptualized as activity that provides a sense of fulfillment, satisfaction, and enjoyment. This approach is consistent with Tirone and Shaw's 1997 study, which illustrated immigrant women from India found the concept of leisure as time free from obligations to be problematic. The women in their study perceived North Americans to be selfish for wanting free time that takes them away from care-giving and home-maker roles. Some leisure theorists who have studied leisure and ethnicity have taken a similar approach. For example, much of the early leisure studies of ethnic and racial minority groups focused on differences in activity participation, particularly in outdoor recreation settings between African Americans and dominant, white Americans (Kelly 1980; Washburne 1978). These and other studies provided the basis for leisure theorists to begin to understand leisure preferences and differences in activity participation.

Using marginality theories, some aspects of under-participation were explained as being the result of the marginal position some people held in society due to poverty, discrimination, and lack of services (Gramann and Allison 1999). Ethnicity theories have also informed leisure theorists. These theories explain differences in activity participation as the result of values and beliefs held by minority groups and serve to prioritize activities that are different from dominant groups (Gramann and Allison 1999). Other theoretical perspectives draw upon theories related to plurality, lack of heterogeneity among immigrant and ethnic groups, and the need to avoid "false universalisms" that focus on few dimensions of the experience of leisure for immigrants and minority groups (Flemming 1994; Hall 1996).

For many Canadians the basis for knowing and understanding the lives of non-western, non-Caucasian immigrants rests in how past groups of immigrants coped with life in this country and how they were treated by society and by government. From the 1920s through the 1960s, assimilation frameworks guided our thinking about how, with time, immigrants and minority people learn to be like the dominant group and that in so doing their lives would be better (Hebert 2001). The notion of assimilation rests on the assumption that it is best to shed one's minority cultural traditions because dominant cultural practices are better. In many cases immigrants who were viewed as being different from the dominant groups because of language, accents, clothing, skin colour, and religious practices were feared or marginalized by dominant groups. For example, the following quote from a female participant in a study of second-generation young Canadians whose parents immigrated from India, Pakistan, and Bangladesh demonstrates the importance she places on wearing traditional clothing and how some dominant group Canadians have reacted to her clothing preference:

I love Indian clothing. And I am proud of them [saris]. And I even wore, like a traditional outfit to my graduation and to my athletic banquet and stuff. Like I don't prefer dresses. I hate to wear dresses. I have all these Indian outfits and that's what I prefer to wear. I wore them at university and just when I was hanging out at the house. And I wear it to the store and stuff. And I have had people come up and say, "That's so beautiful. You look so nice. It's good that you are wearing that." But then you get some people staring at you and saying "What is she wearing?" and stuff like that. I think that when I was younger I had a lot of problems. As I grew older it got better. (Tirone and Pedlar 2000, 157)

The experience of the young woman quoted above illustrates her preference for traditional clothing and inconsistencies and the unpleasant opposition she occasionally experienced as a result of her choice of clothing.

Using a neo-Marxist framework to analyze multiculturalism, immigration and leisure provides a way to see the state as a mechanism by which dominant classes ensure their ability to accumulate private capital and legitimate those in power through the creation of policy (Panitch 1977). In examining federal government policies from the time of nation-building, the capital accumulation function of state policy is clearly evident. The way in which immigrants were recruited and admitted to Canada is indicative of how the dominant class of the day ensured both wealth accumulation and leisure at the expense of a poor immigrant class. For instance, many people came to Canada as invited immigrants, such as Chinese labourers who were recruited to work on building the Canadian Pacific Railway, which opened the west to settlement as well as Eastern Europeans who were recruited to settle and farm the Prairie provinces (Elliott and Fleras 1990; Kordan 2002). What is important for this discussion is that capital accumulation imperatives also ensured that leisure of dominant groups would be enriched by the early immigrants who became the labourers in leisure industries. This point is explained more fully below.

Legitimation refers to the means by which governments attempt to gain the support of all constituents by creating policies that give the impression that the needs of all people are addressed, not just those of the ruling class (Panitch 1977). For example, policies like the ones we know in the field of leisure service delivery aim to ensure equal access and freedom from harm for all participants in sports and recreation. These policies legitimate governing bodies (whether state or non-profit groups) who are responsible for ensuring the well-being of the population and for those most vulnerable. While the accumulation and legitimation functions of government should occur in some kind of balance, they are often in opposition to one another. Critics argue that while governments aim to play the middle ground, their attempts to ensure that the needs of both dominant and subordinate classes are addressed may instead perpetuate social inequities. Mahon (1977) argues that policies reflect how governments exert power over vulnerable people in a capitalist system. Immigration policies reflect the tension between the accumulation and legitimation functions of government, but few have considered the role of leisure in this process.

Poverty and discrimination are two significant challenges immigrants continue to face, and these have a direct impact on quality of life and, as is discussed below, on leisure. Canada attempts to recruit immigrants to certain geographic areas where populations are in decline, such as parts of Atlantic Canada, the Prairies, and the north. We expect immigrants to accept low-skilled, low-waged jobs that have been left unfilled by Canadian-born workers, regardless of their expertise, qualifications, and training prior to immigration. The Longitudinal Survey of Immigrants to Canada (LSIC 2003b) undertaken by Statistics Canada, reports that only 42 per cent of immigrants who arrived in 2000 and 2001 had obtained jobs in their intended occupation. While most of the others found work, other studies indicate that finding adequate employment is very challenging, particularly for visible minorities (Kazemipur and Halli 2001a). In their analysis of the 2002 Ethnic Diversity Survey, Reitz and Banerjee (2007) found that visible minorities perceive they are discriminated against in their job searches, a perception that increases the longer they remain in Canada and is even higher among their Canadian-born children. Our multiculturalism policy, regarded by many as the best in the world, ensures entry for some immigrants but has failed to ensure equity once they begin to live in Canada.

Immigration policies are primarily designed to address Canada's need for skilled and experienced workers. Many of our assumptions about immigrants' skills and training are based on stories of immigrants from past generations who tended to assimilate over time, i.e., as they learned English or French, gradually climbed into jobs that paid well, and gradually became like dominant group Canadians. Over time they reduced the likelihood of experiencing poverty throughout their lives (Kazemipur and Halli 2001a). However, Kazemipur and Halli describe the deepening poverty among racial and ethnic minority immigrants in the last twenty-five years and the unusually severe poverty experienced by adolescent-aged immigrants.

LSIC (2003b) reports that, although education levels of newcomers are generally higher than those of the average Canadian-born resident, they have less employment success, resulting in lower wages. Little research has been conducted to specifically explore the history of poverty among immigrants, which has led to a lack of theory about immigrant poverty (Kazemipur and Halli 2001a). However, theories such as John Porter's vertical mosaic thesis remain valid as we note persistent inequities in occupations and income status among immigrants, a fact often explained by assimilation and discrimination theories (Kazemipur and Halli, 2001a; Porter 1965). Our inability to address the issues of poverty and discrimination among immigrants and minority Canadians may be indicative of the residual ways we have of knowing about immigration. That is, our understanding of what it is like to be an immigrant in Canada is often based on assumptions about assimilation. Kazemipur and Halli (2001b) describe Canada's "new poverty" in which some immigrants, i.e., those who live in large cities and are recently arrived visible minorities, are over-represented. This and other studies provide evidence of deepening poverty among new immigrants and their growing discontent over experiences of discrimination in the workforce and in the communities where they live.

There appears to be a significant disconnect between the reality of life for newcomers and minorities in Canada and how Canada has responded to their needs. Most Canadians think that official policies on multiculturalism and human rights address discrimination sufficiently (Reitz and Banerjee 2007). However, multiculturalism is highly idealistic and provides little direction for how it can be implemented at the service delivery level. This is also problematic for the leisure delivery system.

Leisure, Newcomers, and Minority Groups in Canada

Although we are very much accustomed to receiving newcomers, Canada has a long history of exclusionary policies that inhibit and at times exclude the participation of newcomers and minority groups in society (Abella and Troper 1982; Burnet 1986; Li 1990). Leisure is an aspect of social life that newcomers and minorities have not always enjoyed. At times their leisure has been fulfilling, and alternatively it has been problematic (Kidd 1996; OCASI 2005; Tirone 2000). Leisure is considered here in the three different contexts: how the labour of some immigrant groups has served to enhance the leisure of dominant group Canadians, how leisure has been used as means for controlling the behaviour of immigrant groups and individuals, and how leisure in Canada has been enjoyed by newcomers and minority groups.

Newcomers Providing Leisure for Others

The experiences of one group of newcomers illustrates how federal government policies ensured a rich leisure for wealthy, white, dominant group Canadians, while denying basic rights for some groups of newcomers. The following example of the building of Canada's national parks helps to make this point.

Shortly after Confederation, homesteaders were invited by the government of Canada to settle the Prairies, and many of those who accepted the invitation were identified as German or Austro-Hungarian nationals (Kordan 2002; Knowles 2000). They came to Canada at a time of nation-building, which was aimed at establishing a distinct identity for Canada, separate from Britain, and developing a Canadian economy, social structure, and political system. Part of Canada's nationhood was established when the government officially joined the war in Europe in 1914. A consequence of that move was the way Canada treated 120,000 immigrants, primarily from the Ukraine, and who came to be known as "enemy aliens" because they were born in places at war with Canada. With the War Measures Act of 1914, 7,762 residents were interned as prisoners of war and many of those prisoners are the people who built the first infrastructure for Canada's national parks system (Bella 1987; Kordan). Canada's national parks are a nationwide system of natural areas that represent the diverse geography of the country. The parks system was created over one hundred years ago for the preservation of natural places and for public enjoyment and appreciation (Parks Canada 2008).

The factors contributing to this situation are complex and disturbing. Homesteading was very difficult at that time, and many people migrated to the cities in Western Canada looking for work. The recession of 1913–14 prevented them from finding work, leaving them indigent. The immigrants were destitute at the time when sentiments about protection of the homeland were on the rise. Internment was the solution adopted by the government of Canada to deal with the situation (Bella 1987; Kordan 2002). The government argued its actions were justified because this was a way to provide relief for these indigent people (Kordan 2002). As well, the government of Canada claimed the right to force the internees into work projects because they had been "cast upon the charity of the State" (Kordan 2002, 39). The employment of the internees for building such projects as roads and national parks freed up other men from this work to join the war effort. Park projects that employed interned labourers included the building of ski hills, tennis courts, a shooting range, trails for the Alpine Club of Canada, and a horse pasture, as well as the golf course in Banff National Park, Canada's first national park established in 1885 in the heart of the Canadian Rocky Mountains, in the province of Alberta (Town of Banff 2010).

Banff National Park covers an area of over six thousand square kilo-metres of rugged mountain terrain, more than a thousand glaciers, and Alberta's southernmost herd of endangered caribou. The park attracts approximately four million visitors each year and is a UNESCO World Heritage Site. The following quotation is from the records of Parks Canada, the agency that manages Banff National Park to this day:

> I wired you on Saturday suggesting that you put as many aliens as possible on the work extending the [Banff Springs] golf links. As the aliens will not be at Banff a great while longer this season, and as it is desirable that all possible work in the golf links should be done by alien labour, I hope you will be able to arrange for a much larger gang than you have been operating there in the past. (J.B. Harkins, Park Commissioner to S.J. Clarke, Parks Superintendent, May 8, 1917. National Archives of Canada, Record Group 84, vol. 70, file R313; in Kordan [2002], 112).

The national parks became a significant source of leisure for the wealthy who, in the early part of the twentieth century, were able to afford to travel by train, and later by car, to the mountains. The Canadian state legitimized its use of civilian internees who were forced to work on public works projects because of the belief at the time that these individuals were "outside the community and therefore not quite under the protection of the law. That their fate would ironically be bound up with other political objectives, the building of the national parks in particular, made it all the more remarkable and unusual" (Kordan 2002, xxvi). The use of forced labour to construct parks infrastructure served to legitimate the right to leisure for dominant group Canadians and to exclude from leisure the poor immigrants who supplied the labour for construction of mountain roads and parks infrastructure.

In many ways, this situation persists. Recent immigrants, especially visible minorities, live in poverty far more than white immigrants and native-born Canadians (Kazemipur and Halli 2001a; 2001b; Reitz and Banerjee 2007). Even though immigrants tend to have higher levels of education when they arrive in Canada than their Canadian-born peers, only 42 per cent of immigrants surveyed in the LSIC found work in the field in which they had trained prior to entering Canada, leaving the other 58 per cent to find jobs for which they had not trained, often in the service sector of the job market (Statistics Canada 2003b). Therefore, they contribute to the leisure of more wealthy Canadians by supplying the labour necessary for restaurants, hotels, and many other sectors of the entertainment industry.

Poverty is especially detrimental to the leisure experiences of immigrants living on low incomes. Generally, youth in low-income families miss opportunities to participate in many of the sports, recreation, art, and extracurricular activities enjoyed by their affluent peers. For those youth whose families cannot pay fees required for recreation, some low-cost activities are occasionally provided by youth-serving agencies such as municipal recreation departments, YMCAs, and Boys and Girls clubs. However, recreation programs and policies aimed at addressing the needs of immigrant and minority youth have not materialized (Frisby et al. 2005; OCASI 2005). Ethnic minority youth who live significant portions of their lives in poverty are doubly marginalized by their ethnic status and their poverty. These factors in combination prevent their participation in the activities that might facilitate their acceptance by peers as well as their ability to develop supportive social networks upon which they may later rely for help in securing education, training, and good jobs.

Discrimination further complicates the lives of immigrants and minority Canadians and prevents them from developing adequate and enriching social support networks. Friendship networks are listed as the most important means by which immigrants obtain help in finding housing, health care, training, and jobs (Statistics Canada 2003a). Recreation and leisure are known to be important for developing social supports that contribute to well-being, but unfortunately discrimination far too often inhibits recreation and sport participation by ethnic and racial minority Canadians (see Burnet and Palmer 1988; Kidd 1996; Rosenberg 2003; Stodolska and Jackson 1998; Tirone 2000).

Tirone's (2000) study of young Canadians who are the children of immigrants from India, Pakistan, and Bangladesh described how participants recalled incidents of name-calling and bullying as a result of their minority status as well as the failure of recreation and sport leaders to intervene to help them resolve these incidents. Kidd (1996) discusses how Finns and other settlers in the early twentieth century, when excluded from the sports clubs that served British Canadians, formed their own sports associations such as the Workers' Sports Association of Canada (WSA). The WSA and other ethnic sports groups provided opportunities for sports competition for youth from Finnish, Ukrainian, Czech, Jewish, and other Eastern European family backgrounds. These groups were also important for youth and their families who established social support networks through their club associations and thus were able to preserve and practice their language and to pass along cultural traditions to the next generation (Kidd 1996; Rosenberg 2003). Discrimination, still in existence in the sport and recreation delivery system, ensures access to resources for leisure for dominant group Canadians and is a mechanism to persuade minorities to behave like their dominant group peers (Kidd 1996).

Social Exclusion and Behavioural Control through Leisure

In Quebec, in the winter 2007, Muslim teenage girls were prohibited from playing sports such as soccer and Taekwondo because they wear headscarves (hijab). This is a provocative example of how leisure is used as a means of social control hindering the leisure participation of immigrants and minority group Canadians. According to a report in the Canadian Press, even though sport officials such as the World Taekwondo Federation have permitted Muslim women to wear the hijab in competition for many years, the regulations say that nothing except protective head gear can be worn. Nonetheless, the Quebec officials have chosen to adhere to the rule, thereby excluding the girls from participating because their scarves may be a safety hazard (Canadian Press, April 17, 2007). Photographs of the girls in their protective head gear show that the helmets cover the girls' heads completely and the headscarves they wear under the helmets are not visible. It is difficult for many outsiders to this sport to understand how the wearing of the hijab could pose a safety hazard. Clearly, if the girls in Quebec want to participate with their dominant group peers, they need to shed the traditional cultural practices that are important to them and become like their peers. Alternatively, they may find ethnic sports clubs that permit participation while wearing their headscarves.

Many studies over the past ten years illustrate how newcomers are excluded from leisure, and exclusion is a form of social control. The participants in Stodolska and Jackson's (1998) study of Polish immigrants explained that they experienced less discrimination in leisure than other immigrant groups because their leisure tended to occur within ethnic enclosures. Leisure within ethnic enclosures shielded them from the disparaging remarks they encountered when they attempted to participate in leisure activities with dominant group peers. While they felt excluded from leisure with other white, dominant group Canadians, they enjoyed satisfying leisure within enclaves. The benefits of leisure for immigrants are well known. It has the potential to provide healthy physical activity, assist them with language development, and facilitate social inclusion and networking. These benefits are not realized, however, by youth who are newly arrived immigrants, and other racial and ethnic minority youth report being excluded from activities because of rejection by peers (Doherty and Taylor 2007; McBride 1975; Paraschak and Tirone 2008; Tirone 2000).

McBride (1975) describes leisure activities provided for American immigrant workers of the early twentieth century as "Americanization programs designed to re-culture the immigrant" (McBride, 10). Immigrants were needed to address domestic labour shortages, and the industrialists contracted with the YMCA and other reformers to "re-culturalize the immigrant" through educational and leisure programs that would "promote complacency, docility and industrial efficiency in the foreigner" (McBride, 10–11). The Y's activity was purported to "contribute to the development of a 'happy home' by creating the proper cultural and moral environment" (McBride, 66). Few of the workers had "homes," since most of them were single men who were drawn to the western regions of Canada and the United States for jobs and few had family members with them. Further, McBride cited a YMCA executive's claim that the work of the Y contributed to the economic benefit of "participating industries and railroads," explaining how an investment in the Y provided "care for our men away from home" (66). Reformers like the early members of the YMCA were supported by the government and by industry to develop sport and recreation for men who lived in work camps to keep them fit for work, thereby controlling their leisure as well as all aspects of their lives (Harvey 2007). Fortunately, the YMCA has evolved into one of Canada's leading community recreation agencies. The Y and other community agencies like University Settlement House in Toronto, and Metro Immigrant Settlement Association in Halifax and many other non-profit groups are central to the provision of services, including leisure supports for immigrants and minority groups in Canada. (See Dawson's chapter in this volume for more discussion.)

RICH LEISURE OF MINORITIES AND IMMIGRANTS

Newcomers and ethnic minorities enjoy much of the same leisure as dominant group Canadians do, but certain aspects of their leisure are unique often because the traditional cultural practices they enjoy as leisure are unfamiliar to dominant groups. For example there are well-documented historical accounts of ethnic enclaves, established in the late nineteenth and early twentieth centuries in which leisure was an important part of life (Burnet 1986; Rosenberg 2003). Within those enclaves, sport and recreation associations were developed to serve the needs of newcomer and minority youth who were often excluded from mainstream activities (Kidd 1996). In turn, the residents of the enclaves introduced their own sporting traditions to their Euro-Caucasian friends. Estonians, Finlanders, and people from the former Czechoslovakia introduced modern and rhythmic gymnastics to Canada after World War II, and Southeast Asians have made popular a number of their traditional sports such as tai chi and karate (Burnet and Palmer 1988). Recent studies of the leisure experiences of newcomers and minority group Canadians provide evidence of how recreation and sport associations sponsored by minority ethnic groups continue to provide protective environments in which newcomers enjoy leisure away from the discrimination they often encounter in recreation settings available to the general population (Stodolska and Jackson 1998; Tirone 2000; Tirone and Pedlar 2005).

Tirone and Pedlar (2005) explored the rich leisure of South Asian young Canadians and found that, through their leisure, this group experienced an ease of entry into three different groups of people: those who shared their same ethnic background, people from dominant groups, and people from other minority ethnic groups. Their ability to enter into a variety of social groups for leisure resulted in connections and social networks that enhanced access to education and jobs. However, the study participants also explained that at times they had experienced some degree of discrimination in leisure settings. When this happened, they sought leisure opportunities with friends who understood and appreciated their traditional cultural practices, and those friends were often minority group Canadians and people of backgrounds similar to their own.

The traditional cultural practices of many minority groups and newcomers such as food and diverse musical traditions are widely available in places where they have tended to live in concentrated linguistic groups (Chiswick and Miller 2002). Alternatively, when ethnic minority groups experience their leisure in enclaves, the public is unlikely to have opportunities to share in their cultural practices. For example, ethnic sport and recreation associations provide an opportunity for immigrants and established minority groups to experience many of the same activities that dominant group peers enjoy in their leisure. When these activities occur in enclaves, the participants are sheltered from the adversity they might otherwise experience if they were to participate with dominant group peers who may be insensitive to language or other skill deficits. Leisure is known to be an important context in which newcomers experience healthy physical activity, learn and practice language skills, and develop supportive friendship groups with peers who understand and support one another because of common heritage (Chiswick and Miller 2002; Doherty and Taylor 2007).

The leisure experiences of minority and newcomer groups are diverse, ranging from the coercion exercised by the state to ensure golf courses and parks were built as cheaply as possible, to present-day examples of social control and discriminatory leisure practices, to the experience of rich leisure flavoured by the traditional cultural practices important to ethnic minority Canadians and newcomers. Newcomers and ethnic minority Canadians have for many decades developed and supported ethnic social clubs often located within ethnic enclaves. These clubs meet the leisure needs of many people while others prefer to enjoy the freedom of leisure outside of their traditional community and outside of ethnic clubs. When minorities encounter resistance to their cultural practices, such as was the case for the young women who were not permitted to play sports while wearing their headscarves, people will adapt in a variety of ways. They will change their behaviour and conform to rules to be like the dominant majority or they will retreat into groups that value their cultural traditions or drop out of the activity completely (Tirone and Pedlar 2005). Freedom is one of the fundamental values associated with leisure, and we can expect that ethnic minorities and newcomers will seek leisure venues that allow them the freedom to pursue activities they enjoy with people who are supportive and understanding of their interests and the traditions they value. If these venues are not accessible to dominant group Canadians, then the dominant groups will miss out on opportunities to learn and experience leisure based on rich traditional cultures, such as food, dance, music, and religious traditions.

LEISURE POLICY, NEWCOMERS AND MINORITY GROUPS

Federal immigration policies have an impact upon who gets into the country, and multiculturalism provides clarification about how immigrants and minorities should be treated once they get here. Leisure and recreation policies are designed to enhance the leisure of Canadians. An analysis of leisure policies helps us understand how well the leisure needs of immigrants and minority group Canadians are addressed. Most municipalities have recreation inclusion policies, but few of these specifically address the inclusion of racial and ethnic minorities (OCASI 2005). Provincial and municipal inclusion policies commonly focus on the inclusion of girls and women and people with disabilities in recreation, physical activity, and sports and ensuring services are delivered to low-income children and youth (Connolly and Law 1999; Doe 1999; Frisby, Alexander, Taylor, Tirone, Watson, Harvey, and Laplante 2005; Vail and Berck 1995). Many immigrants and ethnic minorities benefit from these inclusion policies but some issues require additional attention. Language familiarity, barriers associated with traditional cultural practices, and discrimination are among those challenges experienced by ethnic minority Canadians and they remain problematic in spite of leisure inclusion policies.

Several researchers have explored how recreation and sport policies address the needs of minority Canadians. Donnelly and Nakamura (2006) considered how sport policies address the ideals of multiculturalism. They found no evidence of any policy initiatives aimed at multiculturalism other than general statements about inclusion for all people. These generalizations are evident in elite sport and at the provincial government levels. Several local community sport associations had attempted to develop policies and procedures for ensuring the inclusion of minority people but have had little guidance from sport governing bodies or government as to how this should be put into practice. Donnelly and Nakamura found that policies tended to place the responsibility on the potential athlete for finding a way to obtain access to the sports they preferred and few communities had outreach or welcoming policies to ensure the newcomers knew about sports at the local level. Policy statements tended to make the assumption that program provision was sufficient to enable the inclusion of newcomers, and few policies addressed the evaluation of programs to determine outcomes.

A 2007 study of the involvement of newcomers in sports, coaching, and in the National Coaching Certification Program (NCCP) in Halifax (Livingston, Tirone, Miller and Smith 2008) found that sport officials, coaches, and athletes were hampered in their efforts to include newcomers and minority racial and ethnic participants in sports because they did not know how to contact and connect with newcomer groups, and they had little sense of what their role should be in program provision for newcomers. They argued that sport governing bodies would benefit from clear guidelines as to how to establish communications with newcomers and the agencies that support them and how to ensure that special needs are addressed by the sport delivery system. The study participants enthusiastically supported the inclusion of newcomers, recognizing that sport contributes to physical health and to social well-being when people feel included in their communities as members of teams and as coaches (Livingston et al. 2008).

In April 2007, I conducted a review of the websites of nine provincial recreation associations as well as the Canadian Parks and Recreation Association (CPRA) in order to explore how multiculturalism and issues of discrimination are addressed by these groups. A search was conducted on each site using the words "multiculturalism" and "discrimination." The CPRA site search resulted in one link to the *M.A.R.S. project: Making all recreation safe* (Canadian Parks and Recreation Association 2007). This document contains a section on preventing harassment and bullying and recommended that definitions of racial discrimination be posted in recreation settings and that they be reviewed by program participants (11). Later in the report is a recommendation that adults should intervene when incidents occur (37), but the document provides no direction as to what the intervention should entail and how it should be conducted. Searches on the provincial recreation association websites resulted in no links to information on multiculturalism or discrimination. Several of the sites had direct links to the *Everybody gets to play* initiative of CPRA (2007). This initiative aims to ensure access to recreation for low-income children and families. The *M.A.R.S.* and *Everybody gets to play* documents are available for purchase from the CPRA and likely contain specific information about the inclusion of immigrants and minority groups in leisure activities and programs, but because of the fee requirement they may not be purchased by recreation centres.

Many initiatives aimed at involving newcomers and minorities in recreation are carried out by immigrant-serving agencies. Municipal recreation providers and non-profits that serve public recreation interests have been slow to accept the challenge of addressing the needs of immigrants (OCASI 2005). Attempts by OCASI to involve municipal recreation providers and the non-profit sector in the development of recreation for newcomers and particularly for newcomer youth have not yielded much in the way of interest (OCASI 2005).

SUMMARY AND RECOMMENDATIONS

Canadian immigration policies of the past few decades have resulted in the arrival of waves of newcomers from diverse cultures, who have been encouraged to enter Canada to fill labour shortages. Multiculturalism, although an idealistic political doctrine that promotes cultural difference, provides little in the way of specific direction for how it is to be implemented (Elliott and Fleras 1990). However, these policies and policy frameworks have not been sufficient to ensure the social well-being of newcomers and minorities in this country. Since municipal and non-profit leisure service providers look to national and provincial government and professional associations for guidance, senior-level policy-makers should take a proactive role in demonstrating how policies can and should address the leisure of ethnic minorities and new immigrants. Several suggestions are provided here.

Leadership is required for developing evidence-based guidelines for content that should be included in policies for leisure service delivery agencies to ensure participation by newcomers and minorities. These guidelines should include ideas for how to inform and establish communications with newcomers and settlement agencies and how providers can determine how they might address specific and unique needs of culturally diverse potential participants. Practitioners would benefit from guidance for how to provide services to visible minority newcomers who are generally less affluent than their white peers. These guidelines should address how recreation and leisure providers can develop information that will be understood by minorities and newcomers. Also, guidelines should include specific direction for training of recreation and leisure staff and volunteers to welcome minority groups and newcomers who are often challenged by language difficulties and other settlement issues.

Provincial and national recreation associations should provide leadership for developing a contextual definition of racism and discrimination appropriate for recreational and leisure settings. Once definitions are established, guidelines are needed for how leaders, administrators, coaches, and program leaders can implement actions that address racism or discrimination when it occurs. We also need to provide direction for people who encounter discrimination and what they should do to seek help to reach a fair resolution. If organizations do not have their own procedures, they should be offered an opportunity to place a link on their association's website to a central web-based resource that addresses the issue of discrimination and racism in recreation and leisure settings.

Most recreation services provided for newcomers and minority group Canadians appear to be developed and delivered by the settlement and support agencies serving these groups (OCASI 2005). Policies should be developed to address how municipal and non-profit recreation and leisure service providers can connect and partner with the immigrants serving agencies to provide services to minority and immigrant Canadians. These policies should address the ways in which immigrant-serving agencies can access public recreation services and not have to rely solely on their own resources for meeting recreation needs. Examples of policies should be developed and publicized by provincial and federal recreation and leisure associations.

Ethnic enclaves are an important context in which leisure occurs for many newcomers and minority Canadians. We need to develop a better understanding of the leisure that occurs within enclaves and how enclaves enhance or detract from leisure, especially for youth. We need to explore how policy might address the needs of those who live in enclaves and if so in what ways.

People seek leisure with friends who support and appreciate their traditions, and sometimes ethnic clubs are the best source of that leisure. We need to explore the development of the ethnic social clubs in Canada from the perspective of how they serve the leisure needs of minorities and the ways in which they are they advantageous or disadvantageous for immigrants and minorities. Knowing that the leisure of diverse racial and ethnic groups can enhance the leisure of dominant groups, we need to explore how policy can enhance the development of diverse forms of leisure such as ethnic dance and music.

Enriched, healthy leisure experiences are integral to the well-being of Canadians. Unfortunately, accumulation and legitimation imperatives prioritize economic well-being, and as a consequence the leisure of dominant groups is ensured with less regard for how leisure of newcomers and ethnic minorities unfolds. Newcomers and minority group Canadians are not necessarily impoverished, and many individuals and ethnic groups have the means to create leisure they enjoy, within their ethnic communities, if and when they are not included in leisure with dominant groups. Ethnic social clubs are important in institutionally complete ethnic communities, and they have the potential to enrich the lives of all Canadians when they share their traditions with Canadians who identify with different ethnic groups. Social inclusion in our diverse communities requires more consideration of the potential for leisure policy and the leisure delivery system to enhance cultural and ethnic diversity.

References

Abella, I., and H. Troper. 1982. *None Is Too Many*. Toronto: Lester and Orpen Dennys.

Bella, L. 1987. *Parks for Profit*. Montreal: Harvest House.

Burnet, J. 1986. *Looking into My Sister's Eyes: An Exploration in Women's History*. Toronto: Multicultural History Society of Ontario.

Burnet, J. R., with H. Palmer. 1988. *"Coming Canadians": An Introduction to a History of Canada's People*. Toronto: McLelland & Stewart.

Canadian Parks and Recreation Association. 2007. http://www.cpra.ca.

Canadian Press. 2007. "Hijabs rarely a problem, world taekwondo officials say." *Halifax Herald* April 17: A9.

Chiswick, B. R., and P. W. Miller. 2002. "Do enclaves matter in immigrant adjustment?" *Discussion Paper 449*. Bonn, Germany: Institute for the Study of Labour.

Connolly, K., and M. Law. 1999. "Collective voices: People with disabilities shaping municipal inclusion and access policy." *Leisurability* 26(1): 16–24.

Doe, T. 1999. "Getting a piece of the pie: Accessibility as a universal entitlement." *Leisurability* 26(1): 3–11.

Doherty, A., and T. Taylor. 2007. "Sport and physical recreation in the settlement of immigrant youth." *Leisure/Loisir* 31(1): 27–55.

Donnelly, P., and Y. Nakamura. 2006. Sport and Multiculturalism: A Dialogue. Final Report to Canadian Heritage. Toronto: University of Toronto.

Elliott, J. L., and A. Fleras. 1990. "Immigration and the Canadian ethnic mosaic." In *Race and Ethnic Relations in Canada*, ed. P. S. Li, 51–76. Toronto: Oxford University Press.

Flemming, S. 1994. "Sport and South Asian youth: the perils of 'false universalism' and stereotyping." *Leisure Studies* 13: 159–77.

Frisby, W., T. Alexander, J. Taylor, S. Tirone, C. Watson, J. Harvey, and D. Laplante. 2005. *Bridging the Recreation Divide: Listening to Youth and Parents from Low-Income Families across Canada*. Ottawa: Canadian Parks and Recreation Association. September 26.

Gramann, J. H., and M. T. Allison. 1999. "Ethnicity, Race and Leisure." In *Leisure Studies: Prospects for the Twenty-first Century*, ed. E. L. Jackson and T. L. Burton, 283–97. State College, PA: Venture.

Hall, S. 1996. "Introduction: who needs 'identity'?" In *Questions of Cultural Identity*, ed. S. Hall and P. duGay, 1–17. London: Sage.

Harvey, J. 2007. "Sport, politics, and policy." In *Canadian Sport Sociology*, 2nd ed., ed. J. Crossman, 221–37. Toronto: Thomson Nelson.

Hebert, Y. 2001. "Identity, diversity, and education: A critical review of the literature." *Canadian Ethnic Studies/Etudes ethniques au Canada* 33(3): 155–85.

Kazemipur, A., and S. S. Halli. 2001a. "The changing color of poverty in Canada." *Canadian Review of Sociology and Anthropology* 38: 217–38.

Kazemipur, A., and S. S. Halli. 2001b. "Immigrants and 'new poverty': The case of Canada." *International Migration Review* 35(4): 1129–56.

Kelly, J. R. 1980. "Outdoor recreation participation: A comparative analysis." *Leisure Sciences* 3: 129–55.

Kidd, B. 1996. "Worker sport in the new world: The Canadian story." In *The Story of Worker Sport*, ed. A. Kuger and J. Riordan, 143–56. Champaign, IL: Human Kinetics.

Kordan, B. S. 2002. *Enemy Aliens, Prisoners of War: Internment in Canada during the Great War.* Montreal & Kingston: McGill-Queen's University Press.

Knowles, V. 2000. *Forging Our Legacy: Canadian Citizenship and Immigration 1900–1977.* Ottawa: Citizenship and Immigration Canada. http://www.cic.gc.ca/english/department/legacy/acknowledge.html (accessed November 17, 2005).

Li, P. S. 1990. *Race and Ethnic Relations in Canada.* Toronto: Oxford University Press.

Livingston, L. A., S. C. Tirone, A. J. Miller, and E. L. Smith. 2008. "Participation in coaching by Canadian immigrants: Individual accommodations and sport system receptivity." *International Journal of Sports Science & Coaching* 3: 403–15.

Mahon, R. 1977. "Canadian public policy: the unequal structure of representation." In *The Canadian State: Political, Economic, and Political Power,* ed. L. Panitch, 165–98. Toronto: University of Toronto Press.

McBride, P. 1975. "The YMCA and the politics of co-optation." In *Culture Clash: Immigrants and Reformers 1880–1920,* 62–83. San Francisco: R & E Research Associates.

OCASI (Ontario Council of Agencies Serving Immigrants). 2005. OCASI Research on Inclusive Recreation Model for Immigrant and Refugee Youth: Provisional Model. Toronto: OCASI.

Panitch, L. 1977. "The role and nature of the Canadian state." In *The Canadian State: Political, Economic, and Political Power,* ed. L. Panitch, 3–27. Toronto: University of Toronto Press.

Paraschak, V. & Tirone, S. (2008). Chapter 5: Race and Ethnicity in Canadian Sport. In J. Crosman, (Ed.). *Canadian Sport Sociology, 2nd Edition.* pp. 79-98. Toronto: Nelson.

Parks Canada. 2008. National Parks of Canada. http://www.pc.gc.ca/progs/np-pn/index_e.asp (accessed November 15, 2008).

Porter, J. 1965. *The Vertical Mosaic.* Toronto: University of Toronto Press.

Reitz, J. G., and R. Banerjee. 2007. "Racial inequality, social cohesion and policy issues in Canada." In *Belonging? Diversity, Recognition, and Shared Citizenship in Canada,* ed. K. Banting, T. J. Courchene, and F. L. Seidle, 489–545. Montreal: Institute for Research on Public Policy.

Roberts, L. W., and R. A. Clifton. 1990. "Multiculturalism in Canada: A sociological perspective." In *Race and Ethnic Relations in Canada*, ed. P. S. Li, 120–47. Toronto: Oxford University Press.

Rosenberg, D. 2003. "Athletics in the Ward and beyond: Neighborhoods, Jews, and sport in Toronto, 1900–1939." In *Sporting Dystopias: The Making and Meanings of Urban Sport Cultures*, ed. R. C. Wilcox, D. L. Andrews, R. Pitter, and R. L. Irwin, 137–52. Albany: State University of New York Press.

Statistics Canada. 2003a. *Longitudinal Survey of Immigrants to Canada: Process, Progress and Prospects*. Document 89-611-XIE. Ottawa: Ministry of Industry.

Statistics Canada. 2003b. Longitudinal Survey of Immigrants to Canada: Progress and Challenges of New Immigrants in the Workforce. Document 89-615-XIE. Ottawa: Ministry of Industry.

Stodolska, M., and Jackson, E. L. 1998. "Discrimination in leisure and work experienced by a white ethnic minority group." *Journal of Leisure Research* 30(1): 23–46.

Tirone, S. 2000. "Racism, indifference and the leisure experiences of South Asian Canadian teens." *Leisure/Loisir* 24(1): 89–114.

Tirone, S., and A. Pedlar. 2005. "Leisure, place and diversity: The experience of ethnic minority young adults." *Canadian Ethnic Studies* 37(2): 32–48.

Tirone, S., and A. Pedlar. 2000. "Understanding the leisure experiences of a minority ethnic group: South Asian teens and young adults in Canada." *Loisir et Société/Society and Leisure* 23(1): 145–69.

Tirone, S., and S. M. Shaw. 1997. "At the centre of their lives: Indo Canadian women, their families and leisure." *Journal of Leisure Research* 29: 225–44.

Town of Banff 2010. About Banff. http://www.banff.ca/visiting-banff/about-banff.htm. (Accessed March 2, 2010).

Vail, S., and P. Berck. 1995. Walking the Talk: *A Handbook for Ontario Sport Leaders about Full and Fair Access for Women and Girls*. Toronto: Ministry of Culture, Tourism and Recreation.

Washburne, R. F. 1978. "Black underparticipation in wildland recreation: Alternative explanations." *Leisure Sciences* 1: 175–89.

7

Leisure and Social Development in the Context of Women Who *Offend*

Darla Fortune, Alison Pedlar, and Felice Yuen

The federal corrections system in Canada incarcerates people whose crime carries a sentence that places the person under correctional supervision for two years or more. In April 2004, there were 379 federal incarcerated women in Canada, compared to 12,034 federally sentenced men (Correctional Service of Canada n.d.). For reasons which we hope will be apparent, especially in terms of the exceptional marginalization that accompanies incarceration for a woman, this chapter will focus principally on women who are federally incarcerated. As many feminist critical criminologists and others have noted (Bloom, Owen and Covington 2003; Faith 1993; Hannah-Moffat 2001; Hannah-Moffat and Shaw 2000; McCorkel 2003; Pollack 2004; Smart 1995; Sommers 1995; Worrell 1990), to be a woman who has committed a crime carries an enormous and enduring stigma – not only have they broken the law, an *unwomanly* act in itself, they are also women who, in many cases, are mothers. A report profiling women who have been federally incarcerated in Canada indicated that 66 per cent had children, most (67.8%) were single, and typically originated from socially disadvantaged backgrounds; they experienced a high incidence of substance abuse, and had low levels of education. At the time of their arrest, most of these women were unemployed and possessed limited marketable skills (Dauvergne-Latimer 1995). These facts, along with the removal of the women from mainstream society, increases their marginalization and makes virtually impossible their prospects of regaining membership in the community at large following incarceration.

In this chapter, we consider aspects of daily life, including leisure, in which women who are incarcerated in the federal system may be able to obtain some semblance of participation and inclusion within society. In fostering inclusion, however, leisure may be an aspect of life that seeks to normalize women who are in prison. At the same time, leisure is sometimes seen as providing a space where people can exert *the self* unconstrained by the demands of work and other structures of society that require conformity to certain performance expectations and norms of behaviour. As Foucault (1975) pointed out, however, the act of breaking the law means that the criminal is seen as having offended *all* of society and for that must be punished so that society may obtain retribution for the crime. Society thus responds as the victim of the *offender's* crime. The marginalization and social exclusion that ensue are deep and difficult to overcome.

The very idea of fostering inclusion and extending rights of citizenship to *offenders* tends to be regarded as suspect if not simply unconscionable. Why, then, one might ask, would we seek to find ways of enabling *offenders*, in this case women, to gain or regain a place in society? One reason is that we can envisage a society that is willing to recognize that social and economic exclusion lead people to pursue desperate measures, including those that bring them into conflict with the law. Once sentenced and incarcerated, they are relegated to a space that is beyond even the margins of society. In a society that prides itself on the strengths of individualism and an ability to overcome extraordinarily adverse conditions, social exclusion may be deemed the inevitable and rightful outcome for the *offender*. However, crime does not occur in a vacuum; it typically arises out of a definite background of social conditions that render such activity predictable if not inevitable. With this in mind, we may come to see that a society that accepts and even nurtures those conditions must also accept some responsibility for the criminal activity the conditions foster. This is not to say that the criminal is blameless. But it is to insist that society at large shares responsibility for the crime.

These remarks point to the large and difficult issue of personal and collective responsibility, an issue we will not be exploring here, beyond affirming that the view of placing all responsibility on the individual is as untenable and naïve as the opposing view of placing all responsibility on society. Responsibility understood this way suggests a more inclusive and humane vision grounded in social justice, as argued by Iris Marion Young (1990) in her work on the *Politics of Difference*. In the following paragraphs, we shall begin to consider whether, in the case of women who are incarcerated, social justice through the recognition of difference and in the face of oppression is either feasible or useful. We shall further explore whether social development that is sought through leisure can respect difference and at the same time de-marginalize and ultimately foster inclusion of people as valued members of mainstream society.

Over a four year period we collectively spent more than a thousand hours volunteering in one of Canada's six regional prisons for women, Grand Valley Institution (GVI). GVI was opened in 1998 following the decision to close Canada's one central Prison for Women located in Kingston, Ontario. The opening of regional facilities was driven in part by the desire to have women located closer to their home communities. In 2007, there were 121 women in GVI. The majority was classified as minimum and medium security, with a minority (7%) classified as maximum security (CSC 2007a). Our involvement with the women comprised social interaction while engaged in recreation and leisure opportunities that are brought into the facility. These opportunities occur as part of a program called Stride Night, an evening coordinated by a community agency, Community Justice Initiatives (CJI). Stride Night involves citizens from the community who come to Stride Night as volunteers one evening a week. This program was originally conceived as a vehicle to help foster the development of circles of support, Stride Circles, wherein volunteers from the community would connect with a woman in prison. On release, the members of the Stride Circle would then support the woman as she returns to the community and assist in ways that might improve her chances of reintegrating into mainstream society (Fortune, Thompson, Pedlar, and Yuen, 2010).

We have had many informal conversations with the Stride volunteers and with the women in GVI, during the various activities that occur during Stride Nights, such as coffee nights, craft nights, games nights, or sports nights. In addition, we have interviewed many of the women as part of a study we conducted into their experience with Stride night encounters and activities (Pedlar, Yuen, and Fortune 2008). A second study (Pedlar, Arai, Yuen, and Fortune 2008) that brought us into further contact with these women was concerned with determining what the housing needs of incarcerated women are upon release. These conversations and interviews provided us with extensive information on the life of a woman who is federally incarcerated. We have also gained a good understanding of many of the Correctional Service of Canada (CSC) policy directives and reports that affect the lives of these women. The principles of women-centred programming and interventions are reflected in many directives and are intended to form the axis of everything that takes place around incarcerated women, as well as much of what occurs after their release from prison.

THE FIVE FACES OF OPPRESSION AND WOMEN WHO ARE INCARCERATED

In her work on the *Justice and the Politics of Difference*, Marion Young speaks to five conditions or faces of oppression. The five faces of oppression are exploitation, marginalization, powerlessness, cultural imperialism, and violence. In her analysis, oppression exists within a group or population when at least one of these conditions is present. Among women who are incarcerated, all of the conditions are present.

Exploitation

Young (1990) defines exploitation as a relation of power and inequality, which keeps those who are exploited in positions of subordination. According to Young, "social rules about what work is, who does what for whom, how work is compensated, and the social process by which the results of work are appropriated operate to enact relations of power and inequality" (49). Experiencing exploitation in the form of disadvantageous working arrangements is one factor that may start women on the pathway to criminal activity. Many women were either unemployed or underemployed at the time of their offence and those who had jobs often worked in low-paying, unskilled positions (Law 2004). Once incarcerated, women seem to be devoid of opportunities to rise above this type of oppression. For example, a study of federally sentenced women conducted by Delveaux, Blanchette, and Wickett (2005) showed that despite the women's expressed interest in community-based work release programs, almost none of the women in the study had actually participated in such programs during their incarceration. Delveaux et al. also found that the type of employment women participated in while inside the institution was not comparable to work in the community with respect to such factors as work accountability, responsibility, and the hours worked. A report by the Canadian Human Rights Commission (2003) demonstrated that despite policy directives pointing to the relevance of work experiences in the community, work releases are not regularly built into correctional plans for incarcerated women. As a result, these women are not often well positioned to find gainful employment upon their release. A lack of work experience, coupled with a criminal record, can make it extremely difficult for women to escape exploitive work situations when they are released from prison.

Marginalization

Young (1990) defines marginalized populations as "people the system of labour cannot or will not use" (53). She considers marginalization to be the most dangerous form of oppression in that "a whole category of people is expelled from useful participation in social life and thus potentially subjected to severe material deprivation or even extermination" (53). Young further argues that the provision of material goods is not enough to negate marginality. She provides an example of older adults living comfortably in institutions who remain marginalized due to their lack of participation in meaningful and productive activities. The experience of incarcerated women resonates with this, but even more deeply in that they are not only restricted in their access to meaningful relationships and productive roles, they are also denied access to material goods and personal possessions. Restriction of activity and denial of possessions further perpetuates the devalued and marginal status of women who are incarcerated.

Powerlessness

Status or the lack of status is a key element in powerless, another face of oppression identified by Young (1990). The greater resources and social respect that are associated with high social and professional status bring power. Conversely, powerlessness is characterized by a lack of expertise, lack of work autonomy, and lack of respect. As Mahoney and Daniel (2006) explain, powerlessness is ever-present in the lives of incarcerated women since prisons operate as coercive institutions that restrict behaviours and maintain control through rigid regulatory systems. Mahoney and Daniel argue that the structures of the prison system mirror the oppressive conditions these women face on the outside in that the focus is more on their pathology than on ways to empower them. Moreover, as Pollack (2004) explains, power imbalances inherent in institutional program delivery reinforce the professional/client hierarchy. This hierarchy functions to contrast the status of the professional with the powerlessness of incarcerated women and keeps these women in the subservient roles of clients.

Cultural Imperialism

Cultural imperialism involves a dominant group's culture and values becoming the accepted norm, and the repression or devaluing of the ways of life of non-dominant groups. According to Young (1990), people living under cultural imperialism experience themselves in a paradoxical manner. On one hand, they are invisible to the dominant group in the sense that their perspective is not recognized. On the other hand, they are marked out as different and this difference becomes construed as deviance and inferiority.

The issue of cultural imperialism and its effect on incarcerated women is perhaps most clearly evidenced by the racial disparity present inside correctional institutions. As Richie (2001) explains, the racial profile of women in prison represents one of the most vivid examples of racial inequality in our society since the vast majority of women incarcerated in the United States are women of colour. A similar racial discrepancy exists in Canada, with Aboriginal women being disproportionately over-represented in the federal correctional system. Approximately 31 per cent of women in Canadian prisons are Aboriginal, while Aboriginal people comprise just 3.5 per cent of the Canadian population (Sinclair and Boe 2002). The Canadian Human Rights Commission (2003) identified incarceration as being particularly detrimental to Aboriginal women since it disrupts healing opportunities and diminishes their access to spiritual and cultural resources, practices, and programming.

Violence

Violence as a face of oppression includes not only physical violence but also "harassment, intimidation, or ridicule simply for the purpose of degrading, humiliating, or stigmatizing group members" (Young 1990, 61). According to Young, acts of violence become oppressive when they are embedded within a system that makes them not only possible but acceptable. Based on her research, Richie (2001) highlights the nature and severity of violence in the lives of incarcerated women. She explains that the majority of women in her study described how incidents of childhood abuse and acts of sexual violence had a profound impact on their lives and contributed to their illegal activity. Richie also argues that there is a likelihood of women being released from prison with unresolved abuse issues since in most correctional settings such matters are not confronted. The idea that issues of violence can easily go unaddressed seems particularly critical considering that many women continue to live in fear of institutional violence in the form of attacks from other inmates (HM Chief Inspector 2006).

SOCIETAL RESPONSES TO OPPRESSION

Considering the five faces of oppression, Young posits that, within a society characterized by power imbalances where oppression remains a dominant experience in the lives of marginalized populations, distributive justice is less effective than social justice in redressing these imbalances. She notes, "the reification, individualism, and pattern orientation assumed in the distributive paradigm, moreover, often obscure issues of domination and oppression, which require a more process-oriented and relational conceptualization" (1990, 8). In arguing for the relevance of social justice, Young makes an important distinction between material goods with which distributive justice is rightly concerned and goods such as self-respect, opportunity, power, and honour, which are in her view matters with which social justice ought to be concerned. Social justice includes honouring people's positive rights and issues related to decisions and actions, as well as the ability to exercise capacities. Distributive justice cannot redress power imbalances inasmuch as social exclusion and denial of social goods make access to capacities untenable. Accordingly, the conditions Young identifies in the five faces of oppression are those that arise from injustice and "all involve social structures and relations beyond distribution" (9). Hence, social justice is a necessary condition in ending domination and oppression and a precursor to redistribution. It is when domination is identified and recognized that action can begin in the form of a new social movement, which emerges as the collective/

group begins the process of resisting and seeking to become agents in their own lives.

As we stated in our opening comments, the very idea of a woman in prison being oppressed will likely be rejected out of hand: how is it that a woman who has *offended* can be anything but evil, exploitative, bad, or mad? This rejection in itself speaks to the stigma, marginalization and ongoing punishment that these women experience and that make it particularly challenging to envisage a collective response in the formation of a social movement such as other oppressed groups have managed to forge in seeking to end their oppression and domination. The disability movement, for instance, has managed to make considerable progress, albeit far too slowly, in ending oppression and gaining rights of citizenship and social inclusion by invoking the politics of difference.

An Effort to Shift the Paradigm

There have been several policy initiatives over the past decade and a half recognizing difference and reflecting something of a shift in thinking regarding the treatment of federally incarcerated women. Historically in Canada, as elsewhere, women's imprisonment has been managed within a system that was essentially designed for male prisoners. After decades of debate, studies, and reports that underscored the lack of gender sensitive policy and programming in Canada's prison system, the decision was made to close Canada's federal facility that housed women, namely the Prison for Women (P4W) in Kingston, Ontario, and to establish six smaller, regional facilities across Canada.

The closure of P4W was directly linked to the report, *Creating Choices*, produced by the Task Force on Federally Sentenced Women (TFFSW 1990). This document introduced alternative notions of rehabilitation in preparation for reintegration in contrast to retribution, which had characterized incarceration in P4W. *Creating Choices* identified critical aspects of support if women were to successfully reintegrate on release from incarceration. These included women-specific programming, service-user participation in decision-making, and reciprocal delivery/use of services (TFFSW 1990). This shift in the treatment of women – from retribution to rehabilitation and reintegration – suggests that the intent of policy after the long and dark era of the P4W was to encourage a gentler, more humane, and more gender-specific approach to responding to women who had *offended*.

Creating Choices embodies five guiding principles: empowerment, meaningful and responsible choices, respect and dignity, supportive environment, and shared responsibility. Empowerment is seen as a process wherein women can begin to understand their life situation, and with support they are challenged to call upon their own strengths in order to act positively and gain control of their lives. An absence of power to control their own lives is viewed as leading to low self-esteem and feelings of inadequacy. In order to make meaningful and responsible choices about their lives, it is recognized that women need information and resources to help make informed decisions, which in turn are important to building self-esteem and self-worth. *Creating Choices* notes that where supportive environments exist, more equitable access to services exists encouraging such choices. Also, when incarcerated women are treated with respect and dignity, reciprocal relations of respect and dignity are fostered among inmates and staff. Finally, the principle of shared responsibility sees all of society and its formal and informal institutions and associations ranging from government, through to corrections, business and community as a whole, as being responsible for playing a part in the development, implementation, and evaluation of interventions and services for incarcerated women. These principles are intended to provide women with opportunities to gain control of their lives and become productive, contributing members of society (Dauvergne-Latimer 1995). Significant here is the recognition of the importance of ultimately taking responsibility for one's crime.

The range of programs developed in response to this shifting paradigm is very considerable. Self-understanding and acceptance of responsibility for one's criminal actions are central to many of the programs. Recovery and healing begin here. Accordingly, the CSC Program Strategy for Women Offenders (Fortin 2004) indicates that women's institutions are to provide what are called Correctional Programs that include substance abuse programming and anger and emotion management. As well, education, employment, and mental health programs, focusing on behavioural therapy and psychosocial rehabilitation, and social programs that include community reintegration programs, spirituality services, horticulture programs, leisure education, and peer support programs, to name only a portion of the vast compendium of interventions, are to be made available to women in prison. In practice, not all of these programs are systematically and routinely available. The intent of these programs is to "support CSC's reintegration efforts with offenders" (Fortin 2004, 4), which suggests that in principle rehabilitation and reintegration efforts now predominate over punishment.

What is not acknowledged, however, is that with the best of intentions, such programming often leaves untouched the structural conditions faced by these women. Residual powerlessness is exacerbated by persistent systemic barriers to participation within the community at large during their incarceration, denying them access to typical benefits of citizenship. Such outcomes parallel Young's concern – she points out that in today's society, power is exercised in invidious ways through:

> [the] often liberal and humane practices of education, bureaucratic administration, production and distribution of consumer goods, medicine, and so on. The conscious actions of many individuals daily contribute to maintaining and reproducing oppression, but those people are usually simply doing their jobs or living their lives, and do not understand themselves as agents of oppression (41–42).

The Systemic Nature of Oppression in Correctional Institutions

Oppressive practices are considered to be systemic when they are present regardless of the individual views held by members of an institution. Young (1990) asserts that when such practices become embedded in the ongoing structures of institutions, they can go unrecognized or unquestioned by those they may privilege. She further suggests that the systemic nature of oppression means that it can co-exist along with actions that are both well-intentioned and well-meaning. *Creating Choices* could arguably be the most "well-intentioned" report in terms of improving institutional conditions for women who are federally incarcerated in Canada. However, this report has been criticized for creating policy that narrowly defines women as having low self-esteem, an inability to cope or make sound decisions, and a long history of dependence on men, drugs, and the state (Pollack 2004). Though it is intended to lead to the empowerment of women, this report can perhaps be more accurately described as a blueprint for transforming women into responsible individuals who will start to make wise choices. As Pollack argues, placing too much focus on issues such as self-esteem and dependency and how these issues contribute to poor choices leads to false assumptions that good choices are equally available to everyone. Such assumptions influence correctional staff and practitioners to closely follow a programming framework that focuses on changing the way people think rather than scrutinizing the unfair and inequitable societal conditions that have helped shape their lives. Pollack explains that, within this framework, any attempts by women to discuss the impact of oppression are viewed as denial and rationalizations of their offence.

When experiences of oppression are dismissed and women's criminality is reduced to their inability to make sound, responsible decisions, there is a systemic flaw in identifying program needs (Canadian Human Rights Commission 2003). In particular, program categories will fail to address the unique reasons why women commit crimes and will continue to foster oppressive conditions. Specifically, programs that are designed to transform women's behaviours and coping skills, such as those that involve anger management and addiction counselling, may overlook or minimize the centrality of systemic factors such as poverty, racism, and abuse. When these factors are overlooked, women remain powerless against these forms of oppression and less capable of changing their life circumstances.

Recognizing that oppression can be systematically reproduced in correctional institutions, Pollack (2004) argues that there is a need to understand the multidimensional factors that bring women into conflict with the law and to consider the impact of their oppression on the range of choices available to them. She also suggests that it is imperative to acknowledge the strengths and resources of these women and provide them with authority to identify their own needs and to define how best to meet them.

The transfer of authority with respect to identifying and addressing needs can come from the consciousness-raising approach that is not unlike Freire's (1970) *conscientization*. Richie (2001) explains that the use of consciousness-raising with incarcerated women helps to facilitate initiatives that are based on strategies to help women develop critical insight into the structural influences on their personal choices. This approach is seen as a move away from interventions that foster self-blame by focusing too narrowly on issues of self-esteem, and a move toward initiatives that encourage informed decision-making within the context of limited options. As the women become directly involved in identifying and expanding the options they may have, they are far better positioned to engage in the struggle for freedom from oppression. As a part of this process, realizing oneself to be an individual, an agent, with responsibility to self and others, means that the *offender* does not simply blame the self or the environment for her demise but begins to move forward into a space where she may express her individuality and choose a different future.

Notwithstanding the possibility that empowerment and choice are empty constructs in the face of imprisonment (Hannah-Moffatt 2001), the general thrust of the policies governing the rehabilitation and treatment of women while under correctional supervision points to the traditions of individualism of a pioneering nation where success is essentially up to the individual and those who fall by the wayside essentially have only themselves to blame. This line of thinking pays very little or no attention to the structural conditions that may negate individual effort to participate as a contributing member of society who, in turn, is afforded social and economic inclusion. Indeed, as Foucault (1975) would have it, sentencing and imprisonment remain society's dominant approach to punishment, which in turn seeks to *normalize* behaviours before the incarcerated person can be returned to society. Rather than consider the structures and barriers facing the *offender*, policy reduces the woman's crime to pathology.

THE PARADOX OF IMPRISONMENT AND PREPARATION FOR REINTEGRATION

Following *Creating Choices*, policy directives related to corrections for women who are incarcerated in Canada have been crafted with reintegration as a primary objective of all interventions. For instance, the Department of Justice Canada outlines the responsibilities of the Correctional Service of Canada in the Corrections and Conditional Release Act. Section 5b, which seeks to ensure, "the provision of programs that contribute to the rehabilitation of offenders and to their successful reintegration into the community" (Department of Justice Canada 1992, 4). In addition, Section 76 of Programs for Offenders notes that "the Service shall provide a range of programs designed to address the needs of offenders and contribute to their successful reintegration into the community" (Department of Justice Canada 1992, 23). Indeed, one of the most striking paradoxes of the new policies guided by *Creating Choices* is that the primary reintegration efforts are focused on the period in which a person is institutionalized. The programming activity that happens in the prison trains people for an imagined connection with the community, and inevitably efforts to reproduce conditions of community within the institution remain contrived and unrealistic.

Many years of deinstitutionalization for people with disabilities demonstrated the nonsensical nature of getting people *ready* for integration – the question of *readiness* was finally recognized as entirely unhelpful. It begged the question of whose readiness one was talking about – that of the individual or that of the community? Without an opportunity to know the person and to gain a mutual understanding between the person and the community, readiness became a moot point. Ultimately, it was realized that the question of readiness could never be answered and the person would wait forever to be deinstitutionalized (Lord and Pedlar 1991; Hutchison and McGill 1998). A more realistic and effective strategy involved connecting with the community outside the institution and engaging in community life. As part of the new social movement that emerged around the treatment of people with disabilities, the deinstitutionalization movement strove to ensure that institutions were closed. Unfortunately, not all communities were willing to embrace the deinstitutionalization movement and in the face of ineffective policy and limited community engagement, some people remained disenfranchised. More inclusive policies have been identified by a number of people working in the disability field (Nelson, Lord, and Ochocka 2001; Pedlar, Haworth, Hutchison, Taylor, and Dunn 1999). Over time, the politics of difference saw the galvanizing of efforts to ensure access to resources and to include people with disabilities more fully in community life. However, it is one of the sad lessons of deinstitutionalization that, in the absence of strong community support, a considerable number of people with complex mental health issues find their way into another system of incarceration, namely that of Corrections. The Correctional Service of Canada has seen a dramatic increase in the percentage of inmates with a diagnosed mental illness in its institutions during the period 1997 and 2005 (Chartier 2006). With the exception of anti-social personality disorder, women outnumber men in all major psychiatric diagnoses (Laishes 2002). Women who are incarcerated are three times more likely to be moderately to severely depressed, are more self-abusive, and tend to engage in more self-mutilating behaviours, such as slashing, than their male counterparts (Laishes 2002).

Recent work is attempting to respond to the growing number of inmates with mental health needs. Specifically, the Community Health Initiative currently being implemented by the Correctional Service of Canada is aimed at addressing the needs of individuals with mental illness in order to promote their safe reintegration upon release. As reported in the Ten-Year Status Report on Women's Corrections (Correctional Service of Canada 2006), the increase of inmates with mental health diagnoses is even more pronounced for women, with one out of four women in federal custody having a mental health diagnosis compared to only one in ten for men. This speaks to the life circumstances that many women have endured such as years of trauma and abuse, not infrequently culminating in the crimes that lead to their incarceration.

Creating Choices explicitly recognized these circumstances, and, as noted, the intent of policies and programs that exist in women's prisons today is treatment and rehabilitation. For instance, many programs are designed to be therapeutic and engage expertise from professionals to administer programs such as Anger and Emotion Management, and Dialectical Behaviour Therapy (DBT). DBT is described as targeting "skill development to address dysregulation in the sphere of emotions, relationships, cognitions and behaviours while increasing adaptive behaviours" (Fortin 2004, 13). While seen by many involved with Corrections to be effective in altering women's self-understanding and ability to manage stressors, others have been critical of these approaches to supporting women in prison. As Hannah-Moffat (2001) observed: "the feminization of penal regimes does not forgive their punitive and oppressive tendencies, especially when we consider that the subjects of the regimes are involuntary." She goes on to say that "therapy in prison is a contradiction in terms" (196). Foucault (1975) would likely concur, except he would likely go further in pointing out that this is precisely the issue – those with power over the women will exert that power to shape their self-understanding of worthlessness and guilt, again perpetuating the oppression present in the lives of women in prison.

It's Work Readiness That Really Matters

The results of a study by Delveaux, Blanchette, and Wickett (2005) indicated that the majority of women who are federally incarcerated have considerable employment-related needs, both at their intake to federal institutions and on their release to the community. These needs are related to their high unemployment rate, lack of skills, and a low level of education, noted earlier. The women in the Delveaux et al. study considered assistance with employment-related needs to be very important with respect to the desistence of criminal activities in the future. Despite the women's expressed interest in community-based work-release programs, almost none had actually participated in these opportunities during their incarceration. While incarcerated, women are employed in various tasks and may receive up to $6.90 per day for their labour (CSC

1999). The lack of community-based work releases for women and the dissimilarity between institutional work and work in the community was also identified in both the Auditor General's Report (2003) and the report of the Canadian Human Rights Commission (2003).

The lack of connectedness to community employment opportunities further amplifies incarcerated women's social isolation and oppression. However, there is an assumption that work and productivity will provide that pathway into society that has thus-far eluded many who come into conflict with the law. It is quite probable that the job most of these women will secure on release will continue their marginal economic status. For women who have no alternative but to seek social assistance, neo-liberal policies require that they demonstrate they are engaged in an active job search in order to qualify for social assistance. The degradation of possibly failing to secure employment, at any wage, may lead to recidivism and failure to meet the expectations of reintegration.

WHY ACTION BELIES COMMITMENT TO INTEGRATION

It is apparent that, although reintegration appears repeatedly in CSC policy directives and communiqués dealing with corrections for women, the focus of almost everything that happens around programming is concerned with inside rather than outside the institution. Within women's corrections, there is minimal opportunity to experience the sort of community corrections that involves serving one's sentence in the community. Such options are more generally available to males who are incarcerated. One of the recurring themes in the explanation of this lack of options for women is that there are simply too few women under federal correctional supervision to warrant extending community corrections and supervision options. While a higher percentage of men remain incarcerated vs. in the community on conditional release, there are apparently still sufficient numbers to warrant larger numbers of men under correctional supervision in the community. Ultimately community corrections is reduced to an argument based on economies of scale. One outcome of this is that women are placed in prisons at a cost of approximately $170,000 per annum per inmate (CSC 2007b), whereas in contrast a woman on parole or on statutory release in the community costs approximately $20,000 (CSC n.d.).

What we see from these conditions is a continuation of the oppression that characterizes these women's lives. While the Correctional Service seeks to empower and prepare women for reintegration, it does not focus its energy beyond the institution. This begs the question of whether the minimal effort to link to the community reflects an awareness of the challenges that lie in reintegrating this population into the community. From a communitarian perspective wherein individual flourishing or failure is closely aligned to collective responsibility (Frazer and Lacey 1993), the tendency of the service to look inward mirrors the failure of the community to consider its responsibility in reintegration of this marginalized population. Such circumstances again reinforce punishment of the *offender* for what is treated as her crime against society.

As the gap widens between rich and poor in Canada, it is increasingly recognized that poverty can lead to the desperate measures alluded to earlier. People turn to crime as a last-ditch effort to survive. As was noted earlier, the majority of women who are incarcerated are mothers. A mother with children living in poverty sometimes feels she has no alternative but to commit fraud or steal in order to feed and clothe her family. When she is convicted and incarcerated for such a crime, her children may be cared for by extended family members, but in many instances these children will be taken into residential care by the state. Research has shown that children with this sort of history are themselves highly susceptible to criminal activity in later years (Carlen 1988). A recent media report from the Ontario Office of Child and Family Service Advocacy indicated that one third of youth who come in contact with the criminal justice system have been in care prior to their crime (Moore 2007). Clearly, this is exactly the sort of cycle that well-intentioned policy aims to break, but the deep, structural impediments within our society make it the case that, once involved in the correctional system, it is very hard to not have that become a defining characteristic of one's life.

Confronting Oppression: A Role for Leisure?

Identifying the oppressive practices that are systemic within correctional institutions does not suggest an absence of exemplary initiatives designed to potentially minimize the oppression experienced by incarcerated women. For example, Pollack (2004) applauds the peer support services that are being provided in Canadian prisons for women and offers this program as an example of the ways in which institutional programming can combat the power dynamics that exist within the prison setting and minimize institutional oppression. She explains that in the peer-support program, women are trained to be peer counsellors and provide crisis intervention, support, and advocacy for the prison population. According to Pollack, the strength of this program comes from its potential to increase feelings of self-worth and autonomy since there is less of a reliance on professionals and more of an emphasis on women working collectively to confront issues of injustice. The training component of the program is also significant as it conveys to participants that they are deemed capable and can be entrusted with problem-solving responsibility.

Initiatives that involve incarcerated women and that are specifically designed to address issues of inequality, and empower women to challenge their oppressive circumstances, are deserving of attention. For example, Baird (2002) demonstrates how Freire's theory of *conscientization* (1970) was used to help shape an education program for incarcerated women that provided an opportunity for them to "reflect on, discuss, recognize and address, in their own words, how their lives have been shaped" (8). These stories, in turn, provided the context for a theatrical production that put the spotlight on issues of oppression facing incarcerated women. The showcasing of the play to a diverse community audience, including policy-makers and justice officials, served as a vehicle for examining policy issues that either condone or perpetuate oppression. Perhaps the most striking point highlighted in Baird's account of the response to the play came from a prison guard who admitted to not previously being aware of the women's life experiences. Such an admission signifies, not only the need to clarify the misconceptions about incarcerated women, but also the need for those working closely with this group of women to examine how their ignorance about women's lives may be contributing to further oppression. If prison guards do not have a clear understanding of the life circumstances of incarcerated women, how can they begin to help women change these circumstances in order to resist oppression?

In a similar vein to the empowerment that can be realized through the sharing of stories for the creation of a play, empowerment can also result from opportunities for incarcerated women to use personal narratives as a source of self-awareness and personal strength. Mahoney and Daniel (2006) posit that, through the use of language, incarcerated women can describe their experiences and articulate a plan for change. The narrative approach is principally concerned with human dignity, equity, and self-determination, and it is designed to recognize the effect of oppressive forces on individual functioning. As Mahoney and Daniel explain, when practitioners use the narrative approach, they are able to see women in context and they can listen for ways in which gender, culture, and social and economic context shape women's worldviews and experiences. In the process of co-constructing stories, practitioners can assist women to view the outcomes of problem-dominated stories as examples of courage, determination, and strength in the face of continued oppression.

In-depth qualitative exchanges that the authors have had with women in prison, who attended Stride Night, the once-weekly evening of recreation and leisure involving volunteers coming into one of the regional facilities, underscore the importance of contact with the community. While these connections occur within the context of the prison, it is evident that this involvement is central to the women's ability to see themselves as perhaps regaining respect and citizenship. Furthermore, when analyzing the conversations with the women, it became evident that the five principles of *Creating Choices* (empowerment, meaningful and responsible choices, shared responsibility, respect and dignity, and supportive environment) were reflected in the experiences of the women during these weekly recreation and leisure get-togethers with community members.

A critical aspect of Stride Night and the way it was embraced by the women in the prison and community women was the way in which it provided a space for women, no matter what their status, to come together. With women from GVI and community volunteers involved, it became essentially impossible to tell who was who, except that the volunteers wore a badge with a "V" identifier. When people were seated at tables working on crafts, one could not see the "V" badge and then the volunteers along with the inmates were simply a group of women working together. The presence of non-Correctional staff and volunteers was an essential aspect of their participation. Whether it be a craft night or volleyball or a coffee house evening, Stride Night offered *women* (rather than inmates and volunteers) an opportunity to have an enjoyable evening together. In that setting in that timeframe, differences dissipated, and the faces of oppression were lifted.

Through their connections with Stride Night, women noted the positive experience of reciprocity and trust in those social relations. Of concern for many women involved with the criminal justice system is the fact that they can rarely speak openly about their past and their crime for fear that it will jeopardize their reintegration efforts once they are released. As well, on release they will lose the connection they have had with many of the women they have known in the prison, and in some instances they will want to avoid contact with people they associated with prior to incarceration. All of these discontinuities leave former inmates potentially isolated and vulnerable. It was evident from our examination of Stride Night and Stride Circles that when a woman connected with Stride Night volunteers and when a Stride Circle developed through that association, she had greater stability and was able to receive reassurance of her value as a person (Fortune, Thompson, Pedlar, and Yuen, 2010). It is indicative of the systematic barriers to inclusion that this one community initiative to assist women when released from incarceration has ceased at the time of writing due to funding shortages. In general, the barrier between the institution and the wider community remains strong and impervious, which makes reintegration even more challenging when a woman does return to the community.

From a social development perspective, the benefits of the foregoing connections and relationships are clear. The research supports the proposition that when community members and the incarcerated women come together in leisure, there is a recognition of humanity, respect, and growth that occurs for those women who are incarcerated and those who enter the prison to spend time with them in leisure. The stigma that characterizes so much of an *offender*'s life is for a moment forgotten, and the experience of oppression diminishes. And, of course, the growth and development that occur for people in that setting do not cease the moment the engagement ends; it is something that people can carry with them beyond the walls of the institution. What's missing, however, is an opportunity for greater engagement with the community at large through opportunities for women in prison to interact with people outside of the facility. So much of the attention of the correctional procedures and programs is focused on internal day-to-day concerns; any policy directives that speak to engaging the community and ensuring opportunities for temporary absences from the prison for the women get relegated to the very lowest priority and are quickly forgotten. That said, the value of the engagements that happen in the prison cannot be overlooked as they do provide an illustration of how important a sense of belonging and community that happens in leisure is to the well-being and life quality of these individuals. In the following section, we shall consider ways in which these promising practices point to other policy developments that can further the de-marginalization and suggest an alternative future for women who have been in contact with the law.

Social Inclusion and Sustainability

The idea of seeking social justice through access to leisure, which in turn opens the door to a rich and meaningful community life is unlikely to be immediately embraced either by women in prison or by the community at large. Resistance to this prospect rests among other things in the context of a society where members may expect, through productive engagement with the market, to reap the rewards of social inclusion and citizenship. If we accept the "mad or bad" thesis of social exclusion from community, the predominant view will be that women are incapable of such engagement or they are unworthy of the opportunity. The stigma of their status is accompanied by structural impediments that are daunting in their persistence. However, perhaps despite the dominance of neo-liberalism and its reification of individualism, productivity, and materialism, there is beginning to emerge in some quarters a sharing of social responsibility. This response goes beyond distributive justice and is suggestive of a more socially just response and is happening as society faces consumptive saturation and a search for an alternative future – one which is more cognizant and caring of a fragile society.

Sustainability has been shown to be virtually unachievable if we continue current social, economic, and industrial practices, and the issue of poverty takes on an entirely different face when to be disenfranchised is equated with the ultimate state of destitution – homelessness. For our most marginalized populations who have lost their place in the world of work and productivity, and for those whose future is permanently shaped by the fact that they "have a record," regaining access to the basic necessities of daily life becomes increasingly tenuous in a society bent on accumulation (see Reid, Golden, and Katerberg in this volume). Again, to remain outside the prison in the absence of social support and access to the basic necessities of life, not surprisingly, can lead to a re-enactment of those measures *offenders* used to survive in the past. With or without such re-enactment, the conditions of oppression will continue to dominate their life.

We have seen how, in the presence of leisure engagements women in prison were supported in realizing another self, where respect and dignity, empowerment, and supportive environment came together to suggest an alternative future. Where conditions were right, the relational nature of the involvement, which was rooted in leisure between incarcerated women and community women, led to a continuation of connection after incarceration. If policy further encouraged such connection beyond the institution, the likelihood of social inclusion and integration would be further solidified. Indeed, policies like *Creating Choices* speak of the importance and value of openness and connectivity to reintegration, but the will to implement and act on those policies has been lacking. Ultimately, though, community itself must be willing to accept the differences that are present in the experiences and life-worlds of people who have been in contact with the law. Pluralistic societies such as ours depend on diversity for their sustainability and richness. If we deny the contribution that this diversity brings to a society, we continue the oppression and negate the opportunity for people to contribute to the social health of our communities.

In some respects, there are serious limitations to the suggestions made here regarding the fostering of connections between women in prison and the community beyond the walls of the prison. These suggestions beg the question regarding the sort of society that allows the continuation of the oppression that is so often responsible for the offending action in the first place. More significant is the willingness to engage in collective action to redresses the power imbalances and social and economic discrepancies that precede the taking of desperate measures by marginalized and defeated members of our communities. Returning to the earlier example of progress that has resulted through the work of the disability movement, people with disabilities have accepted both the benefits and responsibilities of inclusion. In the process, the community as a whole has grown richer and benefited from the contributions of members of the movement. Economic and social policies recognizing the importance of difference have shifted in ways that try to ensure accommodation and inclusion – a more socially just society. This did not happen without a struggle and without people with disabilities far too slowly being granted the opportunity to contribute and demonstrate their capacities, and gradually moving from a marginal, disenfranchised status to one of respect and dignity.

Moving from a state of invisibility to visibility is a necessary condition of inclusion (Dechman 2003). In order for that to happen, while there needed to be people with disabilities within the movement initiating action, people without disabilities played key advocacy and support roles in the movement, which lead to a change in status for the collective. Similarly, for women who have come in contact with the law, their position will be strengthened by the involvement of others. While the involvement of these others need not be limited to leisure settings, and indeed important opportunity for engagement can occur in other aspects of daily life, leisure has been shown to be an environment conducive to the realization of common interests and accomplishment, as well as celebrating difference. If, in community then, we encourage such connectivity, we may begin to offer an alternative future and a more socially just society.

REFERENCES

Auditor General Canada. 2003. *Correctional Service of Canada – Reintegration of Women Offenders.* http://www.oag-bvg.gc.ca/domino/reports.nsf/html/20030404ce.html/$file/20030404ce.pdf (accessed July 17, 2006).

Baird, I. C. 2002. "Voices inside: Popular theatre and Incarcerated women's lives." *Proceedings of the 21ˢᵗ Annual Canadian Association for the Study of Adult Education Conference.* Toronto.

Bloom, B., B. M. Owen, and S. Covington. 2003. *Research, Practice, and Guiding Principles for Women Offenders: Gender Responsive Strategies.* Washington, DC: U.S. Department of Justice. National Institute of Corrections.

Canadian Human Rights Commission. 2003. *Protecting Their Rights: A Systemic Review of Human Rights in Correctional Services for Federally Sentenced Women.* Ottawa.

Carlen, P. 1988. *Women, Crime and Poverty.* Milton Keynes: Open University Press.

Chartier, G. 2006. "CSC's Mental Health Initiative for Safer Communities." *Let's Talk* 30(4): 13–14.

Correctional Service of Canada. (CSC). n.d. *Basic Facts.* http://www.csc-scc.gc.ca/text/pblct/basicfacts/BasicFacts_e.shtml). (accessed October 26, 2007).

Correctional Service of Canada. 1999. *Commissioner's Directive 730: Inmate Program Assignment and Payments.* http://www.csc-scc.gc.ca/text/plcy/cdshtm/730-cde-eng.shtml (accessed November 10, 2008).

Correctional Service of Canada. 2006. "Ten-year status report on women's corrections." *Community Transition.* http://www.csc-scc.gc.ca/text/prgrm/fsw/wos24/principle_themes_8_e.shtml (accessed June 29, 2006).

Correctional Service of Canada. 2007a. *Fact Sheet.* http://www.ps-sp.gc.ca/media/nr/2007/nr20040420-eng.aspx (accessed October 26, 2007).

Correctional Service of Canada. 2007b. *Women Offender Statistical Overview.* Ottawa: Correctional Service of Canada.

Dauvergne-Latimer, M. 1995. "Exemplary community programs for federally sentenced women: A literature review." http://www.csc-scc.gc.ca/text/prgrm/fsw/fsw27/toce_e.shtml (accessed April 20, 2007)

Dechman, M. 2003. "The four Ps of social exclusion: A predisposed, pervasive, prolonged process." *Perception* 26(1–2): 7–9.

Delveaux, K., K. Blanchette, and J. Wickett. 2005. *Employment Needs, Interests, and Programming for Women Offenders.* Correctional Service of Canada. http://www.csc-scc.gc.ca.

Department of Justice Canada. 1992. "Corrections and Conditional Release Act." http://laws.justice.gc.ca/en/C-44.6/230765.html (accessed March 3, 2006).

Faith, K. 1993. *Unruly Women: The Politics of Confinement and Resistance.* Vancouver, BC: Press Gang Publishers.

Fortin, D. 2004. *Program Strategy for Women Offenders, 2004.* Ottawa: Correctional Service of Canada.

Fortune, D., J. Thompson, A. Pedlar, and F. Yuen. 2010. "Social justice and women leaving prison: Beyond punishment and exclusion." *Contemporary Justice Review* 13(1): 19-33.

Foucault, M. 1975. *Discipline and Punish.* New York: Vintage.

Frazer, E., and N. Lacey. 1993. *The Politics of Community: A Feminist Critique of the Liberal-Communitarian Debate.* Toronto: University of Toronto Press.

Freire, P. 1970. *Pedagogy of the Oppressed.* New York: Continuum.

Hannah-Moffat, K. 2001. *Punishment in Disguise: Penal Governance and Federal Imprisonment of Women in Canada.* Toronto: University of Toronto Press.

Hannah-Moffat, K., and M. Shaw. 2000. "Prisons for women – Theory, reform, ideals." In *An Ideal Prison? Critical Essays on Women's Imprisonment in Canada*, ed. K. Hannah-Moffat and M. Shaw, 11–27. Halifax: Fernwood.

Hutchison, P., and J. McGill. 1998. *Community, Integration, and Leisure*. Toronto: Leisurability Publications.

HM Chief Inspector. 2006. *Grand Valley Institution for Women: Report on Announced Inspection in Canada by HM Chief Inspector of Prisons for England and Wales*. London: Her Majesty's Inspectorate of Prisons.

Laishes, J. 2002. *The 2002 Mental Health Strategy for Women Offenders*. Ottawa: Correctional Service of Canada.

Law, M. 2004. "Federally sentenced women in the community: Dynamic risk predictors." *Forum on Corrections Research* 16: 18–20.

Lord, J., and A. Pedlar. 1991. "Life in the community: Four years after the closure of an institution." *Mental Retardation* 19(4): 213–21.

Mahoney, A. M. and C. A. Daniel. 2006. "Bridging the power gap: Narrative therapy with incarcerated women." *Prison Journal* 86(1): 75–88.

McCorkel, J. 2003. "Embodied surveillance and the gendering of punishment." *Journal of Contemporary Ethnography* 32(1): 41–76.

Moore, O. 2007. "The state is a bad parent: Does child welfare make criminals?" *Globe and Mail*, March 10, M1.

Nelson, G., J. Lord, and J. Ochocka. 2001. *Shifting the Paradigm in Community Mental Health: Toward Empowerment and Community*. Toronto: University of Toronto Press.

Pedlar, A., S. Arai, F. Yuen, and D. Fortune. 2008. "Uncertain futures: Women leaving prison and re-entering community." Available at http://www.ahs.uwaterloo.ca/uncertainfutures/.

Pedlar, A., L. Haworth, P. Hutchison, A. Taylor, and P. Dunn. 1999. *A Textured Life: Empowerment and Adults with Developmental Disabilities*. Waterloo: Wilfrid Laurier University Press.

Pedlar, A., F. C. Yuen, and D. Fortune. 2008. "Incarcerated women and leisure: Making good girls out of bad?" *Therapeutic Recreation Journal* 42(1): 24–36.

Pollack, S. 2004. "Anti-oppressive social work practice with women in prison: Discursive reconstructions and alternative practices." *British Journal of Social Work* 34(5): 693–707.

Richie, B. E. 2001. "Challenges incarcerated women face as they return to their communities: Findings from life history interviews." *Crime and Delinquency* 47(3): 368–89.

Sinclair, R. L., and R. Boe. 2002. *Canadian Federal Women Offender Profiles: Trends from 1981 to 2002* (Revised). Ottawa: Correctional Service of Canada. http://www.csc-scc.ga.ca/text/rsrch/reports/r131/r131_e.shtml (accessed April 11, 2005).

Task Force on Federally Sentenced Women (TFFSW). 1990. *Creating Choices – The Report of the Task Force on Federally Sentenced Women.* Ottawa: Solicitor General of Canada.

Smart, C. 1995. *Law, Crime, and Sexuality: Essays in Feminism.* Thousand Oaks, CA: Sage.

Sommers, E. K. 1995. *Voices from Within: Women Who Have Broken the Law.* Toronto: University of Toronto Press.

Worrell, A. 1990. *Offending Women: Female Lawbreakers and the Criminal Justice System.* New York: Routledge.

Young, I. M. 1990. *Justice and the Politics of Difference.* Princeton, NJ: Princeton University Press.

★   The authors acknowledge the support of the Social Sciences and Humanities Research Council of Canada, General Research Program, without which this research would not have been possible. In addition, we thank the women of GVI who gave so generously of their time and provided insight into the experience of incarceration.

8

Restoring Our Collective Obligation: Exploring Opportunities for Addressing Homelessness and Social Housing

Heather Mair and Dawn Trussell

Recent events in the United States and around the world are pushing us to come to terms ever more directly with the importance of housing to human health. Reports of mortgage foreclosures, the squalid state of much social housing, and the growing ranks of those living on the streets are finally becoming topics of mainstream discussion. How we think about homelessness and social housing is changing. In his investigation of the destruction of Pruitt-Igoe (a modernist housing project built in St. Louis, Missouri, and a long-standing example of the failure of social housing in the United States), Mitchell argues that the destruction of this building "marked the beginning of the end of a societal, *collective*, obligation to assure that housing is decent and affordable" (2001, 61; emphasis in the original). Furthermore, he challenges the "broken window" thesis (a dubious theory about neighbourhood decay begetting neighbourhood decay and thereby encouraging criminal behaviour) to reveal a growing attack on homelessness and poverty. With this chapter, we seek to build on these ideas by engaging the broader debate about social policy and public responsibility for social welfare. After painting a brief picture of the issues relating to homelessness and social housing in the Canadian context, we build upon recent research undertaken with individuals who are homeless (or at risk of becoming homeless) in the Waterloo Region of Ontario, Canada. We seek to develop a critical understanding of access to safe, affordable, and secure private spaces as well as the changing public debate in order to unmask the power relationships at work in the politics of poverty and homelessness. Furthermore, we think through the opportunities presented by leisure in terms of reaching this goal. While working from a critical leisure studies lens offers little chance of immediately "solving" the problem of homelessness and poverty, we argue that leisure can help to create the context where these issues are discussed, debated, confronted, and reconsidered and where our sense of a *societal, collective obligation* might be restored. Furthermore, we argue that recent debates about where and how individuals living in public places are allowed to be are ultimately leisure issues.

This chapter has five major sections. First, we define the key terms of homelessness and social housing as they are relevant for our discussion and paint a brief picture of the Canadian context. Next, we move into a broader, more philosophical discussion regarding our changing notions of social and collective responsibility for the provision of safe and affordable housing – what we call the dismantling of our collective obligation (after Mitchell 2001). Third, we locate this "responsibility debate" within an even broader discussion of public and private spaces insofar as the increasing gap between rich and poor can be seen as a geographical, spatial split, which allows for a see-no-evil approach to avoiding and ignoring homelessness – what some critical geographers are calling the "revanchist city" (Smith 1996). Fourth, in an effort to think about ways through this discourse of blame and avoidance, we put forward a framework for re-building our sense of collective obligation through the creation of a system that focuses on the provision of safe and affordable housing – in other words, to create a "housing system" (after Hulchanski 2002) much like our health care system and our welfare system. Further, we argue that there is a role here for the community development potential of leisure. Not only can leisure be used, as Dawson and Harrington (1996) and others have shown, to mitigate the impacts of poverty, low income, and homelessness, it can provide opportunities to foster shared understandings and even counter-discourses about these issues. Last, next steps in terms of policy recommendations and opportunities for addressing this situation are explored.

KEY TERMS AND CONTEXT

Homelessness

Research into homelessness has long identified its complexity. Homelessness may be the result of an interrelated web of factors from such broad socio-economic forces as gentrification, urbanization, economic restructuring, to a change in life circumstance such as unemployment, family break-up, financial difficulties, illness, physical injury, disability, or drug and/or alcohol addiction. Main (1998) argues that the interrelationship between individualistic factors and broader, structural factors makes understanding homelessness and its causes a difficult task.

While being "without shelter" may be the crassest definition, it hides many levels of complexity. The United Nations General Assembly for the International Year of Shelter for Homelessness (1982 cited in Scott et al. 2006) defines two types of homelessness: absolute and relative. Absolute homelessness means having no dependable shelter and includes living on the street, staying in shelters, or living temporarily with friends or family (e.g. couch-surfing). Relative homelessness, in this view, means having access to shelter but that shelter may be inappropriate, unsafe, unhealthy, or uncomfortable. Researchers, activists, and social workers also often speak of *visible* and *invisible* homelessness. Those who are visibly homeless are in public spaces while those who are less visible (or invisible) live in inadequate private spaces. Shelter must be dependable, affordable, accessible, and safe. Moreover, access to shelter that meets these criteria is often so tenuous that being at risk of becoming homeless is a growing issue. Table 8.1, developed by Mah and DeSantis (2000), illustrates these dimensions.

Table 8.1: Definitions of homelessness.

Literal Homeless	Hidden Homeless	Imminent Risk of Being Homeless
People who sleep in indoor or outdoor public places and/or use emergency shelters	People who live in illegal or temporary accommoda- tion and/or rely on friends and acquaintances for shelter	People are at risk of being homeless if their current housing is considered: • *unsafe* – e.g., sub-standard housing which has been condemned, a family member is being abused; • *unaffordable* – e.g., paying more than 50% of one's income on shelter, has temporary employment, and may not have rent money for the next month; • *overcrowded* – e.g., two or more families living in the same apartment; • *insecure* – e.g., people who are at risk of eviction; • *inappropriate* – e.g., a severely disabled person who is living in a hospital without choice to live anywhere else, a person who needs attendant services and an accessible building but has neither.

Falvo (2003) argues that homelessness is a growing problem resulting from both changes in social support systems as well as the rising cost of homeownership and renting. He writes that, in addition to health problems and the risk of death, homeless people experience high rates of sexual victimization (especially women), physical assault, police harassment, poor food quality, inadequate hygiene facilities, lack of privacy and security, forced movement, and rampant theft (5). Furthermore, he argues, meeting housing needs becomes a preoccupation for those who do not have it, often to the detriment of an individual's safety as well as physical and mental health. Among the most vulnerable populations (i.e., those who are homeless or at most risk of becoming homeless) are single-parent families, individuals living with disabilities, Aboriginal Canadians, recent immigrants, visible minorities, elderly women, and, increasingly, youth (Miller et al. 2004). Sev'er's research (2002) illustrates that, for a woman being abused by her spouse, becoming homeless is often the only option. Bunting et al. (2004, 365) captured some of the many and complex factors leading to "housing affordability stress" including economic change, social/demographic change and changes to policy.

According to a recent report by the Wellesley Institute (2006), homelessness has three interrelated costs: health (the death rate for homeless people is eight to ten times higher than housed people of the same age and there is a direct relationship between the quality of housing and quality of health), social (poor housing and homelessness has a dramatic impact on communities), and economic (costs of providing shelter, drain on health care system, etc.).

In 2006, Statistics Canada reported (Luffman 2006) that more than 1.7 million Canadians spend more than 30 per cent of their total household expenditures on housing. Perhaps not surprisingly, people renting apartments or houses in Toronto and other large centres are likely to spend even more on their housing costs. In Toronto, nearly a third of all renters spend more than 30 per cent of their income on housing. For those with low incomes, the percentage spent on housing costs becomes even greater.

Social Housing

As Bryant points out, social housing "reflects a commitment by the state to support affordable housing for all" (2003, 53). Social housing or public housing has long been a policy response across the western world to help ensure that those at the bottom of the income ladder have access to shelter. Authors such as Bryant (2003), Layton (2000), and Hulchanski (2002) have assessed the social housing situation in Canada and argue it has been both woefully under-appreciated and under-supported.

Hulchanski (2002) traces the history of social housing in Canada and argues it has been chequered at best. The National Housing Act (1964) was considered to be effective, creating about 200,000 units over nearly ten years. Further amendments in the 1970s led to the creation of many programs, including assisted home ownership, neighbourhood improvement, and housing for Aboriginal Canadians, as well as non-profit and co-op housing programs (Hulchanski 2002, iii). By the mid-1980s, however, the federally elected Conservative government made immediate and lasting cuts to these programs, fostering a quick retreat from social housing. With the 1990s came the growth of the neo-liberal agenda and the subsequent pull-back of state involvement in all aspects of social services provision. In Ontario, the election of a Conservative government at the provincial level resulted in a reversal of twenty-five years of social housing provision (Bryant 2003) in that province. At the federal level, all housing support was withdrawn by 1993 as the supply of social housing fell from 25,000 new units in 1983 to none in the 1993 budget (i.e., non-market housing owned and managed by non-profits or non-equity co-operatives; Hulchanski 2002).

Having passed the responsibility for the provision of social housing effectively onto the provinces and municipal governments, the federal government ensured that these smaller governments would have to absorb the costs of growing populations unable to access affordable housing. As federal transfers were cut, the provinces followed suit by limiting social assistance and decreased the number and kind of social supports. In the next section, we discuss the underlying ideological assumptions that have allowed for the continuation and acceleration of this disaster.

The Legacy of Neo-Liberalism: The Dismantling of Our Collective Responsibility

By now, it is unfailingly clear that the assumptions underscoring much of the development (and dismantling) of the welfare state and social programs in the western world are grounded primarily within neo-liberalism. As Harvey (1989) has articulated, there has been a shift in the role of the state: from a manager of social development and economic growth to a more entrepreneurial focus where the conditions for capital investment are merely fostered leaving private enterprise to take care of itself (and the rest of society). Based upon an interlocking logic of individual responsibility, reduced government involvement (and expenditure) in the fate of its citizens, and unfettered and/or encouraged privately organized economic growth, the past two decades have seen a remarkable and well-documented retrenchment and reversal of social policy in Canada. Indeed, one can see the same neo-liberal logic throughout the discussion of housing in regard to the increasingly market-dominated language of provision in this country as well as the subsequent withdrawal of meaningful support for those who don't have enough income to own their own home.

Indeed, according to Hulchanski (2002), Canada's housing market has become the most private-sector dominated of any western nation and has the smallest social housing sector, except for the United States. The use of shelters skyrocketed under the Harris Conservative government in Ontario as well as across the country to create our current national housing crisis. Hulchanski outlines the processes negatively affecting the provision of affordable housing in Canada. First, the Canadian government, through initiatives such as the Canada Mortgage and Housing Corporation (established in 1946) encouraged growth in the housing market and made it safer for Canadians to buy their own homes and repay their mortgages through amortization. Homeownership, particularly in low-density areas, was also encouraged and fostered by the car culture. Added to this, however, was the continued support of the private-sector rental housing, which allowed for the development of the rental market, creating, as Hulchanski argues, two "pools of housing consumers with dramatically different incomes and assets" (5). While homeowners benefit, renters are often caught in the trap of not having enough money to enter the housing market. As a result, there is a growing gap between homeowners and renters with the latter having less disposable income and fewer tax benefits. Indeed, as Hulchanski argues: "Although some people are in the rental sector only temporarily, others never leave it. They cannot save enough money for a down payment on a house; nor do they have the type of secure employment that would qualify them for a mortgage. In addition, there is a pervasive cultural and institutional bias against renting in Canada" (6).

The growth in building and selling condominiums has only exacerbated the problem. High-density areas, normally more favourable to renters in the form of apartments, are now options for condominium development and market speculation. Builders and developers would much rather access an upper-level income group for a one-time condo sale than engage in a series of rental relationships with individuals with lower incomes. Furthermore, the market fix of so-called "filtering" (the assumption that new, expensive homes would be occupied by wealthy members of society, leaving older and less-expensive homes for low-income earners to purchase) has not really borne out due primarily to forces of gentrification, location, income insecurity, and a booming housing market (Skaburskis 2006).

In short, as Harris makes clear (2000), while the role of the state in housing has been "an incoherent hodgepodge of activity" (399), one trend is clear: a corporate capitalist economic approach to housing provision has been fostered. Harris calls this a mixed blessing that has been biased in favour of the building industry:

> It has led to the production of safe, energy-efficient, and roomy housing for the majority of Canadians, but it has helped create monotonous neighbourhoods and a mountain of consumer debt, while doing little directly to help lower-income households. (399)

As Moore and Skaburskis (2004) point out, because most Canadians are able to afford "market prices" for shelter, the objective of affordability for those with lower income levels becomes further and further out of reach. In a sense, the issue of affordable housing is the result of our general economic market-oriented "successes." They conclude, "[e]conomic restructuring, coupled with reductions in transfers to the poor is offering the lowest-income households a future framed by Third World expectations" (409).

The growing and harsh inequalities wrought by a neo-liberal agenda are being felt in North America and across Europe, especially in the urban areas, and creates what MacLeod calls a "sharpening of inequality alongside the institutional displacement and social exclusion of certain marginalized populations" (2002, 602). The insights from this and other research into the creation of the housing crisis have led Jahiel (1992), among many (see, for example, Layton 2000) to argue that homelessness is socially constructed:

> In general, the events that make people homeless are initiated and controlled by other people whom our society allows to engage in the various enterprises that contribute to the homelessness of others. The primary purpose of these enterprises is not to make people homeless, but rather, to achieve socially condoned aims such as making a living, becoming rich, obtaining a more desirable home, increasing the efficiency of the workplace, promoting the growth of cultural institutions, giving cities a competitive advantage, or helping local or federal governments to balance their budgets or limit their debts. Homelessness occurs as a side effect. (269)

In sum, by taking away supports to help people find appropriate, safe, and affordable housing, we are forcing many to live out their lives in inappropriate, unsafe and/or insecure private places or, more starkly, in increasingly unsafe and unwelcoming public places. Moreover, the growing focus away from a discussion of the need for a broad-based social net to protect the public's welfare means that homelessness is positioned as an individual's problem, not one for society to address. In the words of Jack Layton:

> Blaming the victim. This deceptively simple but brilliant turn of phrase ... captures the essential problem with definitions that slip into this causal mindset. Take this example from the literature: "there are many words for a homeless person, such as beggar, bum, derelict, drifter, floater, gypsy, rambler, vagabond, vagrant, wanderer, wino." These days, such an approach would add squeegee kid, street hooker and panhandler – the victim-blaming terminology receives constant updating. (2000, 24)

It must be said that turning the blame onto the individual who has made "bad choices" pushes us towards what C. Wright Mills warned us about long ago – the separation of private troubles and public issues (1959). When we turn away from issues such as homelessness by positioning it as a question of private troubles, we are nurturing the dismantling of our collective sense of responsibility for this public issue. In some ways, Mitchell (2001) makes this point forcefully, suggesting that social researchers, by succumbing to the thrills of a post-modernist relativism, have helped create the conditions necessary for this dismantling. For now that the dust has settled, it is clear that by abandoning meta-level or grand-scale approaches to social analyzes or theory building, much post-modern social research became, unwittingly, a handmaiden for the neo-liberal agenda as opportunities for *collective* social struggle were often left on the sidelines. While an adequate approach to social housing cannot be built on the assumption that *all* individuals have identical housing needs, we also cannot lose sight that this is a collective problem needing complex, appropriate responses.

However, and as is made more clear in the next section, even positioning homelessness as an individual's problem has not made it generally acceptable to the broader society. And yet, instead of a national outcry, we are beginning to see evidence of an even more devastating development. Despite the growing recognition (and perhaps even grudging acceptance) that the rising tide of neo-liberalism will not lift all boats, when it comes to the issue of homelessness, particularly in urban Canada, there is a growing effort to deal with this public problem in an unsettling way: by making it invisible and illegal. Indeed, as Waldron, a legal scholar in America, notes,

> Now one question we face as a society – a broad question of justice and social policy – is whether we are willing to tolerate an economic system in which large numbers of people are homeless. Since the answer is evidently "Yes," the question that remains is whether we are willing to allow those who are in this predicament to act as free agents, looking after their own needs, in public places – the only space available

to them. It is a deeply frightening fact about the modern United States that those who *have* homes and jobs are willing to answer "Yes" to the first question and "No" to the second. (1991, in Mitchell 1997)

THE REVANCHIST COMMUNITY: THE CRIMINALIZATION OF HOMELESSNESS AND POVERTY

> Let's face it. The homeless are not an attractive people. It is hard to be around them. They can look frightening, they can smell bad, and they most often want something from you. They make us uncomfortable, fearful and, yes, guilty. – *Why don't they just all go away? But where?* (Thomas Rose, Senior CBC Producer, 2006)

In 1999, the Ontario conservative government took steps towards the criminalization of individuals experiencing poverty and/or homelessness with the Safe Streets Act. This Act, which has been implemented more recently in British Columbia (2004), increased police and public attention to the activities of people who are homeless, particularly youth ("squeegee kids") in downtown urban areas. In effect, the Act made it illegal to solicit "aggressively" and included the prohibition of the following activities:

(a) solicit a person who is using, waiting to use, or departing from an automated teller machine;

(b) solicit a person who is using or waiting to use a pay telephone or a public toilet facility;

(c) solicit a person who is waiting at a taxi stand or a public transit stop;

(d) solicit a person who is in or on a public transit vehicle;

(e)   solicit a person who is in the process of getting in, out of, on or off a vehicle or who is in a parking lot; or

(f)   while on a roadway, solicit a person who is in or on a stopped, standing or parked vehicle.

Punishment for these activities ranges from a fine of not more than $500 for the first conviction to fines of not more than $1,000 and up to no more than six months of imprisonment.

In Victoria, British Columbia, there is a by-law prohibiting the erection of any shelter in a public place and sleeping overnight in parks. Montreal has banned overnight stays in public squares. Mitchell (1997) points out that for those made uncomfortable by the public presence of homeless and poor individuals (i.e., members of the middle class, politicians, and business owners), the solution is clear:

> They have turned to a legal remedy that seeks to cleanse the streets of those left behind by globalization and other secular changes in the economy by simply erasing the spaces in which they must live – by creating a legal fiction in which the rights of the wealthy, of the successful in the global economy, are sufficient for all the rest. (1997, 305)·

Mitchell also outlines the development of anti-homeless laws in the United States. It is useful to include a few here:

- In Santa Cruz, Phoenix and countless other cities, it is illegal to sleep in public.

- In Atlanta and Jacksonville, it is a crime to cut across or loiter in a parking lot if you do not have a car parked there.

- In Reno, Nevada, one may not remain in a park for more than four hours at a time.

- In Seattle, it is a crime to sleep on trains.

- In New York it is illegal to sleep in or near subways, or to wash car windows in the streets. (1997, 305–6; 2001, 66–67)

And what are the impacts of these developments? Research is just beginning to tell us the story. For instance, Gaetz (2004) found that it is this effort to push homeless and poor individuals (particularly youth and women) further and further away from the open, safe, public spaces that leads to their further exclusion, often increasing the risk that they themselves will become victims of crime. A recent study by researchers at Ryerson University found that the Safe Schools Act (a zero-tolerance policy for violence in schools) unfairly discriminates against black youth and, by putting them into conflict with their families as a result of being kicked out of school, is increasing the chance that they will become homeless (Alphonso 2007).

Underlying these events is a more general trend in the neo-liberal arena of economic development and urban restructuring which can help to explain at least some of the impetus for this legalistic response to homelessness. As Harvey argues, in an era of rapidly moving finance capital, certain *kinds* of spaces have become more attractive for investment than others (1989; see also Zukin 1991). For most western nations, the days of attracting large-scale manufacturing facilities are over as cheaper labour and lax environmental laws in other parts of the world are regularly pulling away even some of our most long-standing manufacturing centres. Instead, the point is to attract investment by turning the downtown areas of cities and other communities into *commodities* that can attract investment into services, tourism, or large-scale sports and entertainment facilities (see Friedmann et al. 2004). Of course, the images of homeless people wandering into (and living in) these consumption spaces frightens developers, business owners, investors, and tourists alike.

The sleight of hand at work here is the argument that people who are homeless or otherwise *unwanted* in the public spaces of communities (i.e., those who spend time in the downtown core of cities) are the ones causing the problems instead of being an indicator thereof. Whang and

Min (1999) call this process of blaming the victim an "inverted logic of cause and effect so that cause becomes effect and vice versa" (122). Hence the broken windows thesis mentioned at the outset of this chapter. One broken window becomes an eyesore and attracts more broken windows. One homeless person sends a signal that an area is unclean, unsafe, and unregulated and thereby will attract more homeless individuals, ultimately creating a situation of crime and social unrest. As Mitchell argues:

> Urban decline is seen as the result of homelessness. Detroit is "dead" because people "make bad choices" and panhandle on the streets, urinate in public, or sit on sidewalks, thereby presumably scaring off not only shoppers, workers and residents, but capital too. (1997, 312)

And so we have the creation of social policy that, as Atkinson argues, "celebrates the displacement of social problems rather than their resolution" (2003, 1829). Through efforts of displacement, not only are social problems removed from view by being "pushed along" to the outskirts of the public areas or into jail cells, they grow worse. In the broader scheme of capitalist development, it is hardly surprising that some people become unable to afford to live safely and well in this society. In an age of decreased social support and limited opportunities for unionization and securing a dependable and liveable wage, the most dramatic impacts of economic restructuring can be seen at the food banks, on the waiting lists for affordable housing, in the shelters, on the streets, and, increasingly, in our jails (see Arai and Burke, as well as Fortune, Pedlar, and Yuen, in this volume).

One of the ways to think about this criminalization of individuals who are poor and/or homeless is through a critical framework that builds upon radical political economy as well as the work of some geographers who seek to confront and challenge the underlying assumptions about social change and economic development. In one of the more radical approaches, Smith (1996) describes a revanchist city in order to highlight the growing reaction against the anti-discriminatory social policies developed in the 1960s:

Revenge against minorities, the working class, women, environmental legislation, gays and lesbians, immigrants, became the increasingly common denominator of public discourse. Attacks on affirmative action and immigration policy, street violence against gays and homeless people, feminist bashing and public campaigns against political correctness and multiculturalism were the most visible vehicles of this reaction. In short, the 1990s have witnessed the emergence of what we can think of as the *revanchist city*. (1996, 45)

By illuminating these assumptions, we can begin to see a network of interrelated forces at play. In a sense we have the makings of a perfect storm: (1) the continued pull-out of government responsibility for the social welfare of its citizens; (2) a growing cult of individualism, which leaves little room for collective social responsibility; (3) the ongoing quest to attract capital investment through the commodification and revitalization of our downtown core; and (4) the growing acceptance of policies that criminalize and marginalize people who are homeless, at risk of becoming homeless, or live in poverty, as they move into the public spaces of our cities and communities to meet their needs and to find help. A revanchist community trades on assumptions about individual responsibility, public spaces, and appropriate behaviour. In the next section, we outline the ways in which a critical leisure studies approach, and leisure more generally, can help to begin to reframe and counter these assumptions.

Addressing the "Private Troubles ↔ Public Issues" of Homelessness and How Leisure Can Help

In response to a chronic shortage of housing in the City of Victoria, British Columbia, makeshift communities and tent cities were recently set up in Beacon Hill, its biggest public park. When the city passed a by-law to ban the areas, the B.C. Supreme Court overturned the by-law, saying it must uphold the rights of those without shelter to stay in public places. The reaction against the ruling was swift. For instance an editorial in the *Globe and Mail* argued that the ruling pushed "rights beyond where they should go" (2008). This recent ruling has put the issue of homeless and human rights squarely into the world of recreation and leisure and yet we have been virtually silent.

Indeed, leisure research, with few yet important exceptions, has had little to say about homelessness. However, what it has had to say about leisure and individuals who are homeless can add depth to our understanding of the importance and benefits of leisure for individuals enduring a difficult life circumstance. For instance, Klitzing (2003) assesses the role of leisure as a coping mechanism for women who are homeless and living in shelters. Dawson and Harrington (1996, 1997) argued that leisure has a role to play in providing opportunities for, not only developing a more holistic approach to meeting the needs of individuals who are homeless and living in shelters, but in terms of providing avenues for personal empowerment and to stave-off the effects of being increasingly marginalized by the rest of society.

As such, the findings by Klitzing, Dawson, and others are central to this discussion because they bring to the forefront a direct reconsideration of the day-to-day issues faced by individuals who are homeless or at risk of becoming homeless. Leisure, in its very best sense, becomes a vehicle and is based upon a philosophy that refocuses the human attention away from economics solely and includes issues of life-style and well-being. To this end, it can be part of a formulation of a strategy that is relevant both for helping people "link back in" to "normal social life" and for accepting diversity and difference. Thus, it can aid in the goal of inclusion. However, one of the discomforts that arises with discussions of leisure as a coping mechanism or even as a way to access opportunities necessary to engage society is that it risks leaving the "blame the victim" and "broken window" theses unchallenged. While there are undoubtedly many immediate benefits to be gained from addressing issues such as recreation opportunities for individuals living with homelessness or being at risk thereof, we must always be concerned with not losing sight of why this situation exists in the first place.

To that end, it is important to consider broader opportunities afforded by leisure that might hit right at the heart of the perfect storm described above. Thus, the other dimension that we might begin to consider is the role of leisure in public spaces as it can help to build a sense of understanding and thereby a sense of collectivity and mutual responsibility. We can begin to see how leisure might play a role in both reclaiming public spaces as places to discuss and address social problems and in recultivating a sense of collective responsibility. As Hemingway notes, leisure offers opportunities for people to come together in public spaces to engage, confront, and understand social problems (1999). Indeed, if not leisure, then how? When? Where?

There are signs that this kind of thinking about leisure's potential to help address not only private troubles but public issues as well is taking hold. Authors such as Shinew et al. (2004) are beginning to investigate the power of social interaction as it can only take place in leisure spaces as well as its potential to provide the context for building a sense of shared mutual understandings (see also Arai and Pedlar 1997; Mair 2002/03, 2006; Pedlar and Haworth 2006; Shaw 2000, 2006). In this sense, leisure can be the avenue through which to promote a discussion of what Bauman has called "a shared conception of the good" (2001, 140). Shaw (2006) argues that seeing leisure as resistance offers the chance to reconsider and challenge generally accepted assumptions in society – assumptions based upon building and/or maintaining unequal power relationships. In this sense, leisure, while certainly not the sole answer for alleviating the social housing and homelessness crisis, can offer a context through which we can begin to confront blame-the-victim and broken-window theses and to create a counter-discourse that builds mutual understandings and leads to social change. Furthermore, given that those working in our field are the primary keepers and protectors of public spaces in many communities, especially public parks, are we not morally obligated to weigh in on these issues? If the moral undertone of much of our profession is based on equality of access, why do we sit on the fence when many individuals left out of the housing system turn to our public spaces? What contribution can we make to discussions about the use of public spaces in a world of growing privatization and exclusion?

It comes down to this: Can we revision our cities and our communities in such as way as to prevent their being taken over by these revanchist forces? Can we envision a society that rejects the individualistic emphasis that capitalism creates and the consequent inadequacy of housing and the propensity to blame those without resources to control their situation? Are our city's parks and public spaces going to be the site of "c'mon, move along" politics or will they provide safe places for people who are, at this time, homeless? At the same time that we make these public spaces safe for those who need, at this time, to use them for private living, can we also use them to foster public debates about *why* people resort to using these spaces in the ways we use our private spaces?

Signs of Hope: Public Resistance and Counter-Discourses

Feldman and Stall (2004) argue that among the most serious problems facing the future of affordable housing are: underfunding; concentration and social and physical isolation of poor minority families, typically in undesirable and inaccessible locations; inappropriate building designs; crime and vandalism; lack of tenant selection and income mix and ineffective maintenance and management, and an inadequate mix or inaccessible services and employment opportunities (4). And yet, these authors used hooks's (1990) notion of "homeplace" as a site of resistance to tell the story of women activists in Wentworth Gardens, a public housing complex in Chicago. They outline the public and private efforts of these women to sustain and improve their lives in public housing (including fighting to protect their homes from destruction when a stadium was proposed for the land in the mid-1980s). While Feldman and Stall are loath to hold up their case as a "model for ensuring viable housing" (347) in the absence of, or as a substitute for, broader policy changes and government intervention, their work is instructive. These authors illustrate how discussions of private troubles about private spaces must be ultimately repositioned as public issues in order for them to be addressed.

This case is useful for another reason in that it links us back to the earlier argument regarding a need for a new *post*-post-modern social research agenda. As noted at the beginning, Mitchell (2001 sees the destruction of the Pruitt-Igoe complex as signalling the end of the modernist approach to social justice and social welfare. That is, the quest, however misguided, to take on the societal responsibility of helping to improve the lives of people through the provision of public housing has been dramatically softened. Feldman and Stall's (2004) case of Wentworth Gardens illustrates what can happen when large public-housing buildings are left standing and their residents are empowered not only to improve them but to keep them open and operating. At the end of the day, it was the ability to collectively resist and challenge people's assumptions about how best to address the problems of affordable and safe housing that turned the tide. In our case, the need to bring people together to engage in these issues and to continue the discussion about social justice, equity, democracy, and the common good is imperative to reversing the current revanchist trends.

Recently, a fourth-year student at the Ontario College of Art and Design in Toronto (OCAD) undertook a revealing experiment. In a most interesting art project, Mark Daye challenged the very core of how we see city spaces and their regulation. By placing official looking signs at well-travelled locations with phrases such as "Please keep our streets clean, over 818 people have to sleep on them" and "Quiet: Homeless sleeping," Daye encouraged a rethinking of how public spaces are used. He described his intentions for the project in the following way:

> Instead of re-branding a product, or service for my 4th year thesis project I chose to represent a local population that usually gets overlooked. I re-coded official signage and affixed 30 of them to poles in the downtown core with messages pertaining to an obvious but ignored urban sub culture. The goal was not only to catch people off guard by creating signs that acknowledge the homeless population on a seemingly official level, but to get people to think about codes of behaviour, conformity, acceptance and to maybe spare some

consideration for the homeless who live mostly ignored in the city, blending into the background just like the signs. (Micallef 2007)

These and other so-called "urban interventions" can help us reconceptualize public space and to challenge the ways they are increasingly being controlled and used under the guise of attracting capital investment. Another interesting example is Slum Tourism Toronto. A website that takes visitors to see the poor housing conditions across Toronto with a goal to making public the issue of unsafe housing and shaming those responsible (e.g., landlords) into compliance. These and other efforts help set the stage for broader discussions regarding the need to challenge efforts to criminalize people who are homeless and living in poverty as is done with the Safe Streets Act. As it stands, the primary challenges to these efforts are happening on legal grounds. For instance, a recent report in the *Globe and Mail* (Kari 2006) outlined efforts to have the aforementioned by-law in Victoria, British Columbia, struck down as it violates the Charter of Rights and Freedoms.

THE FUTURE: TOWARDS A PUBLIC HOUSING SYSTEM

Despite our growing awareness of the issue of homelessness, the future is uncertain at best. In 2001, the Chrétien Liberal government created the Prime Minister's Caucus Task Force on Urban Issues. In the interim report, the following comments were made:

> The shortage of affordable housing is one of the biggest challenges affecting economic competitiveness and quality of life. Municipal governments and housing providers cannot meet the demand for affordable housing and emergency shelter. As more and more people migrate to cities, the pressure to find suitable accommodation has a ripple effect on society as a whole. As competitions for exiting housing stock intensifies, tenants at the lower end of the market increasingly have no choice but to turn to shelters or remain in

already overcrowded conditions. (Sgro 2002, as cited in Hulchanski, 2002, 5)

And yet, the Task Force and its reports were widely seen as a public relations exercise with little real intention or teeth for affecting change.

On December 19, 2006, the Harper Conservative government announced its Homelessness Partnering Strategy (HPS), allocating $296.6 million in funding over two years to "prevent and reduce homelessness by helping to establish the structures and supports needed to move homeless and at-risk individuals towards self-sufficiency and full participation in Canadian society" (Homelessness Partnership Strategy 2007). This strategy was set to begin on April 1, 2007. The language used to describe the Strategy indicates that it is geared more toward assuring "accountability," fostering public private partnerships and streamlining programs and supports from the federal to the local level. Furthermore, without adequate funding and support for social housing, this strategy reads more like an effort to reduce bureaucracy than to address the issues that make access to affordable housing inadequate and inequitable.

In Alberta, our wealthiest and fastest-growing provincial economy, it was recently announced that $285 million would be allocated to housing, earmarking $35 million for transitional housing, $7 million to help those at risk of losing their homes, and $100 million for municipal initiatives with an overall goal of creating 11,000 affordable housing units over the next five years (Montgomery 2007). However, the government rejected the idea of implementing rent controls, instead allowing landlords to raise the rent no more than once a year (currently they can do this twice annually). In this sense, the benefit of the initiatives is diluted and the challenge of keeping the homes, however affordable, has merely been pushed forward into the future.

The future looks grim. Two steps forward and three steps back. Bryant (2003) argues for an increase in spending on social housing that is equivalent to 1 per cent increase in overall spending by all levels of government in order to address this national disaster. And yet, it's not clear that without sustained public outcry this will ever change.

A most interesting solution is put forward by Hulchanski, whose report for the Canadian Policy Research Network (2002) is held up by many as a key resource on this issue. He makes the following suggestion:

> Although many Canadians refer to the health care *system* or the social welfare *system*, few refer to the housing *system*. Most people talk only of the housing *market*.... Yet Canada does have a housing system, one that is out of balance, one that is discriminatory in the way it treats owners and renters, and one in which the market mechanism of supply and demand works for the ownership sector but not the rental sector. It has become an increasingly exclusive system. (7)

By repositioning homelessness and housing as issues demanding the same kind of attention as our health and welfare systems (although they too are under constant attack), we elevate the debate into the public sphere. By fostering public debate, encouraging such unconventional and provocative efforts at resistance and rethinking as Slum Tourism Toronto, we can help engage people and reclaim and enhance our societal, collective obligation. Bauman has argued that this retreat into individualism is a misguided and wrong-headed venture, for *"individual liberty can be only a product of collective work* (can be only *collectively* secured and guaranteed)" (1999, 7 emphasis original). An individual's right is only secured if society secures it, and thus the private and the public, the individual and the social, are inexorably interconnected. Private troubles are public issues, and ensuring that every person has access to appropriate, safe, and secure housing is just one piece of the puzzle. Leisure studies and leisure researchers can and must make an important contribution to these discussions.

REFERENCES

Alphonso, C. 2007. "Study links zero tolerance, blacks' homelessness." *Globe and Mail*. February 4.

Arai, S. M., and A. M. Pedlar. 1997. "Building communities through leisure: Citizen participation in a healthy communities initiative." *Journal of Leisure Research* 29(2): 167–82.

Atkinson, R. 2003. "Domestication by *cappuccino* or a revenge on urban space? Control and empowerment in the management of public spaces." *Urban Studies* 40(9): 1829–43.

Bauman, Z. 1999. *In Search of Politics*. Stanford, CA: Stanford University Press.

Bauman, Z. 2001. *Community: Seeking Safety in an Insecure World*. Oxford: Blackwell.

Bryant, T. 2003. "The current state of housing in Canada as a social determinant of health." *Policy Options* 24(3): 52–56. http://www.irpp.org/po/ (accessed April 23, 2007).

Bunting, T.E., R.A. Walks, and P. Filion. 2004. "The uneven geography of housing affordability stress in Canadian metropolitan areas." *Housing Studies* 19(3): 361–93.

Canada. Prime Minister's Caucus Task Force on Urban Issues (Sgro Report). 2002. *Canada's Urban Strategy: A Vision for the 21ˢᵗ Century*. Interim Report. Ottawa. http://www.iog.ca/cityscapes/sep18background urb.pdf (accessed April 23, 2007).

Dawson, D., and M. Harrington. 1996. "'For the most part, it's not fun and games.' Homelessness and recreation." *Society and Leisure* 19(2): 415–35.

Dawson, D., and M. Harrington. 1997. "Recreation and empowerment for homeless people living in shelters." *Journal of Leisurability* 24(1): 415–35.

Falvo, N. 2003. *Gimme Shelter! Homelessness and Canada's Social Housing Crisis*. Toronto: Centre for Social Justice.

Feldman, R.A., and S. Stall. 2004. *The Dignity of Resistance: Women Residents' Activism in Chicago Public Housing*. Cambridge: Cambridge University Press.

Friedmann, M. T., D. L. Andrews, and M. L. Silk. 2004. "Sport and the façade of redevelopment in the post-industrial city." *Sociology of Sport Journal* 21(2): 119–39.

Gaetz, S. 2004. "Safe streets for whom? Homeless youth, social exclusion and criminal victimization." *Canadian Journal of Criminology and Criminal Justice* 46(4): 423–56.

Harris, R.S. 2000. "Housing." In *Canadian Cities in Transition: The 21ˢᵗ Century*, 2nd ed., ed. T. Bunting, and P. Filion, 380–403. Don Mills, ON: Oxford University Press.

Harvey, D. 1989. "From managerialism to entrepreneurialism: The transformation in urban governance in late capitalism." *Geografiska Annaler. B (Human Geography)* 17(1): 3–17.

Hemingway, J. L. 1999. "Critique and emancipation: Towards a critical theory of leisure." In *Leisure Studies: Prospects for the Twenty-First Century*, ed. E. L. Jackson and T. L. Burton, 487–506. State College, PA: Venture.

Homelessness Partnership Strategy. n.d. http://www.homelessness.gc.ca (accessed April 25, 2007).

hooks, b. 1990. *Yearning: Race, Gender, and Cultural Politics.* Boston: South End Books.

Hulchanski, D. J. 2002. *Housing Policy for Tomorrow's Cities.* Ottawa: Canadian Policy Research Network.

Jahiel, R. L. 1992. "Homeless-making processes and the homeless-makers." In *Homelessness: A Prevention-Oriented Approach*, ed. R.I. Jahiel, 269–98. Baltimore: Johns Hopkins University Press.

Klitzing, S. W. 2003. "Coping with chronic stress: Leisure and women who are homeless." *Leisure Sciences* 25 (2&3): 163–81.

Kari, S. 2006. "B.C. bylaws targeting homeless face court challenge." *Globe and Mail*, August 29.

Layton, J. 2000. *Homelessness: The Making and Unmaking of a Crisis.* Toronto: Penguin.

Luffman, J. 2006. "Measuring housing affordability." *Perspectives on Labour and Income* 7(11): 16–25. http://www.statscan.ca (accessed April 23, 2007).

Mah, J., and G. DeSantis (in consultation with the Cambridge Action on Homelessness Group). 2000. *So, What's in the Middle? A Brief Report on the Middle of the Housing Continuum in Cambridge.* Cambridge, ON: Social Planning Council of Cambridge and North Dumfries.

Main, T. 1998. "How to think about homelessness: Balancing structural and individual causes." *Journal of Social Distress and the Homeless* 7(1): 41–54.

Mair, H. 2006. "Community development: Creating spaces for deep democracy, social action and resistance." *Leisure/Loisir* 30(2): 447–54.

Mair, H. 2002/03. "Civil leisure? Exploring the relationship between leisure, activism and social change." *Leisure/Loisir* 27(3/4): 213–37.

MacLeod, G. 2002. "From urban entrepreneurialism to a 'revanchist city'? On the spatial injustices of Glasgow's renaissance." *Antipode* 34(3): 602–24.

Micallef, S. 2007. "Homeless signs." http://spacing.ca/wire/?p=1723 (accessed April 25, 2007).

Miller, P., P. Donahue, D. Este, and M. Hofer. 2004. "Experiences of being homeless or at risk of being homeless among Canadian youths." *Adolescence* 39(156): 735–55.

Mills, C. Wright. 1959. *The Sociological Imagination.* New York: Oxford University Press.

Mitchell, D. 1997. "The annihilation of space by law: The roots and implications of anti-homeless laws in the United States." *Antipode* 29(3): 303–35.

Mitchell, D. 2001. "Postmodern Geographical praxis? The postmodern impulse and the war against homeless people in the post-justice city." *Postmodern Geography: Theory and Praxis*, ed. C. Minca, 57–92. Oxford: Blackwell.

Montgomery, S. 2007. "Alberta to spend $285-million on housing." *Globe and Mail.* April 25.

Moore, E., and A. Skaburskis. 2004. "Canada's increasing housing affordability burdens." *Housing Studies* 19(3): 395–413.

Ontario. 1999. "Safe Streets Act." http://www.elaws.gov.on.ca/DBLaws/Statutes/English/99s08_e.htm (accessed April 24, 2007).

Pedlar, A., and L. Haworth. 2006. "Community." In *A Handbook of Leisure Studies*, ed. C. Rojek, S. M. Shaw, and A. J. Veal, 518–32. New York: Palgrave MacMillan.

Rose, T. 2006. "Should having a home be a right? CBC news viewpoint posted 22 September." http://www.cbc.ca/news/viewpoint/vp_rose/20060922.html (accessed April 25, 2007).

Scott, H., S. Alvi, and W. Stanyon. 2006. *Durham Region Homelessness Initiative: Literature Review*. Toronto: Ontario Institute of Technology. http://www.criminologyandjustice.uoit.ca/assets/Social~Science/PDF/Literature_Review_8.pdf (accessed April 23, 2007).

Sev'er, A. 2002. "A feminist analysis of flight of abused women, plight of Canadian shelters: Another road to homelessness." *Journal of Social Distress and the Homeless* 11(4): 307–24.

Shaw, S. M. 2000. "If our research is relevant, why is nobody listening?" *Journal of Leisure Research* 32(1): 147–51.

Shaw, S. M. 2006. "Resistance." In *A Handbook of Leisure Studies*, ed. C. Rojek, S. M. Shaw, and A. J. Veal, 533–45. New York: Palgrave MacMillan.

Shinew, K. J., T. D. Glover, and D. C. Parry. 2004. "Leisure spaces as potential sites for interracial interaction: Community gardens in urban areas." *Journal of Leisure Research* 36(3): 336–55.

Skaburskis, A. 2006. "Filtering, city change and the supply of low-priced housing in Canada." *Urban Studies* 43(3): 533–58.

Slum Tourism Toronto. 2010: http://www.torontoslumtourism.com/.

Smith, N. 1996. *The New Urban Frontier: Gentrification and the Revanchist City*. London: Routledge.

Wellesley Institute. 2006. "The blueprint to end homelessness in Toronto." http://wellesleyinstitute.com/theblueprint (accessed April 23, 2007).

Whang, I., and E. Min. 1999. "Blaming the homeless: The populist aspect of network TV news." In *Reading the Homeless: The Media's Image of Homeless Culture*, ed. E. Min, 121–34. London: Praeger.

Zukin, S. 1991. *Landscapes of Power: From Detroit to Disney*. Berkeley: University of California Press.

9

Hold Gently People Who Create Space on the Margins: Urban Aboriginal-Canadian Young People and Hip-Hop Rhythms of "Leisures"

Karen M. Fox and Brett D. Lashua

Aboriginal peoples[1] in Canada have struggled for self-determination, recognition of sovereignty and treaties, and social justice for generations within imposed Euro-North American legal and political structures. Most Aboriginal peoples are marginalized through dominant discourses, political and economic structures and values, racial and cultural discourses, and cultural and ethical values favouring Euro-North American epistemologies and worldviews. To understand the *leisures* (see Fox and Klaiber 2006; Fox, Klaiber, Ryan, and Lashua 2006) created by urban Aboriginal young people requires re-thinking how traditional and modern Aboriginal practices contest Euro-North American processes of leisure, create alternative, expressive, and resistive sites for Aboriginal identities and practices, and add alternative voices and strategies related to civic governance, public voice, social policies, and social interactions.

In this chapter, we explore the power and promise of leisures as practised and imagined by urban Aboriginal youth and young people through hip-hop musical practices. This cultural and musical focus leads us toward a concept of social cohesion not through similarity and inclusion but through multiplicity of resonances, rhythms, melodies, alternatives, and holding people as they are gently. The typical and widespread Euro-North American concept of "good" implies monolithic static "wholes" and leaves invisible worlds of paradox, change, violence, conflict, and deviance vital for the growth and "happiness" of some peoples if not societies.[2] We find it far from clear that inclusion processes captured under one standard would actually result in positive outcomes for all people.

We want to place alongside of typical and partially positive processes of social cohesion and inclusion, rhythms that hopefully hold gently people who create space on the margins, who are forced to find life on the margins, who sing differently of leadership and expressivity, or who provide the necessary alternatives and pluralistic choices required for a healthy dynamic society with openings for social innovation and critiques of seemingly monolithic hegemonic forces. Inclusion processes typically and predominantly focus on how "to help" people on the margins change without questioning the value, "goodness," and change requirements of the dominant status quo or "master page." Specifically, we listen to the voices and take seriously urban Aboriginal leisures (specifically urban arts such as hip-hop and digital media) as interactive sites that posit alternative conceptions of leisures, leisure programs, activities, societal practices, civic engagement, and leisure values. Interactive hip-hop sites created by urban Aboriginal youth and young peoples invite others to join them, to experiment with identities and different ways of professional leisure practices, and to modify the structure and processes of social policies and governance. These interactive sites invite participation over time and sketch the potential for alternative and emerging forms of leisures, social cohesion, and employment. Relatively static and noun-oriented concepts haunt the Euro-North American concepts of leisure – leisure as a "thing" to be defined, identified, programmed, and structured. Urban Aboriginal hip-hop suggests a concept of leisure sounds, movements, beats, and social rhythms. These terms privilege processes, connections and relationships, and shift our thinking about leisures to social, spatial, and temporal processes – rhythms and movements – rather than the "piece itself."

Attention to these processes and movements has been called "rhythmanalysis" (Lefebvre 2004). A rhythmanalysis remarks upon the interactions between place, time, and patterns of everyday life by which repetition, disruption and resumption, linear and cyclical processes (including natural rhythms such as seasonal changes, day/night), public and private actions, and growth and decline are manifest. This concept resonates with the irreducibility of differences and horizons and the complexity of the lived experiences of urban Aboriginal young people and helps explicate the many concurrent and competing voices and dances of leisure. Lefebvre (2004, 32, all emphasis in the original) explained:

> Just over the horizon, other horizons loom without being present, so beyond the sensible and visible order, which reveals political power, other orders suggest themselves: a logic, a division of labour, *leisure activities* are also **produced** (and productive), although they are proclaimed free and even 'free time.' Isn't this freedom also a product?

When applied to leisure sites and practices such as walking in the city (Wunderlich 2008), a rhythmanalysis can highlight the varied orchestrations of everyday social practices that help to shape and in turn are shaped by the city. When attuned to the leisure practices of urban Aboriginal young people, rhythmanalysis may highlight the entangled relations of social space, politics, and identities (Lashua and Kelly 2008). That is, a rhythmanalysis is useful, not only in terms of noting where, when, and how people move, but also how such movements are both produced by particular power relations and are themselves productive of power relations in social space. These relations, connections, or energies between "things" are always more difficult to identify and interpret because they are literally hard to see. Focusing upon rhythms makes the processes of their production – and thus their social relations – more visible; in Lefebvre's words, "the 'object' of interest must be expected to shift from *things in space* to the actual *production of space*" (1991, 37, emphasis in the original). Our interest in urban Aboriginal young people engaged in hip-hop is therefore concerned with how space (e.g., a "youth" centre) is produced, claimed (e.g., through graffiti or playing loud music in public), how young people move through space (e.g., breakdancing or freestyle rapping in shopping malls), and disrupt some spatial discourses (e.g., young people out of place during the school day or working day) while reinforcing other discourses (e.g., certain spaces, streets or neighbourhoods deemed either "safe" or "dangerous" – but which, and for whom?).

The hip-hop rhythms of leisure spaces labour to re-map understandings of centres and margins, belonging and excluding. At this temporal moment, the inclusion of Aboriginal peoples, practices, and societies within dominant, mainstream Euro-North American society (including leisure practices), even with avowed multicultural values, is problematic and not necessarily in the best interests of Aboriginal peoples, given the dominant economic and political power structures. To consider social policies related to Aboriginal peoples, the intersection of social issues, Aboriginal peoples, and leisure must include attention to social policies that protect and sustain alternative and resistive voices, listen and invite others to participate grounded in their own governance and civic engagement processes, develop reciprocal and mutual power relationships, and include a material commitment to changes *within both systems.*

Even as dominant Canadian[3] processes and structures simultaneously maintain exclusion and inclusion strategies, the Aboriginal perspectives and claims to alternative and creative governmental and societal processes must be made visible within the conversations and policies. Margins emerge as discourse and power are used to support *one dominant identity.* Margins can be fruitful and positive as they provide alternative conceptions of realities, provide "safe havens" for people who are different, and provide sites for creative explorations. On the other hand, margins can also be sites of oppression, discrimination, denial of resources, and violence. Although there is a nod toward concepts of pluralism within Canada, dominant government and economic structures are always presumed as existing, good, and necessary. Furthermore, given the structures and usage of the English language and existing scholarship, imaginary[4] "master pages," of existing political and leisure practices are typically static and monolithic states rather than a dynamic, pluralistic, conflicting, contesting, and changing set of processes and learnings. Therefore, the irreducibility of margins in this historical era require us to engage and profoundly respect how margins are "necessary," irreducible, and nourished for their power and ability to provide alternative understandings, for their ability to sustain differences among people, and for the historical realities of Aboriginal nations within Canadian society.

As such, we are attracted to theories and practices such as rhythmanalysis and "getting to maybe" (i.e., getting to maybe is focusing on relationships and emerging possibilities within relationships not focusing on discrete goals and objectives that demand people to fit within structures and ideals) that posit multiple and dynamic relationships within contexts of uncertainty and ambiguity to imagine how leisures might contribute to various, contesting, and emerging/re-emerging margins that allow for differences, provide resting spots for people who do not fit by choice or design, nourish transitions between difficult life or societal events, challenge dominant conceptions, provide new conceptions of society and life, and posit Aboriginal (as well as other) alternative, community, and organic strategies for living in polyrhythmic Canadian society. We suggest a healthy society requires *both* social cohesion and processes that challenge, move, and change the very understanding of social cohesion if we are to avoid or mitigate the possibility of social cohesion becoming social oppression.

ABORIGINAL HIP-HOP AND SOCIAL JUSTICE

Urban Aboriginal youth and young people are situated amongst numerous boundaries, margins, and forces. As one of the Canadian population groups with growing numbers, urban Aboriginal people are struggling to develop coping mechanisms, appropriate relationships and structures, and facilities and communities of solidarity. Urban Aboriginal identities float between band/reserve and urban, traditional and modern/technological, racism and respect, inclusion and exclusion, economic structures, and familial/tribal and global interactive relationships. Although they may have familial ties to reserves or bands, their lives also revolve around urban rhythms, events, forces, and structures. Differences in standing (i.e., treaty, non-treaty, Metis, Inuit, or mixed heritage) are problematic for provincial and municipal designations and homogenizing categories. The statistics around educational achievement, housing, employment, and health levels all indicate urban Aboriginal youth and young people fare poorly (or problematic even if successful) in processes and structures that are predominantly structured and implemented by non-Aboriginal peoples. Policies of inclusion constructed by non-Aboriginal people around non-Aboriginal policies, programs, and facilities have demonstrated limited benefits for urban Aboriginal youth or young people. These policies and programs are often implicated with subtle and insidious forms of oppression, subjection, racism, discrimination, undervaluation, and underemployment.

Set against this oppression, Canadian urban Aboriginal hip-hop groups are intimately connected with movements of liberation, social justice, and solidarity with other oppressed groups, tribal forms of expressivity and governance, and healing ceremonies (Efron 2001). Aboriginal hip-hop focuses on local expressions and descriptions of life, the struggles of urban Aboriginal youth and young people, and dreams for the future. Creative, artistic forms of leisures particularly connected to Aboriginal ceremonial legacies (e.g., dances, chants, word games, interrelationships, and distributive economics) are avenues for urban Aboriginal youth and young people to express their political critiques and civic engagements and envision alternative methods for enacting policy, public governance, and civic engagement. Private ills (i.e., addiction, homelessness, poverty, racism, and exclusion) become community issues requiring community responses and engagement (Mills & Gitlin 1959). The Aboriginal underground hip-hop perspective connects with a social architecture of self-reliance through community performance among Aboriginal youth and young people within Aboriginal traditional protocols. Such practices revolve around contingencies, hybrid approaches, and incremental universalism. Drumming or rapping their stories opens spaces and creates new "beats" in the rhythms of their everyday lives for healing, inviting others to create differently, questioning the very processes of enacting policies. Long-term socio-emotional growth involves more than current forms of civic engagement reaching to the arts, emotions, and personal relationships.

The international movement of community-based or underground hip-hop provides a medium to voice the lives, experiences, and dreams of urban Aboriginal and young people. The power and potential of hip-hop for healing, political activism, creative expression, and community-building rarely receives attention outside of a small interested group of aficionados and scholars. Furthermore, these musical forms give rise to political critique within the human desire for collective joy expressed in ecstatic celebrations of feasting and dancing (Ehrenreich 2007). Urban Aboriginal youth and young people use, make, and remake public space through graffiti "tagging," breakdancing in car parks, rapping while waiting at bus stops, listening to hip-hop music on personal stereos, or embodying hip-hop style as they move through and sometimes claim what they consider "their" cityscape. The rhythms of urban Aboriginal hip-hop express the life stories and experiences of urban Aboriginal youth and young people and connect to larger international forums and create alternative educational, political, healing, and economic avenues for success, survival, and support networks so other urban Aboriginal youth and young people may survive.

Again, these sites of leisure may be difficult to identify as isolated *objects*, however, when considered as marginal spaces produced through complex webs of social rhythms, new possibilities, or horizons, may emerge. Urban Aboriginal youth and young people (re)create, use, and take up space with particular styles and meanings relevant to their presence and as critique of existing practices. So-called marginalized spaces may represent opportunities for both harm/violence and creative/expression. Soja (1996) thus refers to the conceptualization of "Third-spaces" that transform "the categorical and closed logic of either/or to the dialectically open logic of both/and also" (60). In a hybrid third-space, hip-hop leisures, social rhythms, and identities must be considered as *both* good *and* bad *and also* more.

Internationally, numerous Indigenous[5] groups are establishing parallel education, health, and governmental structures/processes aligned with Indigenous worldviews and perspectives. These emerging groups on the margins of commodified, hegemonic, and globalized processes are necessary for the survival of Indigenous groups and to remind the world that dominant powers and forces are not necessarily what has to be, a good, or inevitable – and that the intractable can be changed. Urban Aboriginal youth and young people are also using hip-hop to embody and address their struggles, marginalization by dominant society, and creatively address globalized forces. Underground cultures of hip-hop, as a political art, may need to be heard and seen in their complexity on the margins for them to be effective and explore identity, political change, and expressivity.

Leisures potentially provide one of the few relatively safe, playful, and joyful spaces and times for people and societies to explore, come to know, and engage in all aspects of what it means to be human, including violence, "harmful and risky" choices, challenging norms, creating alternatives, and foolishness. If leisures are deeply connected to expressivity, choice, and experimentation, the full range of behaviour and differences as well as consequences needs to be protected and not foreclosed with attachment to specific ideas of inclusion, integration, and social cohesion. Sometimes difference, separation, and conflict is essential to knowing who we are and what is valuable even as it may not necessarily be acceptable or contribute directly to productivity and employment.

Sites of leisures may furnish opportunities for exploring choices and behaviours relevant to working through both positive and negative experiences with the world and engaging with dominant and alternative strategies. The move toward conformity and similarity in a world of hegemonic globalized forces leaves less room for creative and different individuals and "dancing with the dark side" of human nature. Violence toward children is a reality that many urban Aboriginal youth and young people intimately understand and find commonality with children affected by war or who come to Canada as refugees. This lived experience of violence and pain is worked through in artistic and creative processes that allow expression, healing, and transformation. And, of course, all creative endeavours are risky. Criminal or illegal activity may be part of experimenting and creating identities that both reflect and resist the violence of dominant society and mainstream "making one's way in the world" (Orlie 1994). Typically, violence or illegal activity enters leisure practices through programs labeled "at risk" or "rehabilitative" and with the goal of standardizing behaviours according to dominant norms. The possibility of deviance as an appropriate function for resisting harmful societal practices and cultural and racial oppression or creating "third spaces" has been overlooked. Furthermore, such leisure practices as body modification (piercing, tattooing, scarification, painting), recreational drug use, or unusual food and alcohol practices which are legal and provide venues for creating identities not constricted by norms are typically viewed negatively and have not surfaced within leisure policies. Each of these leisure practices bring up questions around societal norms, the use of such practices to support healthy identities that must resist the dominant and normative, the purpose and meaning of the complexity of human nature both good and bad, and the necessary human choices for creativity and expression.

Although leisure is surely a part of healing, the role and function is far from clear. Moving the children and youth into "safe and peaceful" environments may be harmful without appropriate processes and connection with the horrors of their life experiences and lead to a sense of being invisible because the violence and horror of their lives and actions have no place in conventional leisure practices and activities. Earlier research in leisure has suggested that when children could play at war during war, the playing was positive for the children. But when the boundary between playing war and being at war is erased, the children are harmed. In some cases, the children and youth may have never learned to play or may never have found leisure as safe. How will we teach them about these spaces and repair the boundaries where playing at war and violence becomes playing again and a relatively safe place to address horrific memories, behaviours, and experiences of war and violence? Inclusion may not be the appropriate strategy even as building connections and community is necessary.

The Euro-North American concept of leisure does not fit easily, if at all, with Aboriginal cultures and values. First and foremost, dominant structures and professional practices of leisure presume the "goodness" of the status quo, restrict choices to activities and programs related to efficiency, excellence, and achievement, and are subsumed within education, economic, and political structures and processes that have traditionally and recently excluded Aboriginal peoples and perspectives. Dominant leisure practices and programs are imbricated in Euro-North American values related to capitalism, excellence, people as expendable resources, and profit lines that ignore the well-being and flourishing of human and non-human communities.

Mainstream cultures retard deviance and support the status quo. These mechanisms that maintain the current practice and profession of leisure along with stability and privilege also maintain marginalization even as population segments are "included" in specific forms of the existing society and for specific needs of that society (i.e., employment). Structural requirements (i.e., placing leisure activities in certain places with certain performance requirements) and attitudinal mechanisms (i.e., viewing these youth as "at risk" or "in need of skills" related to middle-class values) of marginalization by the mainstream can disarm potentially revolutionary movements in ways that support stability in social institutions and practices.

Therefore, moving, assimilating, or integrating underground Aboriginal hip-hop into typical recreation venues depoliticizes hip-hop performances and undermines the Aboriginal political challenges of everyday life that leaves them at the mercy of Euro-North American and globalized processes of racism, exclusion, power strategies, and economic forces. These "marginal" groups and movements challenge how the leisure profession has hijacked expressive, uncontrolled, and ecstatic forms of leisure for rationale, goal-oriented, benefit-producing, controlled, and predictable forms of leisure. What value is inclusion into status quo leisure venues when they leave larger exclusions and racism in place?

Although subsistence and necessary tasks plus spiritual and cultural ceremonies of Aboriginal populations often now appear as leisure, this arena is laced with political forces and may transform, negate, or problematize the traditional powers of elders and Aboriginal community processes. Aboriginal people clearly understand the Euro-North American concept of leisure and struggle to engage with this hegemonic force to protect and sustain their cultural practices, establish Aboriginal identities and voices, and negotiate the modern world with Aboriginal protocols and knowledges. It is far from clear how non-Aboriginal leisure practitioners negotiate this dangerous territory.

Urban Aboriginal youth and young people have been carving out spaces for themselves to live in relative safety and to create their own identities, spaces to consolidate resources, sites of resistance, and physical, political, and economic "presence." Margins may be crucial for their leadership and support of their aspirations for a more peaceful existence. International peace activists such as the Peacemakers, PBI, and others who promote peace-making based upon connection with, respect of, and gently holding people who are violent are also found on the margins. Pragmatic perspectives see such actions and alternatives (e.g., restorative justice, truth and reconciliation processes) as "marginal" and inapplicable to the needs of dominant societies for security and control. Interconnections between urban Aboriginal youth seeking non-violent solutions and actions within a larger society that does not often support or use such strategies (e.g., restorative justice and healing circles are a small part of a punitive justice system in Canada) require rapport and relationships with other marginal groups that live peaceful alternatives and are able to hold the victims and perpetrators of violence gently. Such movements and practices are necessary to provide counterpoints to larger societal forces, open avenues for different ways of being, and boundaries for the pursuit of their lives. Although often labelled different, strange, or "collaborators," these groups and their leisure practices are essential as critiques, role models, and alternatives. Moving to include them into pragmatic, practical, and global processes could possibly destroy their lives and the power of their practices.

Identity construction harbours within itself a deconstruction of the constructed identity and its own mode of self-alteration (Estes, Farr, Smith, and Smyth, 2000). Urban Aboriginal young people struggle with various types of identities (e.g., rural or band versus urban, designated as "at risk" or "troublesome" youth, mixed heritages beyond Aboriginal descent). Rebecca Tsosie (2000, p. 150) argued that Native People's political identities may depend on their ability to demonstrate marginalized status.

"Citizenship may be inconsistent with tribalism in a society founded upon racial, social, and economic stratification and difference, where 'marginalization' is the only way to preserve the values of a different culture and political organization." Hence, margins are crucial for sustaining the history and knowledge of Aboriginal peoples in Canada and their struggles. Furthermore, inclusion within larger societal frameworks dominated by non-Native People undermines Native People's abilities to gather the necessary presence to maintain culture, resist and change subtle but significant racism and exclusion, and create alternatives consistent with their values and political needs and aspirations.

New Leisure Songs in the Key of "Social Policy"

Social policies are needed to support these irreducible "thirding" spaces. It is essential to listen, hear, and see where urban Aboriginal youth and young people are right now as they have created and structured processes and relationships that address violence, cope with racism and violence that surrounds them, create alternative economic, leadership or political patterns, and support numerous types of relationships and healing unavailable through typical, standard, and mainstream structures and epistemologies. Urban Aboriginal youth and young people have struggled for control, voice, influence, and power within the space allotted them and created what "works" in response to exclusion, social injustice, ignoring of their needs, racism, powerlessness, and worldviews that leave them stranded between multiple boundaries.

If leisures are spaces for the democratic imaginary of all peoples and supports creativity and choice for people including urban Aboriginal youth and young peoples, leisures must be intimately connected with larger social issues and forces. The rhythms and connections between housing, employment, choice, creativity, political power, and economic potential are then conceived as a whole, in time with each other, and concurrent harmonies and melodies (although sometimes out of tune and time) to be addressed rather than the separate and apolitical conceptions of leisure that currently exist.

Traditionally leisure scholars and practitioners posit processes and values of inclusion, integration, access, and social cohesion as "goods," as positive objectives connected to leisure programming and leisure values. Rhythmanalysis places urban Aboriginal hip-hop in resonances with traditional and historical Aboriginal practices of economics and governances through ceremonies, dances, creative expressions, humour, and redistribution. Leisures as separate from employment, political, economical, and legal issues are discordant and undermine the very power of urban Aboriginal hip-hop for programming, participants, or facilities. The seemingly straightforward, separate, and transparent positive processes and values become problematized and available for analyzes and critique. The hidden assumptions and imaginaries of "good societies," "good human relationships," "good leisures," and "democratic imaginaries" become visible within their Euro-North American frameworks.

Although the connection between leisure and work is ancient within Euro-North American scholarship about leisure, the relationship has fluctuated over the eras. The emphasis on which beat to strengthen (work or leisure) is highly dependent upon use of space, time, and energy. Within a globalized and corporatized world, Euro-North American leisure emerges as subservient to production and/or a benefit after production is achieved. Given environmental concerns and affects, recent results that indicate populations in highly industrialized and consumer societies are not necessarily happier the more they consume or work, this connection needs to be rethought. Structuring and moving urban Aboriginal youth and young people into employment that denigrates social well-being and environmental health and structures human beings as resources reflects oppressive and harmful forces for Aboriginal practices, traditions, and rights. Urban hip-hop artists seek avenues to strengthen the hip-hop culture and provide a different space for young people to envision themselves and create other social/environmental practices. They give energy and space to leisures or see leisures as having a productive value unrecognized by corporate actors to provide counterpoints, challenges, and critiques of the harmful practice of dominant society. Many of these youth cannot succeed at typical education and certification practices nor are these practices necessarily relevant. So, where does one find a healthy developmental cycle for young people who have lived on the streets? Where are social services that first look to the strengths and rationale for the world that street youth have created – and build on those strengths to provide an alternative concept of development, work, and worth. Native Hawaiians who are committed to the sovereignty movement are not interested in being encompassed within traditional U.S. economic structures. Typical critiques of Native Hawaiian education, which includes traditional skills and cultural practices, revolve around how this type of education does not prepare the young people for today's world. But what if today's economic world is not healthy or desirable? Native Hawaiian education does prepare Native Hawaiians to build on their culture and create alternative economic, political, and social practices. As such, these need to be nourished given the potential for the health of Native Hawaiians and alternative ideas within a pluralistic world that always keeps options in motion.

Social policies that consider pluralistic responses, identities, and economic structures require alternative strategies and concepts. Social entrepreneurship, sheltered employment, redistribution of resources, and environmental protection are part of the knowledge, energies, dreams, and skills of underground urban Aboriginal hip-hop. Creating a society or element of society through leisure that maintains connections to social responsibility values people of all talents and abilities and moves past a definition of success for only the few are part of the margins given the force and power of dominant, globalized forces. Historical efforts related to welfare or enforced employment training for marginalized groups are rarely overwhelming successes and often mean inadequate housing, under-employment, low pay, and poor child care; assimilation of Native People meant geographical displacement, social alienation, and cultural loss among more immediate problems of disease, hunger, and homelessness. Even benignly intentioned and necessary social programs, like desegregation in the southern United States, destroyed neighbourhood schools, small businesses, and recreational areas. Assimilation thus resulted in almost no significant loss or changes within the dominant society, but led to considerable change and destruction for the integrated groups with very little gain. Supporting policies that allow for experimentation by all peoples, including urban Aboriginal youth and young people, is crucial for diversity, critique, choice, and the democratic imaginary.

VARIATIONS AND ALTERNATIVE TRADITIONS TO THE "MASTER SCORE"

When conditions such as poverty, homelessness, marginalization, and underground elements are viewed as affecting or benefiting all of society, the specific conditions (poverty, illness, etc.) move from private medical or enforcement policies to social policies that require a response from the entire community. Lefebvre's concepts around social rhythms in the city provide an entree into thinking differently about leisures and the relationships between centre, margins, social cohesion, and employment. They help conceive of movement patterns as intersections of time, energy, space, and moods. They frame leisures as types of rhythms and situate rhythms on larger stages of economic, historical, political, societal, and conflict processes. Urban Aboriginal hip-hop performances become responses to employment forces, rational and efficient economic processes that disrespect familial, tribal, and human relationships, joyless jobs, and punitive political and legal systems without healing or transformation. Attention to the rhythmic processes of spatialization which cross through a distinct mixture of social relations allows consideration of the struggles over the organization and meaning of space, both literally and figuratively. How are urban Aboriginal youth and young people being placed by non-Aboriginal society? How are social movements framed in artistic performances and how are Aboriginal tribal rhythms placed outside of cognitive, rational debates and political and economic systems? How do these performances challenge the claim of a democratic society in Canada or the efficacy of existing leisure systems?

 Social rhythms (i.e., excluding or including) consist of movement of bodies at particular times in particular spaces and require an expenditure of energy (the triad of place, time, and energy). So, the very designation and design of who is at the centre, who is at the margins, who needs to be included, who gets to define what the master page is are all social

practices or sets of relationships that are entangled in concrete relationships, spaces, and times that create rhythmic patterns over time. They
permeate practice and are permeated by it.

Although centres have boundaries, these borders are malleable
and porous. Furthermore, it is the existence of strong marginal groups
that keep the boundary malleable and porous – whether because of the
commitment of the centre or through resistance and power strategies.
Without margins, social cohesion and the centre become oppressive and
static. The margins are sites for diversity in identities and behaviours but
with substantial costs. Marginalization imposes difficulties and restric-
tions on groups and individuals, but the presence of groups can usurp the
mechanisms of marginalization and initiate moral, social, and political
change. Many theorists, writers, and artists employ these tactics to redefine mainstream conceptions such as beauty, humanity, music, leisure,
political engagement, and disability.

The dominant social institutions of Euro-North American leisure
tend to mark their spaces as concrete and static. The entrenchment of
leisure practices intended to support individual social members and
fundamental social values may fail to reflect the needs and values of
the individual social members. Urban Aboriginal youth and young
people are merging traditional practices and values with urban culture and globalized political and economic forces. Participation in the
international hip-hop movement connects urban Aboriginal youth and
young people across oppressive structures and practices and challenges
the identities, practices, and behaviours constructed and maintained by
traditional recreation practices. Institutional retrenchment and practices
meant to "help" urban Aboriginal youth and young people might have
the odd effect of marginalizing the very people they are working with.
These practices, worldviews, and organizations may need reorganiza-
tion. Inclusion within practices that are not particularly useful for urban
Aboriginal youth and young people may be counterproductive at best
(Estes, Farr, Smith & Smyth 2000). More often than not, many marginalized young people find that participation is oppression, and most sense
it from miles away and steer clear. Many have no desire to participate in
"mainstream" activities – though perhaps safe and structured – that do

not resonate with the everyday realities and exigencies of their lives, or that otherwise rob them of the resistant or transgressive power of doing things differently.

Urban Aboriginal youth and young people through hip-hop are not necessarily individuals or groups who need to be liberated, saved, or helped. People in the centres may view them as undesirable, difficult, or painful. The irreducibility of the margins and the power of the voices of urban Aboriginal youth and young people are a necessary part of the flux of societies and reminders of what dominant society has yet to address. Urban Aboriginal youth and young people demonstrate their strength, claim space, lead through leisure, and create experiences of hope and healing through hip-hop. We may want to think about promoting acceptance because we see people as they are, in their own worlds, and as contributing to society just as they are. Then, a dialogue can emerge about what both of us desire, need, can contribute, and how all relationships require reciprocal change.

TRANSITION OR BRIDGE

If we are to develop social/leisure policies that see beyond "margins" as places to be liberated, people to be helped, or people to be punished, the very frames of leisures need to include dynamic conceptions of leisures and margins – a table of oppositions constituting an ensemble (Grönlund 1998). If leisure is a constructed space (physical, social, and imaginary) where individuals, groups, and societies have relative freedom to choose specific forms of pleasure, civic engagement, activities, happiness, and relationships, then leisure is a right of citizenship, a vehicle or process for multiple identities, community growth, and democratic participation through multiple vehicles.

Aboriginal urban hip-hop invites leisure professionals into the arena of social innovation through participatory and collaborative processes that move us toward, in Westley, Zimmerman, and Patton's (2007) words, "getting to maybe." Aboriginal urban hip-hop sings and beats the dreams of Aboriginal youth and young people. The policies and realities of turning dreams into practices are uncertain, ambiguous, and unknown at this time. Leisure professionals/scholars together with urban Aboriginal youth and young people among others need to come together to see the relationship among all the elements and change our way of thinking about leisures, leisure practices, and programming. Rather than predict or control what leisures are to emerge, social innovation requires all of us to become active participants in shaping the changes – to move with the rhythm and beats of Aboriginal urban hip-hop. To identify elements or "the things" of leisure is more straightforward than identifying relationships of connection, energies, resources, and movement; relationships are harder to see. Social innovation requires all of us to dance together and live with uncertainty but in relationship as we work with interactions that are more likely to result in transformation. Again, Westley, Zimmerman, and Patton (2007) use these words:

> Control is replaced by a toleration of ambiguity and the "can-do" mentality of "making things happen" is modified by an attitude that is simultaneously visionary and responsive to the unpredictable unfolding of events. The successful social innovator is, intentionally or not, a part of the dynamics of transformation rather than the heroic figure leading the charge. (20)

It is a noisy, polyphonic, loosely orchestrated "jam session" of people harmonizing their various instruments of leisure practice and scholarship. It is about "tipping the scales in favour of successful social innovations in the face of seemingly overwhelming odds. Getting to maybe" (21).

Social innovation resonates with Aboriginal urban hip-hop because there is no fixed address. Success often breeds the very institutions that will then become resistant to innovation and critiques from the margins. Hence the necessity to provide space, opportunity, and processes to hold gently people and groups on the margins – they are essential for the health of the centre. So, although Aboriginal urban hip-hop can challenge and change theories about leisures, we are proposing that the dynamics of the margins may be essential for the health of the people and groups who inhabit those spaces. We are proposing that we within the centre seriously consider how we support the well-being of those on the margins as they are – no rehabilitation, no change to normative standards, no improvement of what they do.

Kauffman, a complexity scientist, coined the term "fitness landscape" (1995) to describe the interaction of the external (the larger system) and the internal (the individual agent). Social innovation becomes a movement on a rugged landscape that shifts as we try to move across it – a fitness landscape. Even as we connect and support the dreams and efforts of Aboriginal urban hip-hop artists, the forces of technology, globalization, sovereignty, and economic/environmental change are also changing. Success is ephemeral; if social innovation is successful, it will redefine the leisure landscape in which it has emerged, assuring that its immediate success is short-lived even as the foundation has been laid to take on new challenges – or a process of getting to a new maybe (Westley, Zimmerman, and Patton 2007).

However, we do seek to make deep changes in the culture of ideas, the policies, and the flow of resources in relationship to the role and significance of leisures. To dance with Aboriginal urban hip-hop youth and young people is to ask about the basis of citizenship: What does it mean? How can we reconstruct our definitions of leisure and citizenship to acknowledge the rights and responsibilities of all of us? Hopefully, urban arts as an expression of Aboriginal urban youth and young people becomes, not radical, but as normal as the air we breathe because we can see the significance, the vitality, and the civic engagement in an aesthetic form. Aboriginal urban arts is the counterpoint with an emphasis on are we doing the right things with are we doing things right. It is "forward-toward" (Vaill 1991 & 1996) movement toward an imaginary destination where specific rhymes and performances must be addressed or highlighted along the way. The temporary destinations are not what we expected when we started, but this is not a mark of a failed journey. System transformations often surprise the very people who set out to create them.

REFERENCES

Ehrenreich, B. 2007. *Dancing in the Streets: A History of Collective Joy.* New York: Metropolitan Books.

Efron, S. 2001. Native hip-hoppers rap out their message. *The Georgia Straight.* Retrieved March 16, 2010 from http://www.sarahefron.com/stories/tribalwizdom.shtml

Estes, Y., A. L. Farr, P. Smith, and C. Smyth, eds. 2000. *Marginal Groups and Mainstream American Culture.* Kansas City, KS: University of Kansas Press.

Fox, K., and E. Klaiber. 2006. "Listening for a leisure remix." *Leisure Sciences* 28(5): 411–30.

Fox, K., E. Klaiber, S. Ryan, and B. Lashua. 2006. "Remixing, performing, and producing studies of leisures." *Leisure Sciences* 28(5): 455–66.

Grönlund, B. 1998. "Lefebvre's rhythmanalysis." http://hjem.get2net.dk/gronlund/Lefebvre_Rhythmanaslyses.html (accessed November 13, 2008).

Kaufman, S. 1995. *At home in the universe: The search for laws of self-organization and complexity.* New York: Oxford University Press.

Lashua, B.D. and Kelly, J.R. 2008. Rhythms in the concrete: Re-imagining the relationships between space, race, and mediated urban youth cultures. *Leisure/Loisir: The Journal of the Canadian Association of Leisure Studies, 32*(2), 461–488.

Lefebvre, H. 1991. *The Production of Space,* trans. D. Nicholson-Smith. Oxford: Blackwell.

Lefebvre, H. 2004. *Rhythmanalysis: Space, Time and Everyday Life.* London: Continuum.

Mills, C. W. & Gitlin, T. 1959. *The sociological imagination.* New York: Oxford University Press.

Orlie, M. 1994. "Thoughtless assertion and political deliberation." *Political Science Review* 88: 684–695.

Soja, E. W. 1996. *Thirdspace: Journeys to Los Angeles and Other Real-and-Imagined Places.* Oxford: Blackwell.

Taylor, C.M. 2004. *Modern Social Imaginaries.* Durham, NC: Duke University Press.

Tsosie, R. 2000. Marginalization and political identity: The experience of Native Americans. In Y. Estes, A.L. Farr, P. Smith, & C. Smyth (Eds.). *Marginal groups and mainstream American culture* (pp. 138-152). Lawrence, KS: University of Kansas Press.

Vaill, P. 1996. *Learning as a way of being: Strategies for survival in a permanent white water.* Mississauga, ONT: Jossey-Bass.

Vaill, P. 1991. *Managing as a performing art: New ideas for a world of chaotic change.* Mississauga, ONT: Jossey-Bass.

Westley, F., B. Zimmerman, and M. Patton. 2007. *Getting to Maybe: How the World Is Changed.* Toronto: Random House.

Wunderlich, F. M. 2008. "Walking and rhythmicity: Sensing urban space." *Journal of Urban Design* 13(1): 125–39.

NOTES

1 The use of large Euro-North American categories to encompass Aboriginal peoples with different tribal, geographic, political, and historical contexts is problematic. In Canada, Aboriginal peoples can be identified on the basis of geography, language, tribal affiliations, Pan-Aboriginal organizations, international and national status, class and socio-economic levels, legal status, and political affiliations. Although we use Aboriginal peoples as shorthand for the range of identities and political realities, we are uncomfortable and tentative with this language.

2 There are numerous political, philosophical, and spiritual worldviews that suggest all peoples need to embrace that change is the reality of life.

3 The use of 'Canadian' in this paper presupposes the dominant Euro-North American discourses around democracy, government, economics, civic engagement, and cultural values. Although there are certain aspects, such as the official opposition, that provide a nod to diversity and pluralism, the historical debate around what it means to be a Canadian, immigration, and treaties with Aboriginal nations supports a very cautious approach toward

inclusion in a system built on exclusion and denigration of Aboriginal culture and peoples.

4   An imaginary or social imaginary is a set of values, institutions, laws, practices, discourses and symbols common to a particular social grop and the corresponding society. Charles Taylor a Canadian philosopher addresses the concept of Western imaginaries in his book *Modern Social Imaginaries (2004)*.

5   Indigenous refers to the various Aboriginal, Native, and Aborigine peoples around the world as identified under the United Nations.

Conclusions:
Exercising Our
"Leisure Imagination"

Heather Mair, Donald G. Reid, and Susan M. Arai

Each of the chapters in this book offers a unique piece in a complex and often unclear puzzle. However, by presenting this collection, we've created chances to develop a deeper understanding of at least some of what's at stake. In this way, this book provides a unique contribution to the debate by deliberately inserting leisure into questions and considerations of social policy, public policy, and social welfare.

Ranging widely in methodological approaches and presentation styles as well as presenting a dramatically different array of subject areas, this collection represents a one-of-a-kind endeavour for our field. Poverty, homelessness, federally sentenced women, people living with dementia, Aboriginal youth, new immigrants ... the list goes on. One might be tempted to walk away from a project such as this with a feeling of utter bewilderment and even disenchantment at the range of problems in society. And yet, each of the authors brought together for this collection begins from three key normative and ultimately hopeful assumptions.

Public Policy Is Essential

First we'd all agree that public policy should exist and that it remains the foremost mechanism for addressing collective troubles that affect us all. Dawson takes us through a consideration of policy development and shows us that, while not always obvious, leisure and recreation have indeed had a role to play in social development. Reid, Golden, and Katerberg take policy development head-on and call for a re-orientation of work-dominated approaches to policy to concentrate instead on worth and achievement. Taylor and Frisby argue for more participatory-oriented approaches to policy-making at the local level. Dupuis similarly contends that meaningful policy formation involves the voices of those who are ultimately affected.

Arai and Burke broaden our very definition of policy and seeks to keep the complex nature of poverty (using the metaphor of grains of sand in an hourglass) alive in our minds as they argue for policy that is not merely reactive but rather preactive and sensitive to difference. Tirone argues that multiculturalism, perhaps our most deliberate of social policies, can be strengthened through a deeper understanding of the intended and unintended outcomes. Fox and Lashua call out for complexity and challenge the very nature of hegemonic approaches to policy formation, which seem only able to foster one way of being in the world. Mair and Trussell argue that social circumstances are putting social policy issues, especially in terms of rights and access to public spaces, right at the front door of our field and the time to step into the debate is now. Fortune, Pedlar, and Yuen critique the underlying goals of social development policies from the standpoint of some of the most marginalized individuals in our society.

Leisure Is Essential

We all contend, in our own ways, that we must act collectively, through policy, to actively change society for the better. Being leisure specialists, it is hardly surprising that we all see a role for leisure in this process. The second key assumption, then, is that we'd all agree that now, more than ever, we need to move beyond dominant considerations of leisure as individualized, privatized opportunities for self-expression where leisure policy is implemented merely to respond to market failure (although these considerations are important) to consider ways of making leisure a central quality of our collective social life. No author, however, accepts leisure uncritically.

To differing degrees, each chapter engages the notion of leisure from a critical, sociological perspective as authors tease out the tensions of leisure as a mechanism both for social change and for social control. Dawson introduces us to these concerns and each subsequent chapter builds on his discussion. Dupuis examines the role of leisure as not just an instrumental vehicle for helping people cope with issues of ADRD but also as providing an opportunity for people to come together in communities to foster support networks and build social ties. Arai and Burke echo these sentiments by arguing for a relational-based approach to the social determinants of health that makes leisure a central component in the web of support relationships that can help women overcome the many challenges they face in a patriarchal, racist, and class-based society. Mair and Trussell see leisure as providing a safe space for collective debate on a topic that is beginning to have implications for our field. Fox and Lashua see not leisure but *leisures* and consider how we might embrace and support diversity and marginality.

Taylor and Frisby stay within the realm of leisure and recreation policy to argue that leisure programs need to be taken at least as seriously as other social programs offered at the local level. Tirone sees leisure as a site for helping immigrants gain access to mainstream society and to build connections to the cultures they left, but she is also critical of the ways leisure can be used as a tool for shutting out difference. Fortune, Pedlar, and Yuen consider the double-edged sword presented by leisure programming in a federal institution as it offers a way of connecting to society after incarceration while leaving untouched many of the structural problems that foster law-breaking in the first place. Reid, Golden and Katerberg centre leisure and leisure policy in their model of social transformation and consider its pivotal role in challenging the dominance of work and the market economy in how we value individuals in society.

Third, and perhaps most importantly, we'd all agree that hope for positive change is at the core of the challenges we describe. As social scientists concerned with the human condition, none of the authors would engage in this research if they thought change was impossible. Perhaps it is because leisure research has always been on the margins of social research, often derided and devalued by colleagues in other fields, that we can see opportunities for alternative ways of structuring society. In short, we all see a role for leisure to help society move from blaming individuals for their failings to creating opportunities to collectively embrace difference. Reid, Golden and Katerberg are among the most direct as they present a model and a process for a great social transformation. The present economic and political conditions, particularly in North America, leads many of us to feel that such great change could come. Dupuis works with communities deeply challenged by ADRD, still relatively poorly understood in comparison to other health issues affecting older adults. And yet, like Reid et al., she presents a fundamentally new approach based in a planning framework grounded in respect, trust, reciprocity, and collaboration. Taylor and Frisby introduce one of the most hopeful methodological developments in social research as they argue for participatory approaches to policy development where access to decision-making is an equal-opportunity venture. Fox and Lashua envision not only a new way of seeing leisure as a multiplicity; they consider avenues for keeping complexity, difference, and richness alive in leisure and policy development.

Mair and Trussell bring in some recent examples where hope can be found, at least in terms of sparking public debate about safe and adequate social housing and our collective responsibility. Arai and Burke describe a future where policy-makers and leisure providers overcome the fragmentation in society and a holistic approach to care is fostered. Fortune, Pedlar, and Yuen invoke the example of social movements where individuals with disabilities worked together and with the broader community to win many access and inclusive rights. They consider how these changes might be brought to bear on women who have been in contact with the law to create a more socially just society. Tirone challenges the legitimation and accumulation imperatives underscoring multiculturalism policy in an effort to improve it and to make it more responsive to the needs and challenges faced by new Canadians and to embrace social inclusion in a more critical way.

New Avenues for Leisure (and Social Policy) Research: A Caveat

While these three key assumptions form a sort of scaffolding for this book, that is not to say that the authors here can or should have the last words on the subject(s). By putting our work forward in this way, we call on others in fields concerned with social welfare to help us continue the discussion. In particular, the role of leisure in addressing issues of ethnicity, sexuality, and geography are in need of attention and critical exploration. New avenues for research are opening all the time and the epistemological, ontological, and methodological revolutions reverberating throughout the social sciences offer many exciting opportunities for the future. We eagerly await a new generation of socially committed scholars who will take on these concerns and help us in our efforts to move the leisure/work debate in new directions.

It should be noted that most of the projects described in the chapters of this book are based upon qualitative methods that sit within the overarching paradigm of critical interpretivisim. We certainly feel confident that these approaches have offered opportunities for important new insights without which this book would not have been possible. However, they also foreground concerns about ethics, power and control in social research. Indeed, many of the authors writing in this collection are openly committed to the maxim: *research with and for* communities and individuals as opposed to *research on* communities and individuals. And yet, as the individuals who have agreed to be participants in our studies are among the most marginalized members of our society, this maxim is fraught with ethical considerations. We didn't ask the authors to reflect on these considerations but are very aware of their presence. If we are going to push the discussion about leisure, marginalization, power, and equity to a broader audience, we need to make sure our research is not reinforcing the very structures we are seeking to address. Future researchers, thus, need to come to terms with these issues and more debate in this area is needed.

TOWARDS A LEISURE IMAGINATION

We may collectively see leisure as a space, an activity, maybe even a period of time when we can "be ourselves" and engage in activities that are refreshing, stimulating, and educational. And yet, these activities are not as "freely chosen" as we might like and we must always remain aware of the ways leisure is socially constructed with relations of power strewn through. We began this book by reflecting on language and how we have come to define leisure as something individualized, a response, a reward, a salve, for paid work. If we enlarge our perspective to think of leisure as essential to the "nourishment of the whole person," we still need to keep in mind the forces working to constrain that nourishment. In effect, in asking why leisure has not taken on this role, we are inviting a critique of our present condition. As Rojek has argued, "[it] is in our leisure that we confront our chained existence with the greatest candour" (1999, 92).

C. Wright Mills argued for the development of the sociological imagination. He defined it in the following way:

> The sociological imagination enables its possessor to understand the large historical scene in terms of its meaning for the inner life and the external career of a variety of individuals. It enables him to take into account how individuals, in the welter of their daily experience, often become falsely conscious of their social positions. Within that welter, the framework of modern society is sought, and within that framework the psychologies of a variety of men and women are formulated. By such means, the personal uneasiness of individuals is focused upon explicit troubles and the indifference

of publics is transformed into involvement with public issues. (2000 [1959], 5)

From this perspective, meaningful social change is grounded in the interaction between individual and community; between an individual's private troubles and the public issues that frame them. To that extent, each of the researchers in this book, in their own way, has been exercising their "leisure imagination" by situating their specific concerns and the individuals they work with in the broader historical period in which we live.

This brings to the foreground an underlying tension that runs throughout the book. As we each embrace the ability of leisure to aid in addressing marginalization, we must also consider what happens to the individual. Are we advocating the broadening of "the mainstream" or seeking to change those who are outside of it? We'd argue that the authors we brought together for this collection are each trying hard to dance within this tension and keep alive the beauty and richness of diversity and difference while bearing in mind the role of bigger structural forces. Each is trying to consider how collectivity and diversity (universalism and individualism) can work together. How, they ask, can enclaves offer safety and assurance while being sure that they are not imposed from the outside? How can we be sure that the doors are always open for broader collective activities, learning, sharing, and collaboration? These are fundamental questions; how we endeavour to answer them may determine how and when our field (and leisure more generally) becomes a more serious player in addressing social issues.

REFERENCES

Mills, C. W. 1959 [2000]. *The Sociological Imagination*. New York: Oxford University Press.

Rojek, C. 1999. "Deviant leisure." In *Leisure Studies: Prospects for the Twenty-First Century*, ed. E.L. Jackson and T. Burton, 81–95. State College, PA: Venture.

Notes on Contributors

Susan Arai

Susan Arai is an associate professor in Recreation and Leisure Studies at the University of Waterloo. Her research and practice examines concepts such as social inclusion/social exclusion, therapeutic relationships, empowerment, mindfulness, and health. Central in this work are critical explorations of the reproduction of oppression and marginalization within social systems and institutions, and the processes of healing and transformation, empowerment, and new social movements. Susan has conducted research with hospitals, municipal and regional governments, a federal correctional facility, community health centres, healthy communities initiatives, social planning councils, and disability organizations. Current research has begun to explore performance arts as leisure in processes of individual and community transformation.

Rishia Burke

Rishia Burke (B.A. Physical Health Education, M.A. Recreation and Leisure Studies) engaged in frontline work as a community developer and health promoter in neighbourhood associations and community health centres for more than a decade. Rishia has worked for eight years as a consultant to health-promoting organizations, municipalities, community health centres, and groups addressing poverty issues. Defining situation-specific best practices and facilitating evidence-based learning is a driving force behind Rishia's work as researcher, planner, and evaluator for mutli-disciplinary teamwork initiatives, early year projects, positive youth development programs, seniors' outreach initiatives, and partnership development. Her recent work focuses on recreation as a determinant of health and healthy public policy to increase access to recreation, arts, and leisure programs for low-income families.

Donald J. Dawson

Don Dawson has been a professor of Leisure Studies at the University of Ottawa since 1982. He is concerned with the delivery of recreation and leisure services in a pluralistic society with emphasis on under-served communities. Other interests include social theory and cultural studies within the context of post-modernity and globalization. He is currently participating in an experiential learning program that places university students in local elementary and high schools to act as mentors to at-risk children and youth while providing innovative leisure opportunities.

Sherry Dupuis

Sherry Dupuis is the Director of the Murray Alzheimer Research and Education Program and an associate professor in the Department of Recreation and Leisure Studies at the University of Waterloo. Sherry's research program has focused primarily on identifying ways to improve the quality of the lives of persons living with dementia, their families, and other care partners and to ensuring that the voices of persons with dementia and their care partners are represented in research, education, practice, and policy development. She is committed to the transfer of research into action through the use of participatory action research approaches and alternative representations of research findings.

Darla Fortune

Darla Fortune is currently a Ph.D. candidate at the University of Waterloo. Darla returned to graduate school after spending several years as Director of Recreation Therapy in a long-term care facility. Her research interests include opportunities for community engagement and social inclusion for individuals living in institutional settings such as prisons and long-term care facilities. Her dissertation will examine social inclusion in the lives of federally sentenced women who are reintegrating into the community after their release from prison.

Karen Fox

Karen Fox is a full professor at the University of Alberta. Her research interests focus on leisure practices on the margins, theoretical musings about leisures, and the challenge of urban Aboriginal hip hop for the study of leisures. Her research has included travels to India, the Canadian Rockies, England, and Scotland.

Wendy Frisby

Wendy Frisby is a professor in the School of Human Kinetics and the former Chair of Women's and Gender Studies at the University of British Columbia. She has written extensively on poverty, feminist participatory action research, and leisure services. In 2004, she was awarded the Earle F. Zeigler Award for outstanding scholarship, leadership, and service by the North American Society for Sport Management (NASSM). She is the former editor of the *Journal of Sport Management* and serves on the editorial boards of several journals, including *Leisure/Loisir*.

Leigh Golden

B. Leigh Golden graduated from the Ph.D. program in the School of Environmental Design and Rural Development at the University of Guelph in 2008. Her doctoral research focused on social policy, community development, and leisure planning – particularly the social integration of marginalized individuals. Currently, Leigh works in social services doing social planning, research, and evaluation within a municipal context.

Leah Katerberg

Leah Katerberg has pursued a commitment to address poverty both in Canada and around the world for over a decade. Having worked for leading development agencies in international and local project development, she now provides research and consulting services to the non-profit sector. Her education, combining economics with planning and development, has given her unique insight into the issues that surround poverty, both in Canada and in the Third World. Domestically, her work aims to strengthen the non-profit sector through strategic training and development of public education resources. Internationally, she provides development organizations with services ranging from research and proposal development to project monitoring and evaluation.

Brett Lashua

Brett Lashua is a lecturer in the Carnegie Faculty of Sport and Education at Leeds Metropolitan University. He holds a Ph.D. in Leisure Studies from the University of Alberta and specializes in research involving young people, identity politics, music-making, urban spaces, and ethnographic methods.

Heather Mair

Heather Mair is an associate professor in the Department of Recreation and Leisure Studies at the University of Waterloo. She has published research on a variety of topics. Recent works include a book entitled *Rural Tourism Development: Localism and Cultural Change* (with Donald G. Reid and E. Wanda George) as well as scholarly papers presenting research on tourism in small communities, food-related activism in the context of leisure, the role of curling clubs in rural Canadian life, and broader issues of critical leisure research, civic engagement, and community development.

Alison Pedlar

Alison Pedlar is a distinguished professor emerita at the University of Waterloo. She has broad applied research and practical experience in issues related to disability, aging, and leisure and recreation services in Canada. Her teaching and research activity focused on social policy, planning, and development of human services. Much of her work has been conducted within a participatory and collaborative research framework and has included community development work with older adults, individuals with disabilities, incarcerated women, and other marginalized populations. Her work over the last decade has been particularly concerned with bridging theory and practice.

Donald G. Reid

Donald G. Reid is a University professor emeritus in the School of Environmental Design and Rural Development at the University of Guelph. Don's professional focus is on community development, leisure provision (including tourism and recreation) and social development. He is engaged in researching the impacts of tourism in rural communities, both in Canada and in Africa. Books include *Work and Leisure in the 21st Century: From Production to Citizenship* and *Tourism, Globalization* and *Development: Responsible Tourism Planning*. His research focuses on the critical issues facing rural communities as they attempt to diversify their economies from purely primary-sector-based activity (farming) to service-based industries (tourism). Don is also involved in research that examines the delivery of social service provision in rural communities.

Janna Taylor

Janna Taylor is a former director of Parks and Recreation, a former president of the British Columbia Recreation and Parks Association, and has worked as a consultant in the recreation field for several years. Her master's thesis research involved conducting focus groups with parents of low-income families in Canadian cities to obtain their perspectives on municipal recreation programs and policies. She is currently an instructor in the School of Human Kinetics at the University of British Columbia.

Susan Tirone

Susan Tirone is an associate professor in the School of Health and Human Performance at Dalhousie University in Halifax, Nova Scotia. Her research explores how leisure is experienced, enhanced and/or constrained by societal factors such as immigration status, poverty, race, and ethnicity. She is the principal investigator of several studies of Canadian immigrant families from non-western countries, a study of families and children living in a low-income housing development in Atlantic Canada, and she is a member of a national research team that studied the accessibility of municipal recreation services for children and families in low-income communities. She is the principal investigator for a longitudinal study of second-generation South Asian Canadians and the co-leader on a study of immigrants' experiences in sport and coaching. Susan's recent publications include book chapters and articles appearing in *Canadian Sport Sociology, Canadian Ethnic Studies, Leisure/Loisir,* and the *Canadian Journal of Community Mental Health*.

Dawn Trussell

Dawn Trussell is an assistant professor in the Department of Recreation, Sport and Tourism at the University of Illinois. Her research focuses on diverse social contexts and issues of power and social inclusion, particularly related to constructs of gender, family, age and rurality. She also has a keen interest in methodological issues in the research process when working with vulnerable and socially marginalized populations (i.e., children, youth, and those living in poverty). In her leisure time, you will find her on the volleyball court, hiking backcountry trails in the mountains, or canoeing in Algonquin.

Felice Yuen

Felice Yuen is an assistant professor in the Department of Applied Human Sciences at Concordia University, Montreal. She is interested in leisure as a context for community development and civic engagement. Recent projects include research with the Youth Advocacy Training Institute in Toronto, Ontario, and the Native Sisterhood, a cultural group in a women's federal prison. Felice has presented at national and international conferences and was a recipient of a Canada Graduate Scholarship Award from the Social Sciences and Humanities Research Council of Canada.

Index

relational, 3, 4, 59, 61, 120–21, 126–28, 131, 134, 135–38, 182, 197, 253

relationship, 60, 93, 98–100, 105–7, 109, 111–12, 125, 126–27, 131–32, 134, 136–38, 146, 180, 190, 196, 205, 219, 230, 232, 233–35, 239, 240–41, 243–47

resistance, 80, 134, 166, 196, 219, 220, 224, 239, 244

restructuring, 215
    economic, 205, 210, 216

revanchist city, 5, 147, 204, 213- 17, 220, 221

rhythmanalysis, 231, 233, 241

rights, 13, 37, 60, 67, 100, 105, 130, 136, 152, 176, 182–83, 214, 217, 218, 241, 247, 252, 254
    human, 28, 49, 158, 218
    individual, 10, 100, 153
    See also Canadian Charter of Rights and Freedoms, Canadian Human Rights Commission,

rural, 47, 74, 104, 109, 127, 239
    communities, 36
    See also under poverty

S

Safe Schools Act, 215

Safe Streets Act, 213, 222

serious leisure. *See under* leisure

shelter, 70, 71, 74, 119, 120, 133, 137, 143, 205–7, 209, 210, 214, 216, 217, 218, 222
    access to, 5, 147, 205–10, 223, 224

single-parent. *See* lone-parent

social assistance. *See* welfare

social capital. *See under* capital

social change, 2, 4, 6, 145, 216, 219, 253, 257

social cohesion, 60, 229, 230, 233, 236, 241, 243, 244

social contract, 63–65, 69, 75–76, 79, 80, 82, 83–86
    Rousseau, Jean Jacques, 67

social determinants of health, 60, 120, 121, 126–28, 131, 132, 137, 143, 253

social exclusion, 1, 2, 3, 5, 8, 11, 12–14, 17, 24, 31, 48–49, 53, 54, 60, 63, 120, 121–22, 126, 129, 131, 146, 160, 163, 176, 182, 196, 210, 215, 220, 232, 233, 234, 238, 240, 250

social housing. *See under* housing

social inclusion, 2, 4, 5, 7, 9, 10, 12–14, 16–17, 19, 23–26, 28–31, 36, 43, 52, 54, 61, 63, 69, 83, 94, 122, 126 27, 130, 132, 134, 136, 139, 145–47, 149, 150, 152, 153, 163, 167–68, 171, 176–77, 183, 187, 195, 196–98, 218, 229–30, 232, 233–34, 236–38, 240–41, 244, 250, 255

social innovation, 230, 245–47

social insurance. *See* welfare

social issue, 212, 219, 220, 222, 224, 257

social justice. *See under* justice

social movement, 182–83, 189, 243, 254

social policy. *See under* policy

social problems, 1, 4, 13, 25, 66, 216, 219

social solidarity, 60, 64, 67, 68, 80, 83, 86

social support, 13, 101, 106, 126, 137, 143, 161, 162, 180, 197, 206, 208, 216

social wage. *See under* income
(guaranteed annual income)

social welfare. *See* welfare

socioeconomic status, 89, 137, 191, 240, 249

space:

dialogical, 1, 37, 45, 50, 95, 110, 137, 176, 187, 195, 219

park, 41–42

performative, 230–32, 234–35, 239–41, 243–47

political, 25, 35, 37

private, 204–5, 215, 220

public, 12, 35, 39, 50, 133, 204–6, 211, 212, 214–16, 217–20, 221–22, 232, 235, 252

third, 235–37, 240

state. *See* government

stigma, 2, 74, 75, 97, 103, 110, 122, 127–29, 135, 175, 183, 196–97

substance use 100, 133, 135, 176, 184, 186, 205, 235, 237

systemic, 2, 8, 12, 52, 60, 82, 98, 101, 107, 111, 120, 124, 125, 130, 134, 138, 185–86, 193

T

Taylor, Janna, 2, 3, 8, 35–58, 72, 167, 252, 253, 254, 264

technology, 2, 8, 26, 47, 247

Tirone, Susan, 4, 5, 35, 38, 43, 145, 146, 149–74, 252, 253, 255, 264

tourism, 16, 215,

slum, 222, 224,

transformation, 3, 25, 60, 64, 119–21, 131–32, 134, 138–39, 236, 243, 246, 247, 253, 254

trauma. *See* abuse

Trussell, Dawn, 4, 5, 146, 203–28, 252, 253, 254, 265

U

unemployment, 14, 29, 69, 73, 76, 86, 130, 135, 176, 179, 190, 205

universal, 10, 11–14, 25, 29, 30, 73, 86, 151, 154, 234, 257

urban, 20, 36, 74–75, 104, 129, 210, 212–13, 215, 216, 221–22, 229–50

urbanization, 205

V

victim-blaming. *See* blaming the victim

violence, 85, 125–27, 130, 134, 143, 178, 181–82, 215, 217, 230, 232, 235–37, 239–40

W

wage, 14, 66, 70, 110, 124, 127, 156, 157, 191, 216

See also under income (guaranteed annual income)

welfare, 2, 4, 7, 9–12, 16, 17, 20–22, 26–30, 37, 60–61, 66, 75, 76, 77, 78, 79, 85, 86, 95, 119, 127, 132, 133, 136, 146, 203, 204, 208, 211, 217, 221, 224, 242, 251, 255

well-being, 1, 10, 11, 12, 36, 41, 42, 70, 81, 94, 103, 107, 110, 111, 126, 129, 152, 156, 161, 168, 169, 171, 196, 218, 238, 241, 247

Wellesley Institute, 207

women who are federally incarcerated, 175–202

work, 1, 2, 3, 14, 16, 48, 53, 60, 66, 69, 77, 80–86, 94, 99, 105, 124–27, 134–35, 155, 156,

159–61, 164, 176, 179, 180, 191–92, 197, 241, 242, 252, 253, 255, 256

World Health Organization, 120, 136

worthfare, 60, 77–78, 135

Y

youth, 6, 15, 45, 46, 47, 53, 58, 133, 136, 147, 161, 192, 237–38

    Aboriginal, 1, 5, 147, 229–36, 239–41, 243–47, 251

    homeless, 206, 213, 215, 242

    low income-, 161, 167

    minority, 157, 161–64, 169, 170, 215

Yuen, Felice, 4, 5, 146, 175–202, 216, 252, 253, 254, 265